...th them. correct...

You whenever you come to northern Californi...
I'm very well indeed and I look...

been good

All my best, and again thanks for sending me
JERUSALEM, and I hope that all your holidays
ones... *and always will be*

MOR

M.F.K. Fisher
to
Joan Nathan
'400 Bybrook Lane
levy Chase

of
l
ood
as
by
on't
hing
ble,

ve the
do new
o, that
ing and
want to

RÉPUBLIQUE FRANÇAISE 1,15
LA TRINITÉ-SUR-MER

PARIS 16
13H30
6-1
1970
RJEAN RICHEP

Mr. and Mrs. Ernest Nathan
204 Freeman Parkway
Providence, Rhode Island 02906

nachi...
...et ste...
...rollen,
...mel b...
...neiden...
...t büttu...
...on hellgelb raus.

...offel Omelette

...m Teller voll ro...
...artoffel wird...
...ezogen d.h. a...
...cier dann...

103 Irving Street, Cambridge, Massachusetts 02138 (617) 876-1072
FAX (617) 491-2347

Dear Joan:

Thanks for your note. I have just returned from Italy, where we had a
lovely time. Now I am about to take off for various culinary engagements
and then to California for the winter months.

Here's hoping you have a happy Thanksgiving. Let me know if you will
be in the Santa Barbara area any time this winter. It would be fun to get
together!

Meanwhile, all the best

Julia Child

ings
Fd
s lea

nit
mer

עיריית ירושלים
بلدية اورشليم - القدس

ירושלים

gain. Form into 3 round loaves and let double
n bulk. Bake 45 minutes at 350 degrees. Bake
n piepan for round loaves.

add 1 T anise seeds, crushed and reduce the
amount of white flour and add more rye flour
plus bran - delicious!

lly lovely speaking to you
le! I hope you had a memor...

My car is delightful. I received
ause I have had so many groups of jour...
an oil English journalist last week w...
nel. I felt that no matter what I rel...
osite viewpoint. Took another English
ll the new housing developments in R...
her Loval took us to lunch explaining
-up. Went with Charles Mohr of the N...
ity with an Arab who works here and
...interesting inde...

My Life in Recipes

My Life in Recipes

Food, Family, and Memories

Joan Nathan

Photographs by Gabriela Herman

ALFRED A. KNOPF   New York

2024

The real voyage of discovery consists not in seeking new landscapes,
but in having new eyes.

—MARCEL PROUST

Joan as the sleuth of *zwetschgen knoedel*.
Tracking down its origins in secluded Prague cafés
Or *knafeh*'s history in Nablus and Ramallah.
What was wrong with just a simple book on all things culinary?

—ALLAN GERSON,
"An Ode to Joan on Our Silver Anniversary"

Contents

Beginnings: An Introduction

I learned to make my matzo balls from my mother, skimming off the schmaltz from the top of the finished soup, just as she learned from her mother or *The Settlement Cook Book*. Later, I learned from pre–World War II German Jewish cookbooks about the custom of adding ground nutmeg and ginger to flavor the dumplings. Later still, I added fresh ginger and cilantro to mine, but kept the same al dente consistency that I favor from my mother's.

For a while, my mother-in-law, Paula, lived near us, and then with us. Her feather-light version, I was shocked to discover, came from a box of matzo-ball mix with baking powder—similar to the boxed matzo-ball mix that she first used in Zamość, Poland, just before the war. Paula substituted soda water for plain tap to make them even lighter. After she passed away, in 2007, just before Rosh Hashanah, I had a dumpling dilemma. Should I continue making the heavier ones I liked or, out of respect for Paula, should I make hers? I really did not know what to do. When I asked Allan and my son, David, my sense was that although they liked them both, they liked mine better.

I have made my recipe ever since.

One-Pot Chicken Stew with Peas, Carrots, and Matzo Balls

This recipe began as a one-pot chicken stew with dumplings, shared with me by a parent at my grandchildren's nursery school in L.A. When I made the recipe for the first time, I thought, why not replace the dumplings with matzo balls? And make it a one-pot Shabbat chicken stew? This easy and delicious dish was the result. You can also use the matzo balls in regular chicken soup, or make the stew with leftover turkey after Thanksgiving.

Though this recipe is a relatively new addition to my files, the flavors and feelings it evokes go back to my beginnings. Since it all comes together in one pot, this recipe is my way of adapting chicken soup with matzo balls for the next generations.

---

1. Set a 3-quart heavy pot over medium-high heat, add the oil, and cook the onion, celery, and turnips until the onion is translucent, about 5 minutes. Add the chicken, and cover with 5 cups (about 1.2 liters) water, or enough to almost submerge the chicken. Bring to a boil, reduce the heat, and simmer for about 30 minutes. Cool, cover, and refrigerate for at least a few hours, but ideally overnight, until you're ready to serve.

2. Make the matzo-ball mix at least 3 hours before serving. Stir together the eggs, schmaltz or oil, stock, matzo meal, nutmeg, ginger, and parsley in a large bowl. Season with 1 teaspoon salt and a few grinds of pepper. Cover, and refrigerate until it's chilled, about 3 hours, or overnight.

3. About 45 minutes before serving, skim off any fat that has accumulated on top of the chicken (if you do this earlier, you can use the fat for your matzo balls; otherwise, freeze it for another use), and break the chicken pieces into chunks, removing and discarding the skin and bones as you go. Place the chicken back into the pot, bring the liquid to a boil, then reduce the heat and add the carrots and peas.

4. Add heaping tablespoons of the matzo-ball mix to the top of the soup. Cover, and simmer until the matzo balls are cooked through, about 20 minutes. Serve topped with fresh parsley or dill.

Serves 4 to 6

For the stew
2 tablespoons olive oil
1 large onion, cut into large chunks
1 stalk celery, cut into chunks
1 turnip or parsnip, cut into rounds
1 cut-up chicken, with bones, about 3 pounds
2 carrots, peeled and cut into thick rounds
1 cup fresh or frozen peas
2 tablespoons chopped fresh Italian parsley or dill

For the matzo balls
4 large eggs
2 tablespoons schmaltz or vegetable oil
6 tablespoons chicken or vegetable broth
1 cup (115 grams) matzo meal
¼ teaspoon freshly grated nutmeg
2 tablespoons freshly grated ginger
2 tablespoons finely chopped fresh Italian parsley, dill, or cilantro
1 teaspoon kosher salt
Freshly ground black pepper

A Note on Ingredients

This book includes some of my favorite recipes and the story of my life as it relates to food. After a lifetime of cooking, I've come to prefer unbleached all-purpose flour as well as the high-quality, freshly ground flours made from ancient grains that are more available today. I encourage readers to try these. I always buy yeast in bulk and keep it in the freezer, rather than buying individual packets, which seem to be a waste of money.

For readers who follow the laws of kashrut, I have taken all practical measures to ensure that the recipes contained herein fulfill the Jewish dietary laws and have provided pareve substitutes for milk products wherever necessary, but within the many observant communities there are different views on the dietary laws. Accordingly, although rabbinic authorities have been consulted in the preparation of this text, the ultimate responsibility for ascertaining the conformity with kashrut of any particular recipe remains with the reader.

1.

The Old World:
My Earliest Memories
and My Father's Family

My father, Ernest Nathan, came to this country from Germany at the age of twenty-four, traveling first-class on the SS *Bremen*, a brand-new ocean liner that was among the fastest of its time. He arrived not long after the 1929 stock-market crash, the timing of which he always joked about.

In his pocket he carried innovative formulas for Imprägnol, a waterproof finish for fabric, patented by his family's business, R. Bernheim in Augsburg. Four years later, in 1933, the German authorities expropriated the company and changed the name to Chemische Fabrik Pfersee. Dad used the formulas in a joint venture with the Crompton Company, known for corduroy, at their chemical factory in Wood River Junction, Rhode Island. (Later, during World War II, the company supplied water-proofing chemicals to the government for uniforms.)

My father as a little boy

Dad told me that by 1923, after Hitler's first putsch in nearby Munich, his childhood friends walked across the street to avoid him. Even then, as an eighteen-year-old, he knew that Germany was no place for a Jew, so he joined Blau Weiss, the Zionist youth movement, something he believed in for the rest of his life. Although he did not go to Israel because he was able to come to the United States to work at a family business, he always supported Israel. He was one of the lucky ones who realized early and was able to get out.

Although I was born in Providence, Rhode Island, in 1943—during World War II—three years later, when my father sold his textile chemical business to a larger company, my parents, my older brother, Alan, and I moved to the lovely suburb of Larchmont, outside of New York. Dad commuted to Long Island City, where he ran the company he had sold plus other companies in the buyer's collection. My younger brother Richard was born one year later. It is here that my memories begin.

In one of my earliest recollections, I'm sitting on my father's lap on a pink-and-turquoise-fabric-covered chair that matched the pink flowered wallpaper in my bedroom. I loved listening to Dad read me nursery rhymes from Germany. My favorite was one from an oversized orange-paper-covered copy of the 1844 book *Struwwelpeter*. I still can recite one rhyme by heart: *"Messer, Gabel, Scher' und Licht sind fürgibt man kleinen Kinder nicht"* ("Knife, fork, scissors, and candlelight should not be given to little children"). Dad seemed so at peace then, not his usually stern Teutonic self.

Almost more vivid than my father's nursery rhymes, or the book about Heidi living in the Alps that he loved, was the story about my great-grandmother Rose Bernheim, the matriarch whom I believe I followed in spirit. Her husband, Isak, founded the family chemical business. Every Friday night, Dad told me, her

Sitting on my father's lap during my grandparents' fiftieth anniversary celebration

children and grandchildren gathered at their home in Augsburg to be together and share a meal with traditional German Jewish foods like berches (the potato-based savory challah), sweet-and-sour carp, roast goose or sauerbraten, and an apple or other seasonal kuchen for dessert. This was not so much a religious gathering for the Sabbath as a family-reinforcing custom I have since heard about from other assimilated German Jewish families who came earlier to the United States. The tradition continued once my father and mother married in 1937. Even though my parents did not observe the laws of kashrut in the home, as their grandparents had, they were united in celebrating the Sabbath and all the holidays in their own way, with family gathered around to share some of the same dishes as generations had before us. As I child, I always looked forward to these dinners.

My father with an old car

Sweet and Sour Salmon with Lemon, Ginger, and Brown Sugar

I found this recipe for sweet-and-sour carp, one of the dishes my father recalled relishing in Augsburg, in one of the handwritten, well-worn books of favorite recipes that my grandmother Lina Bernheim Nathan passed on to her daughters. Most Friday nights, when the family would gather at Great-Grandmother Rose's apartment, she would start the meal with a carp dish, especially for Rosh Hashanah. She would use carp or black cod (also called sable); she always used the head and bones to make stock, because they add thickness and flavor to the sauce. And she served it with either a sweet-and-sour or a parsley sauce.

Today I use a large salmon fillet, cutting it raw into individual portions to poach in a fish stock flavored with spices, brown sugar, lemon, gingersnaps (added to give a sweet gingery flavor and dark color, and to thicken the sauce slightly), and then some crystallized ginger to spike the dish even more. It is easy to make, a real crowd-pleaser, and, in a modern way, reminds me oh so much of my childhood.

---

1. Season the salmon with salt and pepper to taste in a large heavy-bottomed skillet or Dutch oven large enough to hold the fish in one layer. Add the stock, plus water if needed to barely cover the fish, arrange the lemon and onion slices on top, then drop in the bay leaf, raisins, and cloves. Simmer over medium heat, uncovered, for about 10 minutes, or until the fish is almost cooked through.

2. Add the brown sugar, ground ginger, gingersnaps, and crystallized ginger, and continue cooking for about 5 minutes, taking care not to overcook. You'll know the fish is cooked if it is firm to the touch; sometimes I pierce a fork into the center to make sure. Once the fish is cool, remove the bay leaf, then transfer the fish to a serving plate. Scatter the onion and lemon slices on top. Boil the liquid over medium-high heat until it has reduced by half, then pour it over the fish.

3. Taste, and drizzle with the juice from the third lemon. Refrigerate until serving, then serve at room temperature, sprinkled with dill.

Makes 12 small slices for an appetizer or 6 servings as a main course

One 3-pound (1⅓-kg) salmon fillet, skinned and cut into 6 or 12 portions
Kosher salt and freshly ground black pepper, to taste
About 6 cups (1.4 liters) fish or vegetable stock
3 lemons, 2 thinly sliced and seeded, the other juiced
2 medium onions, sliced into thin rings
1 bay leaf
½ cup (80 grams) raisins
½ teaspoon whole cloves
⅓ cup (71 grams) light- or dark-brown sugar
1 teaspoon ground ginger
6 gingersnaps
2 tablespoons diced crystallized ginger
2 tablespoons chopped fresh dill

Unlike many immigrants of the 1930s and '40s, my father was not hesitant to talk to my brothers and me about his childhood in Germany, such as his earliest memory of the mailman, who blew a French horn in his Bavarian hometown to announce the delivery of a letter, conveniently arriving as soon as the family cook took the buttery breakfast schnecken, which we call sticky buns, out of the oven.

He loved Jewish geography, especially when it related to his ancestors: Samson of Baiersdorf, the court Jew, and another very distant ancestor by marriage, the Glückel of Hameln, who wrote a series of wonderful memoirs between 1691 and 1719. When I first read them, many years ago, what struck me about this treasure of regional writing was the role of the weekly market for the Jewish community throughout history. A market was more than a place to buy food. It was a place where Judaism was taught, where matchmaking took place, where people socialized. Those books, more than almost any other, taught me so much about the everyday life of the Jewish woman at that moment in time.

Although the first Jews came to southern Germany with the Romans, my ancestors came much later. According to family lore, they arrived from Italy, possibly through Vienna, in about the ninth century. In the Middle Ages, Jews lived in cities, until they were expelled in the fifteenth and sixteenth centuries. We know that after that they lived in tiny towns, like Ullerichten in southwestern Germany, until they were permitted to live in larger towns like nearby Laupheim—where the municipal records show that the Nathan and Samson branches of my family were living in 1754—or Buchau, where the Bernheim part settled in 1577. My grandfather and grandmother met in Augsburg when Jews were allowed to move to even larger cities.

When Jews were forced to leave most towns in Bavaria in the fifteenth century, they traveled either east to Poland, where they brought the Ashkenazic cooking traits with them, or lived in tiny little villages closer to Württemberg, where they stayed until the nineteenth century.

In 1879, Jacob Bernheim, my distant relative and the shochet (ritual slaughterer) of the Jewish community of Laupheim, was accused of stabbing to death a barber's apprentice. This precursor to modern anti-Semitism sent shock waves through the Jewish community. He was exonerated, but died shortly afterward.

When the Nathan side of my family came to Ulm from Laupheim in 1851, they lived right next to the cathedral at 33 Münsterplatz, above my great-grandfather Alexander Nathan's cigar store. Today visitors can see it: a branch of Deutsche Bank! They can also see my great-great-grandfather Samson Nathan's Haggadah, the text recited at the Passover Seder including the story of the Exodus from Egypt, at the Ulm Archives.

In 1950, Albert Einstein, whose family also came from Buchau, though he was born in Ulm in 1879, happened to share a compartment with my father in the sleeping car of a train from New York to Atlanta. Einstein told my dad that he remembered Alexander Nathan's Cigar Store from when he visited his relatives. Einstein also said that his grandfather and my great-great-grandfather Simon Bernheim were business partners who owned a grocery store in Buchau during the nineteenth century. This is something I have not been able to confirm.

Alexander Nathan's cigar store, on the first floor of the building next to the cathedral in Ulm

Albert Einstein's Strawberries Mixed with Whipped Cream

Serves 6

Zest of 1 lemon

½ cup (100 grams) sugar

2 pints strawberries, hulled

1 cup farmer's cheese,
   pot cheese, or labneh

1 cup (236 ml) heavy cream

About ⅓ cup (79 ml)
   Grand Marnier, other
   orange liqueur, or crème
   de cassis (optional)

A few years ago, I visited the Albert Einstein Archives at the Hebrew University of Jerusalem. Before I got there, the archivist found out that I was interested in food, so he gathered a few documents—and there are only a few—in which the genius, who had a weak stomach, mentioned what he ate. Einstein was known for writing letters, most often dictated to his secretary at Princeton. I should know: my father received at least two letters from him.

In 1917, Einstein wrote a postcard to Elsa, his cousin and soon-to-be second wife: "I live like a cow in the Alps. I am devouring zwieback, butter, honey, and milk in incredible amounts." In another letter, he thanked Erich Cohen of A. Goodman & Sons for sending him matzo: "I thank you very much for sending your excellent matzoth. It is probably the only religious stimulation, with me, that falls on fertile ground. With best regards and wishes, yours, Albert Einstein."

According to his live-in housekeeper, Herta Scheifelbein Waldow, who was with him in Berlin from 1927 to 1933, he started each day with fried or scrambled eggs. He also loved asparagus and ate such things as lamb chops and string beans, clear bouillon with a savory egg custard, and salmon with mayonnaise.

His favorite dessert was strawberries, a fruit he was known to eat by the pound according to *Janos: The Story of a Doctor* by John Plesch. Herta recalls his usual dessert at dinner parties in *Einstein at Home*. "Afterward a strawberry dish with whipped cream mixed with strawberries to make 'strawberry snow.'" The archives kindly provided me with the recipe, with which I then tampered just a bit. It is delicious, especially when strawberries are in season.

1. Put the lemon zest, sugar, ½ cup of the strawberries, and the cheese or labneh in a blender, and process.

2. Whip the cream, fold it into the strawberry mixture, and refrigerate.

3. Cut the remaining strawberries into 1-inch pieces, divide them among six bowls, and spoon the sauce over the strawberries. If you like, drizzle the top with a few tablespoons of Grand Marnier or other liqueur.

German Potato Salad with Peppers and Caraway Seeds

Although my father loved the all-white, bland potato salad with a boiled dressing of his childhood, I rarely make it. Instead, I make a more exciting version I tasted when Allan and I visited Augsburg a few years ago. When my German cousins invited us to have brunch at the Augsburg Textile and Industry Museum, I thought it was a strange choice at first. But the museum, located in an old stone mill, was quite fabulous. And textiles were the industry in which my German forebears participated.

The brunch included food that reflects the new Germany. Sure, there were wursts, simmered in water, that could be eaten alone or with bread or pretzels. But there was also hummus, a bulgur salad with lemon and mint, and all kinds of vegetables. The potato salad we ate that day was both colorful and delicious, a real keeper—and a reminder of my father's favorite dish. I serve it sometimes with tuna fish or olives on a bed of lettuce, making a delicious lunch dish. It is also a perfect accompaniment to roast chicken or wurst, something we all love.

---

1. Fill a large pot with salted water. Bring it to a boil, add the potatoes in their skins, and boil until they are cooked but not mushy, 20 to 30 minutes. Drain, and let them cool slightly.

2. Make the dressing by stirring the vinegar and mustard in a large bowl, then whisking in the oil and adding salt and pepper to taste.

3. Peel the potatoes once they are cool; the skins should slip off easily. Cut them into 1-inch chunks and add them to the dressing. Mix gently.

4. Scatter the onion and peppers over the potatoes, and mix in. Sprinkle with the caraway seeds and the parsley. Serve immediately.

Serves 4 to 6

Kosher salt and freshly ground black pepper, to taste

2 pounds (907 grams) russet or other floury potatoes

¼ cup (60 ml) apple-cider vinegar

1 tablespoon Dijon mustard

⅓ cup (79 ml) olive, vegetable, or preferably pumpkin-seed oil

½ red onion, diced

1 red, yellow, or orange bell pepper, cut into 1-inch squares

1 jalapeño or other hot pepper, diced

1 tablespoon caraway seeds, toasted

2 tablespoons chopped fresh Italian parsley

In 1932, the family of Hans and Sophie Scholl moved into the same building in Ulm where my family had their cigar store. The brother and sister became members of the White Rose, a student group in Munich that was active in the nonviolent resistance movement in Nazi Germany—especially in distributing flyers against the war and Hitler's dictatorship. (By that time, the Nathan family had moved to Augsburg.) Hans and Sophie were both decapitated by the Nazis for their resistance movement on February 22, 1943, twenty-seven days after I was born.

When Dad first came to the United States, despite all that he knew and didn't know was going on in Germany, he charmed Rhode Islanders, bowing and kissing women's hands as he had been taught in Bavaria. In 1934, when he became a U.S. citizen, he wrote letters to the American government, signing affidavits for his relatives to immigrate in the 1930s—before the State Department put more restrictions on immigration in 1941—promising that they "would never be a problem for the government." He was able to bring over his parents and sisters, their families, and many others, but some were reluctant to leave; they could not believe that the Nazi treatment of the Jews could last, especially those who had fought for Germany in the so-called Great War.

Since I was born right in the middle of the war, it was only as I got older that I realized what was omitted from the family stories. Dad never told us, for example, about his aunt or his distant cousin, the ones he could not save. His aunt, Marie Nathan Bernheim, one of the beauties of the family, perished in the Theresienstadt concentration camp in 1942. His cousin Kurt's son, Wolfgang, joined the high school of a Dutch Benedictine monastery just across from the German border. The Nazis, threatening the monastery for hiding Jews, took revenge on the Catholic clergy. The head monk was afraid of retaliation against the whole monastery so, to keep them at bay, he sacrificed the nineteen-year-old Wolfgang, who first tried to escape, then turned himself in. A few weeks later, he died in Sakrau, a labor camp on the way to Auschwitz. He has recently been declared a martyr by the Catholic Church.

About twenty-eight people from just the Nathan line of my family perished in various death camps. I only learned these stories after my father's death at eighty-six, in 1991, from relatives still living in Germany. It may have been too painful for him to tell these parts of our story, or maybe he didn't know the full extent of the truth. But I often saw a sad look on his face, perhaps the frustration of someone who had been unable to save his family.

Cooking was an important activity for my father's sisters, Trudel Bloch and Lisl Regensteiner. In the early twentieth century, when they were growing up in Augsburg, they learned to bake with a miniature Nuremberg kitchen that had been their mother's.

Grandmother Lina received the kitchen, made in Pfersee, Bavaria, on her sixth birthday, Christmas Day 1880. There were miniature replicas of tube pans and kitchen molds. Every December, my great-grandmother brought out and assembled the kitchen, adding new pieces of furniture or kitchen utensils each year. My grandmother told me, in her halting English, about the parties she and my aunts gave using this tiny kitchen. They dressed up in uniforms with white aprons and bonnets; they baked miniature fruit and nut kuchen and torten in the copper molds. When my aunts played with it in the twentieth century electricity fueled the functioning stove, like an intricate and carefully designed Easy-Bake oven. At parties, they used the tiny cups and saucers for tea and coffee. Even my father and his male cousins found cooking fun—not a male thing to do at home in those days—in this doll kitchen.

In 1933, when Hitler became chancellor of Germany, the charmed lives of Dad's sisters, Trudel and Lisl, their husbands, and their children changed forever. Although my uncle Ludwig believed that Nazi rule would only be a passing nightmare, his wife, Lisl, realized, by 1937, shortly after the brownshirts beat up Ludwig, that the time had come to leave. With my father's urging, the two sisters insisted that their families go to America.

Before she left Germany and came to America, Trudel filled a shipping container, called a "lift," with the doll kitchen, as well as beauti-fully penned family cookbooks, children's costumes, furniture, candlesticks, and pewter and silver platters. Trudel's things came with her to White Plains, where she first lived. I played with the kitchen as a child, first at her home, then, when my father bought it from her, at my house in Larchmont. Now my grandchildren play with it. Besides the kitchen, I also have much of her kitchenware from Germany, including the pewter platters and plates and my father's Bar Mitzvah cup, which sit on a wooden hutch in my dining room.

In 2000, a woman with a German accent left a voicemail on my telephone asking if I was a relative of Trudel Bloch. "I hope this is the right Joan Nathan," she said. "I have a handwritten cookbook in German, written by Trudel and Lina Nathan, which I thought that you might be interested in having." The message caused my heart to skip a beat. When I called her back, she explained to me that she was a Swiss Christian, in her late eighties, and lived in Vermont, and that her husband, who was somehow connected to Trudel, had recently passed away. She knew me from my PBS cooking show and cookbooks, so she took a chance on calling me.

As a writer of cookbooks, I was eager to see what I would learn from the old leather volume that arrived, in mint condition, carefully wrapped in cellophane. It was easily divided into annotated chapters: baked goods, egg dishes, meat dishes, fruit, vegetables, and so on. Although there were no smudges from butter or gravy, the book came alive for me, with the handed-down recipes for the dumplings and baked goods that were—and are—the pride of so many southern German cooks.

Zwetschgenkuchen (German Plum Tart)

1 cup (125 grams) unbleached
   all-purpose flour, plus more
   for dusting

Dash of kosher salt

¼ cup (50 grams) granulated
   sugar

½ cup (1 stick/113 grams)
   unsalted butter, chilled,
   cut into small pieces

1 large egg yolk

⅓ cup (107 grams) apricot
   or any fruit preserves

2 pounds (907 grams) Italian
   plums, or other sweet-tart
   plums

½ teaspoon ground cinnamon

¼ cup (29 grams) slivered
   almonds, for sprinkling

Confectioners' sugar,
   for sprinkling

Fall is the season for zwetschgenkuchen, a southern German and Alsatian tart with a muerbeteig (shortcrust pastry) crust filled with prune plums that ripen at that time of year. (When I cannot find them, I use whatever sweet-tart plum is available, cut into slivers.) Each year, as I carefully assemble the plum slices in a circle inside the crust, I remember sitting on top of the chest freezer in our kitchen, watching my mother do the same. This family recipe is just as good during the summer made with peaches, or sprinkled with raspberries or blueberries. I also like to brush the top with a little bourbon. And now I sometimes turn it into a crisp by scattering the cut fruit in a baking pan, adding a little jam, dotting the fruit with the raw dough, and baking in a 400-degree oven for about 40 minutes. So easy! But never for the Jewish New Year. Then I want the traditional tart.

---

1. Pulse the flour, salt, and 1 tablespoon of the granulated sugar in a food processor fitted with the metal blade. Add the butter, and pulse until the mixture is crumbly; then add the egg yolk, and pulse until a dough forms, mixing in more flour if necessary. I prefer the processor for pie crusts, but you can use a stand mixer or your fingers in a bowl, as my mother did.

2. Remove the dough, dust it with flour, and pat it into a disc. Put it into a container, cover, and refrigerate for at least 30 minutes.

3. Preheat the oven to 450 degrees. When you are ready to bake the crust, dust your hands and the dough with flour. Place the dough in the center of a 9-inch pie plate, and gently pat it out to cover the bottom and up the sides. Trim the crust, and prick the bottom in several spots with a fork. Bake for 10 to 15 minutes, until it's pale golden. Let it cool slightly; then spread the preserves over the crust.

4. Reduce the oven temperature to 350 degrees. Pit and cut the plums into fourths (or into six slices if using larger, rounder plums); then arrange them on the crust in concentric circles, starting from the outside and working inward, so that each overlaps the last one, into the center. Sprinkle with the cinnamon and the remaining sugar. (At this point you can wrap the tart in aluminum foil and freeze to bake it later; be sure to remove it from the freezer 1 hour before baking.)

5. Bake for about 30 minutes, or until the crust is golden brown and the plums are juicy. Just before serving, sprinkle it with the slivered almonds and confectioners' sugar.

Isak and Rose Bernheim, my father's grandparents. The stories about Rose inspired me to discover Jewish food.

Once I had Lina and Trudel's cookbook in my possession, I brought it with me to our home on Martha's Vineyard for the summer. I asked Trude Lash, who was an advocate for children and a political activist born and brought up in Germany, if I could visit her once a week to go through the book and translate the recipes. Trude was the widow of Joseph Lash, a biographer of Franklin and Eleanor Roosevelt. The couples were close friends, and the Lashes stayed frequently in the White House. I brought freshly baked cookies for this fascinating woman, who was in her nineties at the time, and she, in turn, told me stories about growing up in Germany as a Protestant who actively opposed the war. It was Trude, not her husband, who brought the concentration camps to the attention of President Roosevelt.

I learned from Trude that the cookbook was written during World War I, when my aunts were in their teens and all the young Jewish boys of their age were off in the war defending Emperor Wilhelm II's German Reich. The wartime recipes included an oat porridge and kuchen, with the advice either to use a potato base or to reduce the amount of butter and eggs, to help the war effort.

As I read, familiar names popped out at me: kuchen from Paulina, the cook of my great-aunt Marie. Here was the sweet-and-sour carp my father loved, the sauerbraten, stuffed goose, dumplings, and all different kinds of cookies and Sacher torte, the birthday dessert in my father's family. And here, too, was an elaborately written recipe for a gefilte Indien, a stuffed turkey, with instructions to first pluck the feathers from the bird and then stuff it with truffles and schmaltz. Through this book, and the printed nineteenth-century and prewar German cookbooks for Jewish women, I learned how our family shared recipes through letters with nearby friends and those who had already immigrated to America.

All these years later, I still think about how my father's past must have continued to churn inside him. His secure life in Germany, where his father was a respected citizen, was torn apart by Hitler; his teenage rejection by his Christian friends pushed him to work at a family business in Milan and then, as soon as the opportunity opened, to start a new life in the United States. Despite all his life's richness, he still retained the insecurity and trauma of an immigrant.

In my professional life, I looked back on the stories my father told me when I was a young girl and held on to the family recipes that I uncovered. But at the same time, I am also my mother's daughter, adapting these recipes to modern times so they remain relevant, and so that we can, I hope, pass them on to the next generation.

2.

The New World: New York City and My Mother's Family

When I was a little girl, my parents gave me a double deck of cards, one portraying a beautiful ballet dancer and the other a beautiful figure skater. I thought the person depicted was my mother—never mind that the woman on the cards was blond (Mother had black hair). Although she was a golfer and an archery pro, she never danced ballet and only took me skating occasionally, at Rockefeller Center or at the pond near the Larchmont train station. But to me, she was perfect and glamorous, just like the cards.

While my father tried to cling to the Old World that he left behind, my mother, Pearl Gluck, born in 1913 (seven years before women could vote), embraced the New. Her parents both came to America as immigrants and raised her as an "American" girl, albeit one entirely aware of her Judaism.

My mother, Pearl, on a banana boat on her honeymoon

Her maternal grandparents, Wolf and Hannah Kops, were born in Kraków, then moved to Vienna, where my great-grandfather worked as a tailor to earn enough money to cross the ocean. Their daughter Martha Kops Gluck, who became a hatmaker, was born in London, where her family lived for about five years, again to make enough money for the passage to America. They first went to Brooklyn, where my great-grandfather worked in a shoe factory, then moved to the Lower East Side, like so many others.

Grandpa Henry Gluck, on the other hand, was born in 1876 in Sečovce, Slovakia (then called Gálszécs, Hungary), and came to the United States as a toddler in 1879, with his parents and two younger siblings; they probably traveled in third class, where the ships transporting emigrants of the time packed them in like sardines.

His father was a seltzer man in Sečovce, selling fizzy water in glass bottles from a horse and wagon, going from house to house, replacing empty bottles with more bubbly. A local factory turned still water into seltzer with a gadget invented in England in the eighteenth century, infusing the water with carbon dioxide gas under pressure. Since the fizzy fad spread quickly from Europe to New York, my great-grandfather did the same in America. In the 1880s, when both my mother's parents were growing up in tenements, one on the Lower East Side and one in Harlem, they must have enjoyed a "two cents plain" of soda with an egg cream for a cent more, or with fancy flavorings like a bit of orange or raspberry. These drinks cooled everybody off, especially those who lived in overcrowded, hot tenements in the summer, before air-conditioning became available to those who could afford it, after World War II.

The oldest of thirteen, Grandpa was able to go to City College in New York before marrying my grandmother. Although they had only been in America for one generation, my mother's family seemed more American than my father's, because they had no foreign accent—just a New York one.

My grandmother's tiny hat store, called Kops, moved from the Lower East Side to the Upper West Side and then east to 550 Madison Avenue at Fifty-fifth Street. In the 1920s, the heyday of handmade hats, *The New York Times* announced when my grandmother went to Europe looking for new designs. The only memories I have of their style are the few hatboxes that were in my childhood attic and are now at the New-York Historical Society, and the old photographs of my mom, her sister, and their mother wearing the creations.

My mother as a little girl

Kops was located right next door to Henry Halper's Pharmacy, where as a child I would sit at the green marble counter. Mr. Halper—he was always called Mr. Halper—would serve me dainty white-bread sandwiches with the crusts removed, filled with egg salad, tuna fish, or with the combination of cucumbers, watercress, tomato, and butter. Why did they taste so very good? Perhaps because they were upper-class, which in those days meant Anglo-Saxon American. When Mr. Halper wasn't around, a liveried waiter assisted me into my chair. I learned later that Halper's was the preferred pharmacy of such personages as Winston Churchill, who always stayed at the nearby Waldorf-Astoria.

Every day at noon, my grandfather would go with friends in the millinery trade to the King Cole Bar in the St. Regis Hotel for a drink and a sandwich. "It catered to gentlemen only until

4:00 p.m.," he wrote me in a letter in 1973. "The drink at that time was Scotch and water. The bar was more like a club with conversation, jokes, kidding around and having lunch. It was relaxing." According to my grandfather, "The bartender just poured the Scotch into the glass with no jigger. Just a gentleman's drink." But there were more—a dry martini, gin, vodka, or a martini on the rocks. The head bartender, Pete (the nickname for Fernand Petiot), claimed to have invented the Bloody Mary in 1934. If Grandpa Henry did not show up at the bar, Pete would call to see if he was okay. Grandpa so loved his Scotch that he carried around a medicine bottle of Chivas Regal: he didn't trust other brands.

On Fridays, after work, Grandpa and Henry Halper would go to the bar for a second drink, then saunter up to Temple Emanu-El on Sixty-fifth Street to attend services. And even in the early 1970s, when Grandpa was in his nineties, he would take me to the King Cole Bar—when women were finally allowed in before 4:00 p.m.!

⊰────◉────⊱

So many of my memories of my visits to my Gluck grandparents in Manhattan are centered on food. But although my friends talked about their "bubbie's" great food, my grandmother worked and never cooked. Instead, I remember eating roasted chestnuts from peddlers on the street and raspberry Linzer cookies from Hungarian bakeries on Madison Avenue near the Metropolitan Museum of Art. My grandfather took us to Hungarian and German restaurants in Yorkville, and my father to French restaurants like his favorite, La Potinière, on Fifty-fifth Street. (It originally catered to the Michelin tire workers who came to New Jersey in the 1930s.)

My grandfather, who worked with Grandma at her hat shop, would also take me to the Horn & Hardart Automat on Fifty-seventh Street, where I loved putting a coin in the slot of the chrome box and miraculously watching the creamed spinach or macaroni and cheese come out, piping hot. As a young child, I never realized that a person was right behind the window putting in the filled plates. Horn & Hardart was a boon for people who needed to spend less than one dollar for a meal. It wasn't gourmet food, but it was delicious.

Limpa (Swedish Rye Bread)

I love to use this bread to make sandwiches, reminiscent of the ones I had as a child at Henry Halper's Pharmacy, only with a slightly more robust flavor. Use Persian cucumbers, with their skins intact, cut paper-thin. Spread labneh on a slice of bread, top it with the cucumber, a little dill, some watercress or alfalfa sprouts, sliced ripe summer tomatoes, and chopped roasted peppers.

When I lived in New York City in the 1970s, I adored this bread. I remember that Zabar's, the famed store founded by Louis and Lillian Zabar in 1934, procured it from a home cook or bakery in Bay Ridge, Brooklyn. Fortunately, they gave me the recipe years ago.

---

1. Add the yeast to 1¾ cups warm water (115 degrees), and stir until it's dissolved. Add the buttermilk, salt, molasses, brown sugar, butter, orange zest, anise seeds, and rye flour. Beat in a stand mixer fitted with the dough hook until the batter is smooth, then gradually add enough all-purpose flour to make the dough pull away from the sides of the bowl.

2. Transfer the dough to a large greased bowl, cover with a towel, and let it rise in a warm place for 1 to 1½ hours, or until the dough is almost doubled in bulk.

3. Sprinkle a little flour on a marble slab or wooden baking board. Punch the dough to deflate it, divide it in half, and shape it into two oblong loaves. Then put them on a baking sheet sprinkled with cornmeal. Using a sharp knife, cut four or five slits crosswise in the tops of loaves. Cover with a towel, and let the loaves rise for 45 minutes to 1 hour, or until almost doubled again.

4. Fifteen minutes before baking, preheat the oven to 375 degrees. Bake the loaves for 30 to 35 minutes, until lightly browned and hollow to the tap. Remove them from the oven, and cool them for 5 minutes. Set them on a wire rack to cool completely before slicing.

Note If you don't have buttermilk, use kefir, milk, or even water. It will still be delicious.

Makes 2 loaves

2 tablespoons active dry yeast
1 cup (236 ml) buttermilk (see note)
1 tablespoon kosher salt
¼ cup (85 grams) molasses
½ packed cup (100 grams) light-brown sugar
2 tablespoons unsalted butter, at room temperature
2 tablespoons grated orange zest
1 tablespoon anise seeds, crushed
4½ cups (540 grams) rye flour
3½ to 4 cups (455 to 520 grams) unbleached all-purpose flour, plus more for dusting
Cornmeal, for dusting

Creamed Spinach

1 pound (453 grams) raw
    mature spinach, kale,
    or Swiss chard (remove
    stems if using kale or chard)
2 tablespoons butter
¼ cup chopped shallots
1 tablespoon unbleached
    all-purpose flour
1 cup (236 ml) milk
1 teaspoon kosher salt
½ teaspoon ground white
    pepper
¼ teaspoon freshly grated
    nutmeg
Dash of Espelette pepper

I've always loved creamed spinach. Of course, I knew spinach from my home when I was growing up; we must have eaten it at least once a week. We kids all wanted to be strong like Popeye. But creamed spinach was another animal, and I loved its mild taste and texture; I've ordered it throughout my life at steak houses like the Palm, Morton's, or Ruth's Chris. Recently, Lisa Hurwitz, the director of *The Automat*, a documentary about Horn & Hardart, shared with me the original company recipe, reduced way down in portions for the *Daily News* in the 1960s. It is a simple dish, varied through the years with cream cheese and other products as they came on the market. Today you can make this dish with spinach, kale, or Swiss chard, or even make an entire meal out of it with pasta. I have added both nutmeg and Espelette pepper to my version to give the dish a little kick.

1. Wash the spinach, kale, or Swiss chard. Place it in a wok or other pan, covered, and cook over medium heat for a few minutes or until it has shrunk but is still green, using only the water that clings to the leaves. When it's done, plunge it into an ice bath, drain well, and chop fine.

2. Melt the butter in the same pan. Add the shallots, and cook until they're translucent. Gradually add the flour, stirring constantly until the roux is smooth. Slowly add the milk, and cook, stirring, until the sauce has thickened. Add the salt, pepper, nutmeg, and Espelette pepper. Then fold the spinach into the sauce, and serve.

Hungarian Chicken Livers with Onions and Red Peppers

A bon vivant, Grandpa Henry loved good food almost as much as he loved a good drink and, I imagine, a pretty woman. When I lived in New York just after college, working as a telephone girl in the NBC newsroom, Grandpa and I visited his favorite Hungarian restaurants on the Upper East Side, including Tik Tak, and discovered the Red Tulip, where I tasted delicious chicken livers, onions, and peppers for the first time.

When I tried to re-create this recipe, I emailed Mimi Sheraton, the longtime *New York Times* food writer and one of my mentors, who remembered the Red Tulip and their fish soup, but not the chicken livers. While testing the recipe on Martha's Vineyard, I was able to get very fresh, totally natural livers without the metallic flavor and mushy texture that keep many in my children's generation from loving them as I do. Cooked quickly at a high heat, they had a delicious meaty flavor that complemented the caramelized onions and red peppers, reminding me of my restaurant adventures with my grandfather. When trying to find takers for chicken livers, I was surprised at how some people remembered them from their childhood and were willing to try them again. And how meat eaters of the next generation loved this dish!

Serves 4 to 6

¼ cup (60 ml) olive oil

2 large onions, sliced into thin half-moons

2 red bell peppers, cut into 1-inch squares

1 pound (453 grams) fresh chicken livers, fibers removed, each cut in half

2 tablespoons sherry or white wine

2 teaspoons sweet paprika

Kosher salt and freshly ground black pepper, to taste

1. Heat the oil in a large nonstick pan, then sauté the onions until soft. Add the red peppers, and cook until the onions are caramelized, about 20 minutes. Remove the onions and peppers with a spatula, and set them aside.

2. Heat the pan again, and quickly sear the livers on one side, cooking for just a few minutes. Add the sherry or wine, and deglaze. Season with the paprika and salt and pepper to taste, then turn the livers and cook another minute, or until they are just pink in the center. Add the peppers and onions, adjust the seasonings, and serve alone or with rice.

My mother and me

My mother lived a charmed life until she was about to go to college. Bright and modern, she was the apple of Grandpa Henry's eye. She went horseback riding in Central Park and spent summers at the Raquette Lake Girls' Camp in the Adirondack Mountains. But in 1929, when she was in Julia Richmond High School, waiting to start at Barnard College, my grandparents' business crashed at the beginning of the Great Depression. Fortunately, she received a scholarship.

My parents met in 1934 at Copake Camp, a *Marjorie Morningstar*–like camp for twenty- to thirtysomethings in Craryville, New York, where Dad and some other bachelors from Providence went in search of wives from New York. It became famous for its entertainers, such as Liberace. Mother, who had recently graduated from Barnard, was freshly returned from a trip abroad with her father, the purpose of which was to try to talk some sense into her for being

involved with a much older man from Armenia who wasn't Jewish. Ernest and Pearl married during the Depression, in 1937, at my grandparents' apartment, which was then on Central Park West; they spent the night at the Hotel Pierre, took their honeymoon in Panama, where they traveled on a banana-shipping boat, and then settled in Providence.

Like so many immigrants, my mother's family seemed transient, trying to take part in the American dream and, in so doing, leaving the past behind. My mother used to say to me, when I was in my twenties and living in New York after college, that she and her parents had no nostalgia about either Europe or Broome Street on the Lower East Side, where my aunt Mildred was born from my grandmother's previous marriage. Once the family moved uptown to the Hotel Theresa on 125th Street, where my mother was born, they never returned downtown, not even for a visit.

The only job my mother ever had before she married my father was as a salesperson at Bloomingdale's. Mother did not cook much, at least in the early days. She even joked that she had made an agreement with Dad that she would never have to cook—an agreement that she could not keep, because new financial conditions eventually compelled her to cook our meals herself. But during my early childhood through the Larchmont years, Mother guided our cook to make her favorite dishes, the ones that she had learned from her aunts and instinctively wanted to pass down to the next generation, such as matzo-ball soup and sweet-potato casserole, and, from my father's family, sauerbraten and zwetschgenkuchen, German Jewish recipes she found in *The Settlement Cook Book* (my mother's cooking Bible, even after I had written eleven cookbooks!).

Mother was quite a character. She lived to the ripe old age of 103 and kept all her faculties until the very end. She attributed her good health and longevity to having a five o'clock strong rye on the rocks in winter, and a stronger gin and tonic in summer. In later years, she would not let me mix her drinks: according to her, I made them too weak. She seemed as American as my father was German. A great athlete, a star student, and a lifelong learner, my mother kept a tiny notebook in which she listed aphorisms to help her through life, a gift from her rabbi when she started college.

More than anything else, my mother set a great example of how to live. Just recently, I found a quote she wrote in a book given to her when she was eighty-eight: "I am one of the lucky ones," she wrote. "I enjoy every single day." As I near eighty, I think of her every day.

As I look back on my early life, I realize that I learned to love exploring the world of New York's foods from my mother's side of the family, while from my father's I learned the importance of knowing my own roots and the family recipes that kept memories alive.

My grandmother's dollhouse kitchen, circa 1865

3.

My Childhood Years: From Providence to Larchmont

February 16, 1956

Dear Diary,

   Today Judy Shuebruk and I went downtown because I needed some wax paper for Home Ec. We had hot fudge sundaes at the Candy Shop. Mrs. Morrison drove us over to Judy's. Ricky & Jeff walked home with me from there & then came over.

   After dinner on the phone Elly and I had a discussion on segregation. We think it's terrible.

February 18, 1956

Dear Diary,

   Judy & I woke up at 10:00 then she had to go to dancing school, so I came home.

   Then Steve, Tommy, Herb & Peggy came over. Then Judy. We played ping pong, played with the trains, & had a play fight. Some boys called up (I don't know who). I made dinner. Everything burned. I made chestnuts & attempted fudge (burned & didn't taste good!)

I n Larchmont, we lived in a large, stately white Tudor Revival house with wood trim, with our Southern Black housekeeper and cook, Susie Marbry, whom we adored, and who unintentionally taught me how to cook as I watched her make soul food, including corn bread and Southern fried chicken, and a one-egg chocolate birthday cake. My lifelong love of the Brooklyn Dodgers came from her, too; my mother was a Yankees fan.

   Susie slept in a two-room apartment above the garage; a few steps led to our bedrooms and a longer back staircase down to the kitchen, so we children could easily spend lots of time with her, especially at Christmas. I am sure that my mother paid for Susie's Christmas tree so that she could put gifts from Dad's Christian clients under it, and so my brothers and I would not feel totally deprived of celebrating Christmas the way our friends did.

Our kitchen featured a system of bells that we never used, except for the one in the dining room. (I can still see Susie sitting at a table under the kitchen bells as she snipped beans or shelled peas.) During dinner, my mother would press her foot on the carpet where a silent butler button was hidden—I could never understand how she found the button—to let Susie know when each course was over. When my parents were not there, we kids ate at a round table in what we called "the breakfast room." I have that table on my back porch today; my husband and I would eat there when we were alone in the spring and early summer.

The cocktail hour, and the time leading up to it, remains a vivid memory of Larchmont. My parents would retreat to the wood-paneled, book-lined study to watch the news on our Zenith television, a rarity at the time, with a cocktail glass filled with Scotch for my father and rye for my mother. In those days there were only ABC, NBC, CBS, and WNEW, and then WNYW before it became Fox. In those days, everyone thought the revered newsmen were totally trustworthy and neutral.

I can't remember what appetizers my mother served with the drinks, but I am sure there was Progresso canned eggplant caponata, one of the earliest tasty processed foods, introduced in 1942; or herring and cream sauce, probably on Ritz crackers. Before cocktail hour began, my brothers and I were allowed to watch the *Howdy*

Our Larchmont house in the winter

Doody show, beginning in 1947. Two years later, we watched *Captain Video, I Remember Mama,* and *The Goldbergs. I Love Lucy* didn't start until 1951. All the neighborhood kids would gather around to watch our black-and-white TV. I remember the box as being quite large, but it was really a tiny television screen. I often wonder if my parents thought that this new invention was a special way for us to integrate into the neighborhood.

During those early years, we'd go to New York every Thanksgiving Day to visit my mother's parents at 240 Central Park South, where my grandparents had moved to the orange Art Deco building at Columbus Circle where the restaurant Marea is today.

On Thanksgiving, my mother carried a freshly cooked turkey on a silver tray with stuffing made from a box bought at the local A&P grocery store in Larchmont. (I found some A&P spices from many years ago in Mother's kitchen in Providence—forty years after we had moved there.) As Dad parked the turquoise-and-white Oldsmobile, my brothers and I followed Mom, carrying homemade cranberry sauce, the classic string-bean casserole with canned mushroom soup and canned fried onions, and a marshmallow-topped casserole of sweet potatoes and canned pineapple. Dad finally arrived, carefully carrying Mother's double-Crisco-crusted apple pie. A perfect example of a homemade meal, but one made with the novelties of the postwar period.

After we deposited our food in the kitchen, we watched the Macy's Thanksgiving Day Parade from the twelfth-floor terrace, transfixed by the large rubber figures of Howdy Doody, Mickey Mouse, and other Disney characters simply floating in air, almost reaching our fingertips.

Many years later, I got into some trouble with a recipe I included in *The Jewish Holiday Kitchen*. A reviewer for *Kirkus* thought it was a stretch that I called such an essentially American dish as the sweet potato casserole with marshmallows an Eastern European tzimmes. The reviewer, who still gave the book a star, was correct: the dish was invented in 1917 by Janet McKenzie Hill, founder of *The Boston Cooking School Magazine*, who developed the recipe for the Angelus Marshmallows company as a way to market the newly mass-made confection to Americans.

In Providence, where we moved later, the Thanksgiving menu was the same as in New York, but we watched the Macy's Parade on television. The cast of characters changed through the years, with my father's relatives coming for lunch the day after the holiday, when my mother made franks and sauerkraut to go with the leftover turkey. Then, when my older brother, Alan, got married, the menu changed again slightly: he added creamed onions and mashed potatoes from his wife Ginny's family. When Allan and I married, in 1974, the menu changed yet again, with the addition of my mother's family recipe of chestnuts and prunes (in *The Jewish Holiday Kitchen*), and vegetables like Brussels sprouts replacing the canned-green-bean casserole.

Throughout my life, Thanksgiving has been a favorite holiday. We have always opened our doors to friends and new family members, and I watch as each new immigrant or new member of a family integrates spring rolls from Vietnam, pupusas from El Salvador, and yalanchi from Armenia into the meal, all surrounding the traditional American turkey. It is also a holiday that reaches all of us in this country. With so many things fragmenting our lives, what we eat, and the fact that we all sit down together on this day, is sometimes the only thing that connects us.

My Mother's Beef Stew

Throughout the rest of the year, on Sundays and Thursdays, Susie's days off, if we were lucky Mother would cook the one dish she knew—my grandmother Martha's beef stew. I remember its whiff so distinctly, redolent of the little bit of wine it was cooked with, and can still taste those big chunks of meat, carrots, potatoes, and sweet turnips.

As children, my brothers and I loved this dish, as much for the aroma and the plump carrots as for the memories. Now, whenever I smell a similar stew, I have a Proustian moment of thinking back to this part of my childhood. I've updated it by adding Aleppo pepper, which I adore, and by cooking the meat first, usually a day in advance, and then, before eating, adding the vegetables. This method yields tender meat and vibrant, almost al dente vegetables. Use bright-green Brussels sprouts and string beans, and, since this is a winter dish, add roasted chestnuts.

---

1. Put the flour, 1 teaspoon salt, ½ teaspoon pepper, and beef in a paper bag, as my mother did, or just mix the flour, salt, and pepper on a plate and use your fingers to toss the beef around in it. If you're using a paper bag, shake it to coat the beef, then remove the beef to a plate, shaking off any excess flour mixture.

2. Heat a Dutch oven or other heavy pan over medium-high heat; then add the olive oil and the onions. Cook for a few minutes; then add the meat and brown it on all sides. Add the beef bone or broth, wine, bay leaf, and a few thyme sprigs, and pour in enough water to barely cover. Simmer, covered, for about 2 hours, or until the meat is tender. Make sure you adjust the seasonings of the beef, and sprinkle with a little Aleppo pepper or paprika to give it some bite. If you like, you can do this step a day ahead.

3. When you're ready to serve, or when the meat is fork tender, bring a pot of water to a boil. Add some salt and the potatoes, turnips, carrots, and Brussels sprouts, and simmer for about 15 minutes; add the string beans and chestnuts after 10 minutes, and cook about 5 minutes more, or until the vegetables are tender. (You can save this water to use when making bread, a pot of beans, or even vegetable broth.) →

Serves 4 to 6

2 tablespoons unbleached all-purpose flour

Kosher salt and freshly ground black pepper, to taste

2 pounds (907 grams) stewing beef, cut into 2-inch chunks

3 tablespoons olive oil or vegetable oil

2 large onions, sliced

1 beef bone, or 1 cup (236 ml) beef broth

1 cup (236 ml) dry red wine

1 bay leaf

A few sprigs of fresh thyme

½ teaspoon Aleppo pepper or hot paprika, or to taste

4 medium russet potatoes, peeled and quartered

4 small purple hakurei or white turnips, quartered

4 robust carrots, peeled and cut into 2-inch rounds

4 to 6 Brussels sprouts

1 cup trimmed string beans

1 cup roasted and peeled chestnuts, sliced in half

4. If you cooked the meat the day before, reheat it; if just cooked, remove it from the Dutch oven with a slotted spoon to a serving platter. Reduce the gravy if it's too thin by heating the pot and scraping the bottom. Then pour half of it on the meat and put the rest in a gravy server.

5. Remove the vegetables with a slotted spoon and surround the beef with them; season the stew with salt and pepper to taste, and serve.

I also loved the dinners we had when we ventured out. We ate hamburgers and curly French fries at Cook's, on the Boston Post Road in Mamaroneck, with its giant arcade and a windmill outside. When my brother Alan started high school, we would often eat at Walter's Hot Dog Stand, located since 1928 in a Chinese pagoda-style building, which in 2010 was added to the National Register of Historic Places. No matter that the hot dogs were an "exclusive" blend of beef, pork, and veal. All we knew was that they were split down the middle, grilled in a "secret sauce," and served on a toasted bun with Walter's mustard: a mix of mustard seeds, relishes, and spices.

On most Sunday evenings, we would go for Cantonese food to Tung Ho, "the" Chinese restaurant in Larchmont. There was no Szechuan food then—that came later, after Richard Nixon's trip to China in 1972. My father loved the chop suey, moo goo gai pan, and egg foo yung, while we children preferred the egg rolls and the silky almond cookies at the end of the meal, which were probably made with lard (we never asked). On some Sunday mornings, for a special treat after Sunday school, Dad would take my brothers and me to Behrman's, a Jewish deli in New Rochelle.

At home, meals and menus were not negotiable, nor were good manners or proper dress. No jeans at meals, and no ketchup bottles allowed. Napkins—always cloth—must drape across laps. (To this day, I can't eat a meal without a napkin on my lap.) My mother sat at one end of the mahogany table covered in a carefully ironed cloth and my father at the other, with my big brother, Alan, on one side, between my parents. I sat on the other side, near my dad, and later, when my younger brother, Richard, came along, he would sit between my mother and Alan. Susie would bring dinner out from the kitchen on a cart, and my father would serve the food.

Dinners were always formal, with set menus, mostly from a 1950s edition of *The Settlement Cook Book*, put out by Lizzie Black Kander, a volunteer for the Settlement House of Milwaukee at the turn of the last century; the Dione Lucas cookbook of 1947; and *Thoughts for Buffets*, which came out two years after we moved back to Providence, in 1958. I also remember eating American dishes like tuna casserole with mushroom soup, what we called exciting noodles with onions, liver and onions, and Salisbury steak or flank steak. Every Friday night, we had bakery challah, though the menu varied—but mostly it was chicken soup with matzo balls, Grandmother's roast chicken seasoned with paprika and garlic salt, rice, vegetables, and a homemade pie or cake for dessert.

Savory Noodle Kugel

Serves 6

Butter, for greasing
8 ounces (227 grams) medium
    or wide egg noodles,
    preferably high-quality
    pappardelle
1 large head broccoli,
    cut into florets
1½ cups cottage cheese
    (with curds, not creamed or
    whipped), farmer's cheese,
    or ricotta cheese
1½ cups sour cream or labneh
1 large shallot, finely minced
1 clove garlic, chopped
1 tablespoon Worcestershire
    sauce, or a bit of fish sauce
Dash of hot sauce,
    such as Tabasco
1 teaspoon kosher salt,
    or to taste
Freshly ground black pepper,
    to taste
¼ cup grated Parmesan
    cheese
¼ cup sliced fresh chives

When Allan and I were in Budapest in the mid-1990s, I tasted a simple dish of noodles and túró, the Hungarian farmer's cheese, which reminded me of what my family called exciting noodles. Clearly, my mother liked the American rendition of this homey dish, one her own parents probably ate during their childhood in the Austro-Hungarian Empire, because she included it in the 1950 collection she edited, *Regard Thy Table, A Cook Book of Treasured Recipes,* from the Sisterhood of the Larchmont Temple. Today Jews would call it a noodle kugel, but it was known in Yiddish simply as "lokshen mit kaese" (noodles with cheese), eaten everywhere in Central and Eastern Europe.

In the 1940s, on the U.S. West Coast, the dish gained celebrity status. Hershel Geguzin came to America from Lithuania at age ten, eventually changed his name to Prince Michael Alexandrovitch Dmitry Obolensky Romanoff, and opened Romanoff's Restaurant in Beverly Hills. He adapted the recipe for this simple dish of poverty that he must have eaten in his home country, bestowing on it the lofty name of Noodles Romanoff. Soon his restaurant was so popular with the Hollywood crowd, such as Humphrey Bogart, Marilyn Monroe, and David Niven, that by 1952 the simple preparation was included in *Dishes Men Like,* a Lea & Perrins pamphlet with recipes that used their Worcestershire sauce. After the restaurant closed in 1962, Noodles Romanoff became a freezer-aisle staple marketed by Stouffer's, along with their Spinach Soufflé and Macaroni & Cheese, dishes that are equally as comforting. It was so popular that Betty Crocker also had a boxed version.

I've made a few changes to my mother's recipe—adding greens, something we always need more of—but I try to keep the same comforting feeling. In the 1940s and '50s, this was served as a side dish but, with the broccoli, it can also be served as a main, with a side salad.

1. Heat the oven to 350 degrees. Butter the inside of a 2- or 2½-quart casserole or gratin dish.

2. Meanwhile, bring a pot of water to a boil, add the noodles, and cook until they're al dente, about 7 minutes. After 4 minutes, add the broccoli. Drain the noodles and broccoli, put them into a medium bowl, and toss them with the cottage or farmer's cheese, sour cream, shallot, garlic, Worcestershire, hot sauce, salt, and pepper.

3. Spoon the mixture into the buttered dish, and sprinkle with the Parmesan and chives. Bake until golden and crusty on top, 35 to 40 minutes.

Note I like broccoli, but you could use spinach, chard, collards, kale, or even red or yellow bell peppers instead.

Rugelach

If I could list one of the most popular American cookies today, after chocolate-chip, snickerdoodles, and maybe gingersnaps, it would be the exotic jam-filled, crescent-shaped European rugelach. I can still see my mother, not necessarily a cookie baker, making a circular dough, spreading it with apricot, raspberry, or chocolate filling, then slicing and rolling up little crescents for Hanukkah each year.

The elegant cookbook writer Maida Heatter, whom I visited whenever I was on a book tour in Miami, popularized the recipe when it made star status in *The New York Times Magazine* on May 22, 1988, when Craig Claiborne and Pierre Franey introduced it to the larger American public as "a crisp, sweet Jewish delicacy called rugelach," and said that "one of the finest, most easily made pastries we know is a recipe from our friend Maida Heatter." She had seen the recipe in 1950's *The Perfect Hostess Cook Book,* written by Mildred O. Knopf, the sister-in-law of the publisher Alfred Knopf. Mrs. Knopf mentioned that the recipe came from Nela Rubinstein, wife of the famous pianist Arthur Rubinstein. I wouldn't be surprised if my mother clipped that same recipe.

It could have originated from many places, mostly in Central and Eastern Europe, where a yeast-risen (later made with baking powder) circle of dough with farmer's cheese was rolled out, cut like a pizza, smeared with jam, then rolled up, revealing little corners of jam- or chocolate-flecked dough. The word "rug" comes from the Polish *rog,* meaning "corner" or "horn." On this side of the ocean, Philadelphia Cream Cheese, butter, and flour became the normal crust, replacing the dryer yeast version, and the cookie became what we all love today.

Hazelnut Chocolate Meringue Torte with Strawberries

In 2017, when we were visiting our daughter-in-law Liv's family in Copenhagen, Eva, her mother, made a delicious meringue torte for us, similar to the schaumtorte of my childhood, a dessert the German part of my family served at Passover, but one that I always thought was too sweet. I loved that the hazelnuts and the dark bitter chocolate of Eva's recipe cut the sweetness of the meringue. Now it is part of our Passover Seder menu, though it also works beautifully throughout the year, especially for gluten-free friends. During the pandemic, when I was in New Orleans, I substituted local pecans for hazelnuts.

Serves 8 to 10

4 large egg whites
½ cup (100 grams) granulated sugar
1 cup (about 135 grams) hazelnuts, toasted and roughly chopped
6 ounces (170 grams) dark (70%) chocolate, cut with a serrated knife into bite-sized pieces (1 cup)
1 to 2 cups (about 180 to 360 grams) strawberries, hulled and sliced, for garnish
1 cup (236 ml) heavy cream, or one 15-ounce (443-ml) can full-fat coconut milk, chilled (do not shake)
Cocoa powder, for dusting (optional)

1. Preheat the oven to 350 degrees, and cut a parchment circle for a 10-inch springform pan, or line a sheet pan with parchment.

2. Whip the egg whites in a stand mixer at medium speed; after peaks begin to form, then slowly add the sugar. Beat until the mixture is shiny, with stiff peaks. (It is ready when you can turn the bowl upside down without having the egg whites fall.) Carefully stir the nuts and chocolate into the meringue, then spoon it into the prepared springform pan or in a rustic large circle (or six smaller circles) on the sheet pan.

3. Bake for 10 minutes at 350 degrees; lower to 300 degrees and bake 20 more minutes. Turn off the oven, and let the meringue cool in the oven.

4. Carefully move the meringue to a serving plate. Just before serving, cover it with sliced strawberries. Then whip the cream and spoon it on top. (If using coconut milk, scrape the layer of chilled cream from the top of the can, and whip it until fluffy; save the liquid remaining in the can for smoothies or soups.) You can also just dust the strawberries with cocoa, or serve as is.

Note If you live in a humid environment, your meringue is more likely to weep. To avoid this, stir 1 teaspoon potato starch or cornstarch into the sugar before slowly adding it to the egg whites.

Rhubarb Cream Sauce

Makes about 2 cups

2 medium stalks rhubarb
  (enough to make 1 cup),
  cut into 1-inch pieces
¼ cup (50 grams) granulated
  sugar
½ teaspoon finely grated
  lemon zest, plus
  2 tablespoons fresh
  lemon juice
1 cup hulled and quartered
  strawberries
1 teaspoon vanilla extract
1 cup (236 ml) heavy cream,
  chilled, or one 15-ounce
  (443-ml) can full-fat
  coconut milk, chilled
  (do not shake)

The hazelnut-chocolate cake is also delicious with this tart, creamy sauce when rhubarb is in season.

1. Heat the rhubarb, sugar, lemon zest, and juice in a small saucepan over moderate heat, stirring and mashing the rhubarb with the back of a wooden spoon until the sugar has dissolved and the rhubarb breaks down, about 10 minutes. Remove the saucepan from the heat, and stir in the quartered strawberries and vanilla. Let the mixture cool completely.

2. Beat the cream in a mixer until moderately firm. (If using coconut milk, scrape the layer of chilled cream from the top of the can, and whip it until fluffy; save the liquid remaining in the can for smoothies or soups.) Stir ¼ cup of the whipped cream into the cooled rhubarb, then fold the mixture into the remaining whipped cream.

Now, all these years later, I realize the fore-sightedness of my parents during this post-war period. Along with other couples in which one spouse was born in Germany, they became founding members of the Larchmont Temple.

Outside the classic American temple was written a quotation from Micah 6:8: "Do justice, love mercy and walk humbly with thy God." We discussed this in Sunday school at a time when Reform Judaism in America was prophetic Judaism—more than following the scriptures, Jews tried to lead an ethically moral life. I have carried those words with me every day, as well as the Shema, called the watchword of the Jewish faith, saying that there is one God, we must love him with all our heart, with all our soul, and with all our might, and we must teach these words to our children. I am so delighted that, from the day they brought their children home from the hospital, my daughter Daniela and her wife, Talia, have sung the Shema to their twins before putting them to sleep.

In the early days of the Larchmont Temple, Mom chaired a fund-raising project that became *Regard Thy Table, A Cook Book of Treasured Recipes,* with illustrations by Gertrude Blue, the mother of Anthony Dias Blue, the famous wine writer. When I first became a food writer, I could never understand why Anthony always reviewed my books for CBS Radio. When I finally thanked him, he said he was Andy Blue, my brother Alan's friend from Larchmont, and we had something in common: our mothers wrote a cookbook together.

It always seemed odd to me that my mother agreed to take on the chairmanship of this project, because she prided herself on not knowing how to cook. But she included lots of her family recipes as well as those from Susie and other women from Larchmont; all the recipe authors were, of course, referred to by their husbands' name, so hers were from Mrs. *Ernest* Nathan.

Larchmont had a reputation of trying to bridge the gap between people, even back then, but there were often slips of anti-Semitism. My first-grade boyfriend announced to me one day that he hated Jews (he probably didn't know what they were or that I was one of them). A seventh-grade teacher waxed nostalgic about a time when there were no Jews in Larchmont, and a classmate told me about a teacher asking "one of you Jewish children to talk about Hanukkah."

Because of this atmosphere, in those days not everyone in Larchmont advertised their Jewishness. One day, my father suspected that a neighbor who lived behind us was also Jewish. Dad, who knew nothing of bagels when he was growing up in Germany and only learned of them in America, decided to go to the Bronx, where we went to the dentist, who was also my mom's cousin. There Dad picked up some bagels—a rarity in those days—and brought them to our neighbors with some whitefish salad. If the neighbors knew what these foods were, they were Jewish, and if not, they weren't. They were so excited to see the bagels. This was just before the 1951 Broadway hit *Bagels and Yox.* Three years later, when Murray Lender came back from the Korean War at the time when freezing became a fad, his bakery—founded as a small bagel bakery in New Haven in 1927—started freezing bagels during the week. Lender's introduced their frozen bagels to the world in 1962. Today bagels have become so American that some of my children's and grandchildren's generation don't even know that today's large, mass-produced bagels have a Jewish origin.

Whitefish Salad

Makes about 2 cups

2 cups (473 grams) flaked
   smoked whitefish
1 stalk celery, minced
2 sprigs fresh dill, minced
½ small onion, minced
Freshly ground black pepper
Juice of 1 lemon, or more
   to taste
1 tablespoon mayonnaise,
   or more to taste
Bagels or crackers,
   for serving

At almost every Jewish celebratory or mournful gathering throughout my life, there has been some sort of whitefish. Unfortunately, most of them are smothered in mayonnaise. I want to taste the smoky, salty flavor of the fish, as well as the texture of the celery and the diced onion. I imagine the salad was once made this way in Central and Eastern Europe, purchased before the Sabbath from the appetizing store. And, of course, just as peanut butter and jelly went with sliced white bread in my childhood, this whitefish salad goes with sliced bagels.

---

1. Put 1½ cups of the whitefish into a medium mixing bowl. Finely mince the remaining ½ cup, then gently stir it into the flaked fish along with the celery, dill, onion, pepper, lemon juice, and mayonnaise.

2. Taste it, and adjust as you like, with more lemon or mayonnaise. I like this to be very light on the mayo—it shines with a lot of lemon. Serve with bagels or crackers.

January 21, 1955

Dear Diary,

  Today, Mommy, Bobbie Noble and I went to see "The Pajama Game" as a birthday present for me. It was marvelous. Before it we had a delicious lunch at a place called the Stage Delicatessen. I had a triple-decker corned beef, tongue, and turkey sandwich with chocolate cake for dessert.

Most of my life centered on friends and school in those years. In the seventh grade, at Mamaroneck Junior High School, one of my favorite subjects was home economics. Besides the tastes, I loved the math of measuring cups and tablespoons, and the easy results of making food. I can't remember what we made besides chocolate-chip cookies. While girls were taking home ec, boys were taking woodwork. Whenever I mention my love of home economics to Alice Waters, she frowns upon the title and says I should call the class "edible education," because home economics is so rooted in the 1950s, and it meant girls making cookies. She may be correct, but I still liked it.

Here I am, holding the Bluebird sign in the Memorial Day Parade in Larchmont in the early 1950s.

My Moment with Marilyn Monroe

One of the most unforgettable moments of my life came a week after my thirteenth birthday, in late January 1956, when my friends and I shook the hand of Marilyn Monroe, whom we met with Arthur Miller. It was after a surprise birthday party for me at a friend's during the day. In the late afternoon, a group of us were hanging out, as we often did, on the bridge at Brookside Drive and Fernwood Road, when Joel Braziller—son of George Braziller, the publisher—arrived, and excitedly bragged that Marilyn Monroe was vis-iting his parents and that she would be willing to say hello to us. Since she was then the most famous sex symbol in the world, we followed Joel to the house, where we filed in two by two to say hello and then leave.

Maggie Cammer—now a retired New York State Acting Supreme Court Justice—remembers that Marilyn was sitting at a dining-room table with her back toward the outside windows, wearing an off-white turtleneck top. The white shirt I remember, too, and her face looked so milk-white and soft. We went up to her to shake her hand, and she said to each of us in a breathy whisper, "It's so nice to meet you." We all remember her being just as she appeared in the movies. As we stood there, we thrust hastily torn scraps of paper that she signed in pencil, "Love & Kisses! Marilyn Monroe." Luckily, in those days I kept an autograph book, so I saved the signed piece of paper; I think I may have been the only one who did. Many years later, my husband, Allan, framed the autograph beneath an Elliott Erwitt photograph of the movie star.

The boys were so nervous, so starstruck that they did not wash their hands for days; while the boys swooned, I was thinking that Judy Shuebruk, one of our gang, was prettier than Marilyn Monroe. (Judy, whom I tracked down in San Diego, remembers Marilyn as perhaps a bit tipsy that night.)

All these years, Joel kept secret what happened after we left. "Later in the evening, I had gone to bed," he revealed to me recently. "The grown-ups were partying in our upstairs living room. There was a knock on my door, and a high-pitched female voice asked me if I would come and dance with her. I said yes and went into the living room and had my dance with Marilyn. She was wear-ing a bright-red deep-cut dress with spaghetti straps. I was before my adolescent growth spurt, so my head was on a level not with her head, but with a lower part of her anatomy, whose plainly visible absence of sag impressed me greatly. She was so physically radiant that I thought she might have been a higher order of being, an angel or something. That's about all I remember from our dance, after which I went back to bed. She and Arthur slept over, and I remember she looked great in the morning in a white top with bold horizontal stripes. She seemed genuinely friendly. I think she was impressed with people she thought were cultured or intellectual and wanted to associate with them."

A few hours later, the two drove away in their black Thunderbird, probably not thinking that all of us would remember this event for the rest of our lives.

Not long after, when Elvis Presley's versions of "Hound Dog" and "Don't Be Cruel" were all the rage, my idyllic childhood in Larchmont ended: we had to move back to Providence, because my father bought a chain of army/navy stores called the Gob Shops.

To this day Daniela, now in her forties, says that, in spirit, I never left Larchmont!

4.

Back to Rhode Island

For months before our move to Providence, I had been romanticizing this new city. I loved the idea of living in a more urban environment, with a drugstore and its soda fountain right around the corner from our new house. And I read in *The Bobbsey Twins* about towns with sidewalks—there were no sidewalks in Larchmont. But the day we arrived, I walked into the entry of our wooden-frame 1920s house on Providence's East Side . . . and I walked right out again. A somewhat spoiled thirteen-year-old, I did not want to be there because I had left all my friends behind and the house was so different from where I lived in Larchmont. So I let my poor parents know it. Change has always appealed to me, but not, I discovered, such long-term change. I am fine once I get accustomed, but initially moves leave me shattered. I have never forgotten the visceral reaction I had on that day.

Soon the Gob Shops turned out to be a financial disaster, so, to help out through my high-school and college years, Mother took some education courses at Brown. Eventually, she taught English at the Barrington High School, where she had a reputation for being very tough.

Susie came with us, but soon we couldn't afford to have live-in help, and she really missed New York. Consequently, Mother learned to cook, and to cook well. She made bread-and-butter pickles, her mother's Friday-night roast chicken, and many recipes that she clipped from *The New York Times* or *The Providence Journal* and that I found years later in her metal recipe box.

Although Mom was so proud of my cookbooks, if she wanted real authority, she turned to Donna Lee, the food editor of *The Providence Journal* as another real authority. After we moved from Larchmont, and until my mother's death in 2017, we always celebrated Thanksgiving in Providence. Once, I was assigned to bake a pumpkin pie. When I suggested substituting fresh pumpkin for canned, Mom literally stood over me, insisting that Donna Lee did not do that. I told her that I had written nearly a dozen cookbooks, but it didn't matter. I wasn't Donna Lee. It was the same with other recipes, until the day she died. *The Settlement Cook Book* was her cooking Bible—not my *Jewish Cooking in America*. How surprised and proud my mother would have been had she lived a little longer to see my book honored as a culinary classic by the IACP (International Association of Culinary Professionals) in 2017.

The move to Providence changed my mother's life for the better, even if she didn't have everything she had treasured before. As I sat on the chest freezer watching her cook, I learned that enjoying the daily process of living—including cooking—is what counts most in life. Mom delicately set the plums in concentric circles on top of the German butter crust for plum pie before Rosh Hashanah, or rolled out dough on a pastry board, smearing it with jam for Aunt Eva's cookies. And, of course, we kids put marshmallows on top of the sweet-potato casserole at Thanksgiving.

Fortunately, in the late 1960s, Dad bought Elmwood Sensors, a company that made thermostats for coffee machines as well as airplanes, helped by a Small Business Administration loan. He later told me, after his Gob Shops mishap, not to put money in any enterprise I didn't really understand.

Today, as I recall my childhood, I realize that my mother was a constant presence, whereas my father was kind of a shadow, but one to whom she always pandered, and whom she seemed almost to fear. But we kids relished our time with Dad, going to a golf range or a restaurant with him. In those days, mothers were such ever-present nourishers that we sometimes took them for granted.

When we moved, Dad's parents also left New York, where they had lived since coming from Germany before the war, to live with one of his older sisters, Lisl, in Rhode Island. Once a week, Dad ate lunch at Aunt Lisl's home in nearby Cranston. Whenever I accompanied him, I tasted German dishes like sweet-and-sour tongue, brains with capers, sausages sent from Schaller & Weber in New York, and the delicious Nuremberg butter cookies that my aunt Lisl would make in the winter, each batch nestled in a tin in the breezeway between the garage and her kitchen. These were early, very important meals for me, each one coming with a story of a long-ago, faraway place.

The adults reminisced about life in Germany before the war and then, speaking in German so I could not understand, related the horrific stories that had gradually come after the war. And we always listened to the Metropolitan Opera, my grandfather Rudolph smoking a big fat Cuban cigar after gingerly removing the label for me to wear as a ring.

When I reflect on my life growing up, it has seemed to me that multiethnic Providence was easier to navigate for all of us, especially my father. Although Jews were restricted from country clubs in both Larchmont and Providence in the late 1940s and '50s, Providence had its own Jewish country club and several synagogues. We went to Temple Beth-El, a Reform synagogue with a beautiful new building designed by the architect Percival Goodman. My father eventually became its president. I got confirmed there, but Reform Jewish girls did not get Bat Mitzvahed until the 1960s.

Ethnic enclaves were fascinating to someone like my dad, especially on picturesque Federal Hill with its Italian community, and at Ming Garden, our favorite Chinese restaurant in Providence, where we replicated the Sunday-night tradition of eating out that we had started in Larchmont.

My Mother's Chicken Cacciatore

When we lived in Providence, my mother learned to make chicken cacciatore. I do not know where she got the recipe—perhaps from an Italian living on Federal Hill. But it was and is delicious, a great everyday dish to which I have added French Basque Espelette pepper, Moroccan preserved lemon, and bright-green Castelvetrano olives for a festive, colorful, and delicious touch. I always use whatever leftover wine I might have in the kitchen, and try to make the dish a day in advance so the flavors meld.

---

1. Season the chicken with salt and pepper, and set it aside.

2. Heat the olive oil in a Dutch oven set over medium-high heat, and add the onions; cook, stirring often, until they're translucent, 10 to 15 minutes. Add the garlic, and cook until the onions take on a little color, about 5 minutes more. Remove them to a plate, and brown the chicken on all sides in the pan.

3. Add the onions back to the pan with the tomatoes, red peppers, Espelette pepper, oregano, 2 tablespoons of the parsley, the wine, and the chicken broth. Bring the liquid to a boil and simmer, covered, for about 40 minutes, or until the meat is so well cooked that it is tender and falling off the bone. Add the olives and the preserved lemon, and continue cooking, covered, just to heat through; then sprinkle the remaining 2 tablespoons of parsley on top. Serve alone or with pasta or couscous, something to sop up those juices.

Serves 4 to 6

4 to 6 bone-in, skin-on
    chicken thighs, breasts,
    or a combination
    (about 800 grams)
Kosher salt and freshly
    ground black pepper,
    to taste
4 tablespoons olive oil
2 medium onions,
    roughly chopped
2 cloves garlic, finely minced
One 15-ounce (425-gram) can
    whole tomatoes,
    or about 5 fresh tomatoes
    (18 ounces/510 grams),
    peeled and roughly chopped
2 large red bell peppers,
    cut into 2-by-½-inch strips
½ teaspoon Espelette pepper
1 teaspoon dried or
    2 tablespoons fresh oregano
4 tablespoons chopped fresh
    Italian parsley
1 cup (236 ml) white or
    red wine
1 cup (236 ml) chicken broth
1 cup green Castelvetrano
    olives, preferably pitted
1 preserved lemon
    (see page 251), seeded
    and diced

My father also discovered dives like Tweet Balzano's in nearby Bristol, where they sold spaghetti by the pound and clams by the bucket from a converted chicken coop. I loved accompanying him and Mother to these finds. My father, often aloof with us, opened up to the waiters, usually in their native language: he grew up in Germany, learned French in school, and worked in Italy for a few years before he came to the United States. Thus began my love of finding restaurants and studying languages.

In Providence, my mother became a docent at the Rhode Island School of Design Museum, eventually having the distinction of being their longest-serving volunteer. When she was a hundred, the museum opened a coffee bar and restaurant, naming it Café Pearl in her honor. She loved the museum and lunch café so much that that was where she had her last meal before she died, at the age of 103.

My father with his two sisters

Egg Salad with Smoked Salmon, Avocado, and Pickled Red Onions

My mother passed away shortly after my last book, *King Solomon's Table*, came out. Always impatient with the long incubation periods of every single book, she would say, "Enough is enough. Give birth to it already."

Before my last visit to her, I debated whether I should carry on the airplane the one advance copy that Knopf had sent me—it was so heavy. How glad I am that I did. When I arrived at Tockwotton, the nursing home in Providence to which we moved her at the age of a hundred, I gave her the book before she took her afternoon nap. At about five o'clock, I called her, because she hadn't called me yet. She said that she was reading the book and loved it. She was especially effusive and thankful that I had put in her mother's egg-salad recipe, a dish that she had never mentioned to me. I knew that Mom had not gotten along well with her mother, and that she had grown sad about that as she got older. I realized, then, that this 103-year-old woman thought that a recipe with hard-boiled eggs and spinach from the island of Corfu—a very different recipe from one from Kraków, Poland—was her mother's. I also realized she was happy that her mother would continue to be in our hearts and minds whenever we tasted the recipe.

The next morning, we visited the RISD Museum, where from her wheelchair she waved hello to all the guards and the museum's president, who was having coffee in the café. Mom and I ordered their smoked-salmon-and-avocado sandwich with delicious pickled red onions.

That night, she passed away.

Recently, I visited Australia and tasted a version of my grandmother's egg salad at three different Shabbat dinners, served with challah as the first course. Like my grandmother, the cooks were descended from Polish Jews. Their egg salad was as simple as I imagined my grandmother's to be, hard-boiled eggs with onions cooked in schmaltz, chicken or goose fat. When I came home, I updated the recipe, adding tarragon and/or chervil, two herbs that go well with eggs. I love this recipe, and I only regret that my mother could not have tasted it, to give me her always frank opinion, as she did for every single recipe in my books. I also think, knowing her as I did, that she would have incorporated Café Pearl's pickled onions, smoked salmon, and avocado into a →

Serves 6 to 8
(about 3 cups egg salad)

6 large eggs
¼ cup (60 ml) schmaltz, chicken fat, or olive oil
1 medium onion, diced
¼ cup chopped fresh chives or scallions
2 tablespoons chopped fresh tarragon or chervil
Kosher salt and freshly ground black pepper, to taste
6 to 8 ciabatta rolls, for serving
Watercress, for serving
Pickled onions, for serving (recipe follows)
Smoked salmon, for serving
Avocado, for serving

sumptuous sandwich with these eggs. Jews in Melbourne and Sydney serve this egg salad every single Friday night, usually alongside avocado salad, carrot salad, and hummus.

---

1. Put the eggs into a pot with cold water and bring the water to a boil. Simmer for 8 minutes, and leave the eggs in the water to cool until you can handle them. Then tap them against the side of the sink and peel them.

2. While the eggs are cooking, warm the chicken fat or oil in a small frying pan set over medium-high heat. Add the onion, and sauté it until it's golden, sprinkling with the chives or scallions in the last minute or so of cooking. Scrape this into a medium mixing bowl.

3. Chop the eggs, then add them to the bowl along with the tarragon or chervil, and salt and pepper. Taste, and adjust the seasonings.

4. Cut the ciabatta rolls in half, then spread with some of the egg salad. Add watercress, pickled onions, smoked salmon, and avocado to make a most satisfying sandwich.

Café Pearl's Pickled Onions

Makes about 3 cups

2 large red onions
2 cups (473 ml) apple-cider vinegar
⅓ cup (66 grams) sugar
1 tablespoon sea salt
1 tablespoon yellow mustard seeds

1. Using a very sharp knife, cut the onions in half vertically and then into long, thin slivers. Pack them into a 2-quart glass jar and set them aside.

2. Put the vinegar and 2 cups of water in a saucepan, and bring it to a boil. Add the sugar and the salt, and stir until they are dissolved. Remove from the heat, add the mustard seeds, and pour this over the onions. Put a lid on the jar, let it cool, then refrigerate overnight before using in salads, on avocado, on smoked salmon toast, or whatever you like. These keep in the fridge for weeks.

I went to Classical High School, which required an entry exam to get in. Providence natives liked to think it was their Boston Latin, the oldest public school still in existence. In those days, we had to take a test in every subject, every single day. Although I liked the academic rigor it gave me, I didn't like that we had no gym class at all. As far as I can remember, the only exercise I ever got was walking through the city up to Classical after taking the bus from my house on the East Side.

I remember all my teachers but Al Morro in particular, the football coach and ancient-history teacher. He taught us the concept of animus and anima in human beings, that each of us has both masculine and feminine traits. This made it so much easier for me to navigate my life, without always conforming to what my mother wanted of me.

In my high-school years I was occupied with many typical teenage pursuits, including boys. It seemed that I developed a type: Italian football players. One in particular asked me to wear his cleat around my neck, a matter of great significance. He was a terrific football player, quite handsome, but a lousy student. When the vice-principal of the school heard whom I was dating, he called my mother out of concern (he was also Jewish). She asked if my suitor was a nice young man and if I was acting, as far as he could see, as a young lady should. He said yes, but the boy was Italian. My mother stopped him by saying that as long as he was a decent human being she was quite content with whatever I did. That was that.

Senior year, 1961, I worked on the yearbook as layout editor and became one of two Miss Caduceuses, the highest honor for our class. The caduceus was a staff borne by the Roman god Mercury (or Hermes in the Greek version), messenger of the immortal gods. The yearbook text for Miss Caduceus read, "Joan, a distinctive and well-liked member of our class, has enlivened our class clubs, and parties, with her spirit and sophistication. Her many successes in activities, her large circle of friends, and her warm humor have made her more than worthy of the title, Miss Caduceus."

I also sang in the a cappella choir, volunteered at the John Hope Settlement House, and was president of Councilettes, the junior arm of the National Council of Jewish Women. The council was founded in the fall of 1893, and by 1900, there were 7,080 members in fifty-five cities, helping support the rights of women, especially to vote, as well as schools for poor Jewish children.

I learned later that chapters of the National Council of Jewish Women also wrote some of the first local Jewish cookbooks at the end of the nineteenth century. And, of course, they held cooking classes in the settlement houses, such as Lizzie Black Kander's in Milwaukee. Local council cookbooks were published nationwide, with the proceeds used to help support local projects. Like *The Settlement Cook Book,* these books often had a German slant and included many goose recipes as well as more typically American dishes of the period such as chicken chow mein—often made from leftover chicken soup—and Saratoga chips, turn-of-the-century potato chips. I am sure my mother learned to make her coleslaw from *The Settlement Cook Book* with tips from our cook, Susie.

My Mother's Coleslaw

☞·

Serves 6 to 8

☞·

For the Slaw

½ medium cabbage

6 Brussels sprouts

1 medium kohlrabi bulb,
    peeled (optional)

1 medium carrot

1 green bell pepper

½ small red onion

½ jalapeño or other hot
    pepper

1 teaspoon kosher salt

½ teaspoon freshly ground
    black pepper

For the Dressing

⅓ cup (79 ml) fresh orange
    juice

2 tablespoons mayonnaise

1 tablespoon yellow or Dijon
    mustard

2 tablespoons sweet pickle
    juice, plus 5 pickle chips,
    chopped (preferably from
    bread-and-butter pickles)

1 teaspoon celery seeds

Up to 1 tablespoon sugar,
    if needed

I can still see my mother carefully slicing cabbage by hand into paper-thin shreds, even after the Cuisinart entered our lives in the early 1970s, advertised as a machine that would make coleslaw and potato pancakes a breeze.

This is my take on Mom's delicious coleslaw, with her secret ingredients in the dressing of orange juice and the juice from sweet bread-and-butter pickles, which perk it up and make it slightly sweet, but not too much. Letting the sauced slaw sit for a day helps the flavors meld together and the cabbage to wilt nicely. Every summer, Mother would make sweet pickles out of the cucumbers in her garden, but any sweet pickle juice will do. She used the food processor to slice them ever so thin, a recipe she learned from a World War II pamphlet sent out to housewives to promote the war effort at home by making their own foods.

I am very glad I asked her to tell me the dressing for this dish, because it is a flavor that I remember so fondly from my childhood. Although I have not tampered with that memorable sauce, I now pulse all sorts of vegetables like Brussels sprouts and kohlrabi from the cabbage family, adding them to the slaw, as they are so fresh in the summer.

---

1. Thinly shred the cabbage and Brussels sprouts with a sharp knife or the shredding blade of a food processor, and put them into a large bowl. Using a food processor fitted with a steel blade, pulse the kohlrabi (if using), carrot, bell pepper, onion, and hot pepper, each separately, for about 8 to 10 pulses each, just to finely chop them—don't go too far. (You can also finely chop them with a knife.) Tip each into the cabbage bowl as you go.

2. Sprinkle the salt and pepper over the vegetables, and toss to mix. Let the mixture sit while you prepare the dressing: Stir together the orange juice, mayonnaise, mustard, pickle juice and pickles, and celery seeds. You should have about ½ cup of dressing. Pour it over the slaw, and toss to coat. Taste, and, if you'd like it a little sweeter, sprinkle in up to a tablespoon of sugar. Let the slaw sit at room temperature for about an hour; then cover it, and refrigerate for up to 3 days.

5.

Broadening Horizons: From Summer Camp to Summer Abroad

Summers have always been special to me, beginning with family trips to Narragansett Beach in Rhode Island when I was still a toddler. After we moved to Larchmont, my mother had me start at the camp she had gone to and adored—Raquette Lake Girls Camp—at the age of six, which proved much too early. Given the postcards of misery that I sent home to my parents, it is no wonder that they decided to let me stay home for a few years and go to Badger Day Camp, right near my house, then switch to an overnight Camp Fire camp, where I could go for a few weeks instead of a whole summer. For the rest of the summer, we rented a beach house in Bristol, Rhode Island, where I learned the preliminaries of tennis, a love for which I have had ever since.

After we moved back to Providence, my parents sent me to Kiniya, a horseback-riding camp on Lake Champlain, near Burlington, Vermont, where every girl rode every day, in addition to swimming, playing tennis, sailing, and engaging in other sports. Mimi Williams, the gentle yet firm owner, visited the bunks on her palomino horse, coaxing the homesick campers to get out of their cabins and involved in an activity. Instead of forcing us to swim or ride, Kiniya had us choose, the big incentive being a system of acknowledgments of basics and intermediates awarded weekly, and vanguards awarded to the very few who really excelled on Awards Night at the end of the summer.

When I was sixteen in 1959, my parents felt that I should do some public service, and instead of returning to the peace of Camp Kiniya, I was encouraged to volunteer at Hidden Valley, a Herald Tribune Fresh Air Fund Camp near Ridgefield, Connecticut. It was a great experience for me, entering an amazing world of African American children from the inner city of New York, as well as meeting counselors from diverse backgrounds and helping to take care of children with handicaps.

My closest friend at the camp was a girl my age who wanted to become a doctor. Her name was Kathy Boudin, and later, in protest against the Vietnam War, she became instead a member of the Weather Underground. We spent many weekends together the winter of our sophomore year of high school, having sleepovers in Providence and New York. We wrote for a few years during college, and then lost touch. I only learned what she had been up to when, in March 1970, members of the Weather Underground accidentally blew up a house on Eleventh Street in New York City; Kathy and Cathy Wilkerson disappeared for a decade.

Kathy emerged in 1981, with her participation in the Brink's armored car robbery in Nanuet, New York, in which three people were killed. Kathy drove the getaway truck. When she was in prison, for twenty-two years, I wanted to contact her, but I did not. As a young mother I couldn't understand what Kathy had done, so I started letters but never finished them. Years later, after

Kathy got out of prison, a mutual acquaintance gave me her cell-phone number and I called her. The next time I was in New York, we reunited dramatically in Times Square, hugging each other for a few minutes.

Kathy wanted to hear about my career, and told me that while she was in prison she often thought that when she got out she would want to learn to cook. I gave her my latest cookbook, and through the years we reconnected. In prison, Kathy taught inmates how to read, and got a Ph.D. from Columbia; she continued to teach and help others until her death in 2022. There is something about the language of old friends. Either you have nothing more in common after being separated for so many years, or your shared history creates a real bond.

At about the same time I met Kathy, in 1959, my father insisted that I learn French fluently, as he thought every educated young lady should. He wanted me to become truly proficient, and so he sent me to France the summer of 1960, after my junior year of high school.

During that year, I took French lessons from Marie Baghdadi, the mother of a family that came to Providence in 1956 as refugees from Cairo (because of the Suez Crisis, involving Great Britain, the United States, Israel, and France). My dad thought he could kill two birds with one stone: he wanted me to learn to speak French and also to help the Baghdadis, who had just

arrived with the assistance of HIAS, the Hebrew Immigrant Aid Society. So I visited Madame Baghdadi—who grew up speaking French—once or twice a week, finishing off each lesson with the buttery ghoribiya cookies that I love to this day. Although I growled a bit before going each week to work with her, I am so grateful to them both for the expertise I now have in French, something that has helped me throughout my life. Eventually, I became fluent, and I could read French recipes in the original text and speak directly with French chefs who had trouble with the English language—great tools to have in the world of food.

Ghoribiya (Egyptian Butter Cookies)

Makes about 36 cookies

1 cup (2 sticks/226 grams)
    unsalted butter, at room
    temperature, or 1 cup
    vegetable oil

1 cup (114 grams)
    confectioners' sugar

1 cup (100 grams) almond
    flour

2 cups (250 grams)
    unbleached all-purpose
    flour

Pinch of salt

1 teaspoon ground cinnamon

About 20 blanched almonds,
    split in half (may also
    use pine nuts)

So many cultures have their version of ghoribiya, shortbread-like butter cookies sometimes made with crushed almonds, which literally melt in your mouth. Through the years, I've noticed similar confections: when I visited the Greek Orthodox archbishop in Jerusalem and tasted their kourambiedes; at Jerusalem Mayor Teddy Kollek's home, where the signature baked good prepared by his wife, Tamar, was Viennese kupferlin (almond crescent cookies); the Moroccan ghouribi, also with almonds; and polvorones (from Mexico and Spain), which are quickly becoming part of American culture. Fortunately, I was able to track down Madame Baghdadi's son, who shared this beloved recipe with me.

1. Beat the butter and sugar until smooth in a stand mixer fitted with the paddle attachment, about 3 minutes. Add the almond flour, all-purpose flour, salt, and cinnamon, and mix on low speed for about 3 minutes, until the dough is like moist sand and sticks together when pinched. Refrigerate it for 30 minutes.

2. Preheat the oven to 350 degrees and roll the dough into little mounds the size of Ping-Pong balls, and place them on the baking sheets. Press an almond half or a pine nut into the center of each ball. Bake the cookies until they're firm to the touch but still white, 17 to 20 minutes. Let them cool on the baking sheets.

When I come home, we must eat differently. I am going to make you some strictly French meals.—I want to eat loads of yogurt! It is so good and healthy. . . . We had cold artichokes, Mom. They are practically given away here. One night we had the most delicious cheese! Our food will be European 'cause Dad and I are European at heart, n'est-ce pas?

—*Letter to my parents from Grenoble, France, 1960*

I was seventeen when I went to France and had my first adventure abroad. I went to live with a family in Grenoble and studied French language and literature at the university, and this was where I first ate zucchini, learned new ways of cooking eggplant, and sipped a sour citron pressé. For several weekends I also visited the family of Rudolph Moos, my father's distant German cousin, and his family, who had moved from Germany to the beautiful Lac d'Annecy in Haute-Savoie in 1938.

The first time I visited the Moos family, when we sat down to what I thought would be a light meal of a tuna salad and a variety of fresh vegetables, I casually commented that this was a nice light lunch. Robert, the eldest son—who spoke English, having studied at Mercersburg Academy in Pennsylvania—informed me that this was only the first course. Then came meat, potatoes, and another salad. Of course, I ate everything. Although I was shocked that the meal stretched on and on, from that moment I was hooked on the French way of eating. Even the snacks: when Ruth, Rudolph's wife, took me hiking in the nearby Alps with Richard, their youngest son, I learned the pleasure of picking raspberries along the trails, then sinking my teeth into the slightly melted bar of dark chocolate sandwiched into a crackly baguette. As far as I was concerned, French food only got better and better.

I am safely on the train now for Venice. I just finished my breakfast—a huge juicy Italian peach. An old Italian man just jumped across the aisle & asked me why I am writing with my left hand—In Italian of course—Capito—now everyone is staring—oh, the joys of being different!

—*Letter to my family, August 24, 1960*

Ruth, in her quiet way, gave me an education well beyond mere language. In her kitchen she exposed me to dishes such as gratin dauphinois (a local regional potato specialty), creamed spinach with a béchamel sauce, onion soup, the poached local fish (salmon trout from Lac d'Annecy) with a mousseline sauce, and delicious tarts and tortes made with plums, apples, and other fruits.

Because she was one of less than a handful of Jews living in the picturesque town of Annecy at the time, it took a great effort for Ruth to maintain her Jewish identity. She told me that, with no shochet (kosher slaughterer) available, she personally taught the butcher how to prepare local chickens in the kosher manner. Then, at home, her maid would pluck them before cooking. At Passover, the butcher would find her a kid (young goat) to roast.

Each Passover and Rosh Hashanah, her daughter Eveline remembers, they had a carp swimming in the bathtub for days, in the only bathroom for six people. Ruth would make an accompanying sauce with parsley, or one with gingersnaps and lemon, similar to the one the German side of my family served. She also made berches each week for Shabbat. As she got older, she taught the local baker how to twist a baguette or miche—a large loaf made with whole grains—into braids, bringing with her poppy seeds to sprinkle on top. (The bread is still available in Alsace-Lorraine; both versions were less sweet than our American challahs.) I loved all that I was learning from this strong, modest woman.

Since I grew up in the comfort of the United States, the Moos family's story had a profound effect on me. I was taken with the art, architecture, and food of France, but it was spending time with Ruth—and, on subsequent visits to Annecy, visiting the kitchens of North African Jews—that taught me the power of listening to people's stories and writing them down. And because I visited France on so many occasions, I also have seen the changes that have occurred even in small towns in France—immigrants invigorating the mix of the population as well as the food served in French homes.

But on this first visit to Annecy, during the summer of 1960, I was too young to think of anything other than French people and food. The Tunisian and other North African Jewish immigration had begun in 1958 and was in full swing. The memories of World War II were still too raw for the Moos family for them to convey to me the horror of the Holocaust. I was merely a seventeen-year-old American girl on an adventure, exploring the outside world; I did not understand how the nuances of history affect us all.

Gratin Dauphinois (Scalloped Potatoes)

1. Preheat the oven to 400 degrees, and position a rack in the upper third of the oven. Rub a 6-cup oval gratin baking dish with the garlic clove and grease the dish with butter. Then cut up the clove and scatter the pieces of garlic in the dish.

2. Cut the potatoes into ⅛-inch-thick slices, dropping them into a bowl of cold water as you go, to prevent discoloring. Drain and dry the potatoes on a towel, then arrange half of them in the bottom of the dish. Season them generously with salt and pepper, half of the cheese, and 1½ tablespoons of the butter. Top with the remaining potatoes, season the potatoes with salt and pepper, top with the remaining cheese and butter, then finish with the milk.

3. Set the dish in the oven and bake for 30 to 40 minutes, or until the potatoes are tender, the milk has been absorbed, and the top is nicely browned, checking to make sure the potatoes are submerged in liquid.

Note For a special occasion, you can also salt and pepper the potatoes and layer them, standing on their sides, in a decorative manner. Dot with the cheese and butter, pour the milk over them, and bake for 30 minutes or more until they are tender, and the liquid is reduced and golden brown.

Serves 4 to 6

1 clove garlic, peeled
4 tablespoons unsalted
   butter, melted, plus more
   for greasing
2 pounds (907 grams)
   medium russet potatoes,
   peeled (about 4 or 5)
Kosher salt and freshly
   ground black pepper,
   to taste
4 ounces (133 grams) grated
   good-quality Gruyère cheese
1½ cups (355 ml) whole milk
   or, even better, cream

Fifty years later, during a visit when I was researching my book *Quiches, Kugels, and Couscous: My Search for Jewish Cooking in France,* I learned what the whole family had gone through during the war. At the home of Robert Moos and his wife, Evelyne, bordering the beautiful lake, we had a lunch of a lamb and vegetable stew. Afterward Robert took me on a journey back to places where he had lived during the war, a voyage he had not taken since he was a child. We visited a château where he and other children were sequestered, in the hope that they could be smuggled by the Red Cross into Switzerland, and we drove up to a tiny village in the Alps where he was hidden, and where the mayor and the priest made the townspeople promise, no matter what, not to turn in the Jews. He talked with townspeople who remembered his family. I saw these encounters through the eyes of a ten-year-old boy in the body of an eighty-year-old man.

Robert, the eldest of four, told me about nights they had spent with his father as the storm was gathering before World War II, in the basement of their beautiful stone home, also on the edge of the lake, wrapping boxes of sardines, cheese, and anything else that wouldn't spoil too quickly, along with old clothes, and then shipping them off to Jews, many of whom were confined to detention or internment camps. (Nine thousand Jews were held in these camps in France, practically without food, which they were supposed to provide for themselves, despite not being allowed to leave the camps.) Later, when the Vichy government took control in 1942, the Mooses helped Jewish refugees flee to Switzerland, housing up to twenty-seven guests in their home for extended periods.

By September 1943, the Mooses, too, had to flee, moving from place to place to save their lives.

Rudi, Robert's father, worked for the Resistance. After Eveline, Robert's sister, was born, on September 2, 1943, Ruth took shelter in a small hotel near Annecy. The Gestapo stopped at the police station, looking for the Mooses; the police entertained them and warned Rudi that they were coming. "My father headed to the butcher, who protected him under the floor, beneath a trapdoor," Eveline told me. "When my mother saw the Citroën of the Gestapo approaching, she left me, went into the next room, and scurried down the back steps." The Gestapo were surprised to find the baby Eveline. "As soon as they left, my mother snatched me up and was able to steal away; she walked twenty-nine kilometers [about eighteen miles] to La Roche-sur-Foron, where our banker would know how to help us."

Meanwhile, the midwife who had delivered Eveline dressed Rudi like a woman and drove him to La Roche. When they passed a guard, he waved them on, though not before saying, "The next time you need to pass a checkpoint, make sure to trim the hair on the 'woman's' fingers." Finally, the family reunited in La Roche, where Robert became a boarder at the school.

After the war, Rudi became the titular head of the tiny Jewish community. Then, in the late 1950s, when so many people were hightailing it out of North Africa, the mayor came to Rudi for help. Within months, Rudi and the Joint Distribution Committee had helped the practically nonexistent Jewish community burgeon with sixty families, a synagogue, ritual bath, cemetery plot, and jobs in Rudi's hardware business. And, by his side, Ruth helped all these refugees find apartments, get work permits, and lead lives as new French citizens.

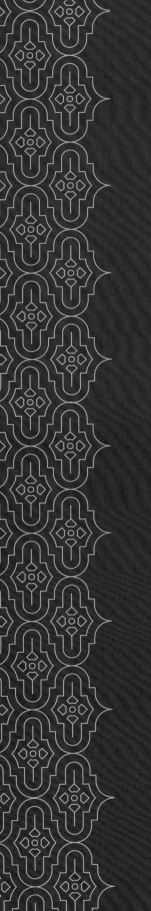

6.

University Years

Ann Arbor Schnecken (Pecan Sticky Buns)

The baker Frank Carollo also tasted the pecan rolls from Drake's when he was a student at Michigan. He later became co–managing partner at the Bakehouse, the second business in the Zingerman's empire. Frank learned to make pecan rolls, as did I, from Michael London of Mrs. London's Bakeshop in Saratoga Springs, New York. Michael learned about these schnecken (their German and Yiddish name) from the greatest of teachers, the late William Greenberg of William Greenberg Desserts in New York. Whenever I make these pecan sticky buns, cutting them into two circles and grilling them with butter, I remember the taste, and the carefree years at my alma mater.

The buns reheat well from room temperature (even if they've been frozen). Make them over two days; the dough is very soft, but that's not a mistake.

---

1. **To make the dough** Combine the milk, yeast, and flour in the bowl of a stand mixer fitted with the paddle attachment, and mix for a minute at low speed. Then add the butter, sugar, and salt, increase the speed to medium, and beat for another minute, until the mixture is creamy, scraping down as needed. Now add the whole egg and egg yolk, mix until they're incorporated, and scrape down the sides of the bowl. The dough will be sticky. Scrape it onto a sheet of plastic wrap, cover, and refrigerate it overnight (or for at least 6 hours).

2. Preheat the oven to 325 degrees, grease a 9-by-13-inch baking dish, and line a baking sheet with parchment paper.

3. **To make the filling** Mix the sugar, cinnamon, and salt in a small bowl.

4. **To make the topping** Beat the butter and sugars in the bowl of an electric mixer until creamy, then mix in the honey and salt.

5. Toast the pecans on the prepared baking sheet at 325 degrees for about 6 minutes, until fragrant. Spread the topping on the bottom of the baking dish, then spread the pecans evenly over that.

6. **To assemble and bake** Unwrap the chilled dough, and put it on a floured surface. Dust the top with flour. Roll into a 9-by-12-inch →

Makes 12 sticky buns

For the Dough
½ cup (118 ml) whole milk, at room temperature
2 tablespoons active dry yeast
2 cups plus 6 tablespoons (320 grams) unbleached all-purpose flour, plus more for assembly
½ cup (1 stick/113 grams) unsalted butter, at room temperature
¼ cup (50 grams) granulated sugar
1½ teaspoons sea salt
1 large egg, plus 1 large egg yolk

For the Cinnamon Sugar Filling
¼ cup (55 grams) packed muscovado or dark-brown sugar
1 tablespoon ground cinnamon
Pinch of sea salt

For the Topping
1 cup (2 sticks/226 grams) unsalted butter, at room temperature
½ cup (100 grams) granulated sugar →

¼ cup (55 grams) packed muscovado or dark-brown sugar

¾ cup (255 grams) good-quality honey

1 teaspoon sea salt

2 cups (240 grams) chopped pecans

Unsalted butter, melted, for brushing

rectangle that is about ¼-inch thick. Brush off any excess flour from the top and bottom of the dough, then arrange it with the long edge facing you. (Since the dough is so soft, it may expand beyond the initial dimensions, but do your best to keep it contained.) Brush melted butter over the surface, then sprinkle the cinnamon-sugar mixture over almost the entire surface, leaving 1 inch bare along the top long edge.

7. Starting with the edge closest to you, roll up the dough, keeping it as snug as possible. Once it's completely rolled, pinch the far edge into the log to make a seam. Roll the log so the seam is on the bottom, then cut it into twelve equal slices. Arrange all the slices on the sticky topping, putting four rolls lengthwise and three widthwise. Press the rolls down until they're ¾-inch thick. Put the pan on a parchment- or foil-lined baking sheet (in case of spillage), cover the rolls with plastic, and let them proof for 1½ to 2 hours, until they've risen by 50 percent.

8. Thirty minutes before baking, preheat the oven to 375 degrees. Bake the rolls for 30 to 35 minutes, until the buns are golden on top and the filling is bubbling below.

9. Cool for 5 minutes, then place a sheet tray or serving platter on top of the pan. Carefully and swiftly flip to invert the sticky buns onto the tray, then remove the pan. Let them cool for a few more minutes. Eat warm. (If necessary, reheat them from room temperature.)

7.

My Junior Year in Paris

Quel bateau! For lunch we had une omelette Lyonnaise, le veau escalope, les haricots verts du fromage du vin du café. We had a discussion about biology and physics. We do have the best table, I would say. At dinner I sat next to one of the French men who explained many of the social amenities to me. We had lobster, duck, les petits pois, le fromage. There are at least 7 courses but it's impossible to choose all of them. We finished with champagne which was délicieux.

—*First letter from Paris to my parents, 1963*

As I stand on my balcony watching all the housewives putting the wine bottles and baguettes of bread on their respective tables, I become hungry. Not wanting to eat until later, I decided to write.

—*Letter from Paris to my grandfather, 1964*

Studying at a cafe on Boulevard Saint-Michel in Paris, 1963

In 1963, I went to Paris for my junior year of college to attend the Cours de Civilisation Française at the Sorbonne. It seems to me that I learned much more about French civilization that year than I did about French language and history. It was such a formative time in my life, and as I write this, almost sixty years later, during the pandemic, I am saddened by so much in all our lives, but especially that students will not have their own experience living abroad and fending for themselves for the first time. During normal times, studying abroad is easier these days, because there are so many programs for students. (But on the other hand, cell phones and the Internet mean students today stay more connected to their homes.)

Before my father would let me go to France, he insisted that I spend the summer taking typing lessons. "No one has to know you know how to type," he told me. (In those days, knowing how to type meant your boss would treat you as his secretary.) "But the skill will come in handy for the rest of your life." He was right. Typing helped me as a journalist and helped me write long letters home from my travels to my family. Now, with the computer indispensable for all of us and typing taught in school, I am surprised to see people who didn't learn to type, still pecking at the keys, using just one or two fingers.

In the fall of 1963, I traveled to Le Havre on the SS *France,* which was packed with students in second class. Lucky for me, I knew several who were going to graduate programs in London and Paris. My roommate, however, was a returning Frenchwoman named Isabelle d'Audiffret, who had been working in New York. On the voyage over, I was introduced to such delicacies as Dover sole, foie gras, and tarte Tatin, the French apple tart. I danced way into the night, and described it all in raptures to my parents.

We met his roommates and drank some creme de cacao! Affreux! One fellow was studying the organ in London and the other was on a Fulbright to London. Then the 5 of us went for a cocktail and the English girl and I went down to wash up for dinner.

. . .

Finally after 2 more drinks I went to sleep at 3 a.m. This morning I woke up at about 8:45 and my roommate and I showered and went for le petit déjeuner—les croissants et brioches et café.

. . .

After I got dressed I went on deck and sat with 2 jeunes hommes—the one from Harvard Law and a phd in history who is on a Fulbright. A Swede joined us and we talked until lunch. We discussed Ingrid Bergman auf deutsch—la guillotine—la mort—le dieu—t'was fun.

—*Letter to my family, September 20, 1963*

During the crossing, a waiter on the boat befriended a few of us who were headed to Paris. He told us that he had an apartment to rent, gave us the keys, and asked us for money in advance. We naïvely gave it to him. When we arrived late at night from a train from Le Havre and took a taxi to the address he had given us, there was no such apartment, it was pouring, and we had no place to go. Finally, after realizing the scam, we were somehow able to find rooms at the Hôtel de Suez, in the Latin Quarter. Not only was it dark and dirty, but we had to pay five francs for a shower. (I understand it gets better marks now.) Mostly, I just felt so completely alone.

That morning, I called Madame Juliette Cerf, as Rudi Moos, my relative in Annecy, had instructed. She introduced me to her daughter, Nanou, a very charming, fashionable, and fabulous young woman who became a lifelong friend, and her son Bertrand, who became like a brother to me. The two escorted me to the pension for "Israëlites" (Jewish girls) suggested by the Mooses for a proper young lady. The moment I arrived at the dreary building in the suburb of Neuilly and met the woman in charge, who told me all the restricting rules, I knew it was not for me.

In desperation, I called Isabelle, my roommate from the boat, who invited me to look at the fifth-floor garret maid's room in her family's *hotel particulier* (private mansion) on Avenue du Général Mangin, in the stylish Sixteenth Arrondissement. Isabelle's erstwhile wealthy noble family, connected to English royalty, had built the house in the nineteenth century. Since then, the family had fallen into hard times and, like so many others, was renting the top-floor rooms to students. I fell in love with the tiny, charming room, with its slightly faded wallpaper pleasantly decorated with roses, and its curtained balcony with a black wrought-iron railing matching the one on the ground floor enclosing the house. It had a single bed, a tiny sink, and a table for writing, which I fortunately did throughout the year—both religiously in my diary in French, and with letters home to my family.

I went to Inno, a supermarket, to buy essentials such as coffee and soap. You can't imagine this place. It has every little shop in one. Huge cheeses, fresh bread, catsup, everything together. It is very stylish to shop there but afterwards we went to a small shop and the woman, seeing our Inno bags, became "enragée" and told us that it wasn't "gentil" to shop there. Then we went to a boulangerie, and the girls had already cut the bread in slices, what the French call "tranche."

—*Letter to my parents from Paris, fall 1963*

I shared a bathroom and a kitchen with other renters. We were lucky that we could use the shower whenever we wanted. In most places, each shower cost a few centimes.

Isabelle's brother, Hugues d'Audiffret, and Karine, his German girlfriend, who later became his wife, lived with me. Hugues and Karine loved good food. It was they who introduced me to escargots à la bourguignonne, a delicacy that my mother loved. I can still see the couple, she twice his size, watching, delighted with their role in initiating me into the rites of the Burgundian dish. Then they patiently showed me how to pour the garlic butter from the snail shell onto a piece of French bread, and awaited the second smile this garlicky dish evoked from me. Pure heaven. That was only the tip of the iceberg for me—tarte au citron, croissants, the list went on and on.

On Friday nights and Jewish holidays, I would often go for dinner at Nanou's parents' lovely apartment on rue des Belles Feuilles, and afterward to the largest Reform synagogue, on rue Copernic. Monsieur Cerf, a very intelligent, rather quiet man, was an industrialist in a large French company that sold building cranes. Madame Cerf was very active in WIZO (Women's International Zionist Organization), so much so that Nanou rebelled and didn't want to hear about it or Israel. Eating with this family, and tasting dishes rather similar to those with which I had grown up—chicken soup with matzo balls, roast chicken with apples or peaches—and listening to the same prayers at the table though with slightly different melodies, connected me to home and to this day, when I reflect on it, always makes me feel the wonder of the Jewish religion. For dessert, the Cerfs would also have charlottes made with ladyfingers and fruit tarts, often bought straight from a nearby bakery. Most French people still buy pastries: the pâtisseries are so good and plentiful that it's not really necessary to bake at home.

And now Saturday night! At 7:45 Bertrand picked me up and we drove to the soirée. I wore my new black dress. It was at his friend's house from the lycée. There were about 50 people there. When we came in, Françoise, the hostess, gave us all glasses with our names on them, filled with whiskey. Mine said "Miss USA" because she didn't know my name. Then there were three different tables with mild, medium, and strong cheeses. Each person was given a plate and a knife and a piece of bread and you mixed while trying cheeses. I guess since I was the only foreign girl, people were extra nice to me, and over the evening I met practically everyone. I learned to dance the Madison and the French boys taught me how to dance French style. It was really delightful. I don't think I have enjoyed myself as much at any party ever. At about 1:00 they served champagne and birthday cake. T'was really good. Although the French drink so much at their parties, the mere fact that they have lots to eat makes them hold their liquor well. Some boys took my name and we left at about 3:30. Late, eh?

—Letter to my family, October 1963

Chicken with Peaches

Although today I really love whole roasted chicken, with fresh garlic and herbs, sometimes, for easier serving, I use a cut-up chicken. This recipe is based on a delicious summer dish made with peaches I tasted in France many years ago; it is made with apples in the winter. I found it by chance on a slightly smudged piece of paper in my favorite recipe file.

Believe it or not, the Alsatian Jewish cook who shared the recipe with me in the early sixties used ketchup. *Quelle horreur!* This addition must have happened when people had started to like American products abroad: it was only five years after the opening of Le Drugstore on the Champs-Élysées, an homage to American postwar modernity, where the French happily dined on cheeseburgers and deli dishes. In those days, they even sold ketchup in supermarkets, and people asked me to bring it from the States, along with maple syrup and peanut butter. Even though I have to admit I am a ketchup lover, I have removed it from this recipe, as well as the canned peaches and their syrup.

Nothing compares to fresh in-season peaches, which is what you should use here. Check your local farmers' markets; local peaches will always taste better than ones from a grocery store. Taste each peach before you use it; it should be juicy, fragrant, and certainly not mealy. I do not bother peeling them. Outside of peach season, I substitute zucchini, or apples and onions sprinkled with cranberries.

Serve the chicken with rice or spaetzle, as the Alsatians do, or with a bulgur pilaf.

Serves 4 to 6

2 whole chicken breasts and 4 thighs, preferably bone-in and skin-on
Kosher salt and freshly ground black pepper, to taste
3 tablespoons olive oil, plus more for searing the peaches
3 large shallots, cut into small pieces (about 1 cup)
1 cup (236 ml) chicken stock
1 cup (236 ml) white wine
2 sprigs fresh thyme
2 cinnamon sticks, or 1 teaspoon ground cinnamon
4 fresh peaches, preferably yellow

---

1. Sprinkle the chicken pieces with salt and pepper.

2. Heat the olive oil in a heavy-bottomed skillet with a lid, add the shallots, and cook over medium-high heat until they are golden, about 5 minutes. Remove the shallots to a plate, then add the chicken pieces, skin side down, and cook for 5 minutes on each side, until they're browned. Add the shallots, chicken broth, white wine, thyme, and cinnamon. Cover, and reduce heat to maintain a simmer; cook for about 30 minutes. Remove the chicken from the skillet and set it aside. You can do this ahead of time, and refrigerate it until you're ready to finish with the peaches. →

3. Cut the peaches in half and discard the pits, add a little olive oil to the pan, and sear them on the cut side for several minutes, until caramelized. If you refrigerated your chicken, add the chicken to the peaches and cook for 5 to 10 minutes, to reheat. Otherwise, add the chicken back to the pan and cook just until heated through. Serve right from the skillet, or arrange on a beautiful platter.

Jacques picked me up after my course and we walked to the Marais which is an old section of Paris. There, we found the old Jewish Quarter and wandered into an Orthodox synagogue—way upstairs in an old building. The rabbi, with a long beard, was teaching the little boys at a table way in the corner of the room. It was out of Sholom Aleichem. We wandered by bakeries with "chola" and strudel. Unfortunately, due to my diet we did not go in. We ended up near les Halles and found a small café called Pied de Cochon. There we ate soupe à l'oignon and omelette des herbes. It was really delicious and fun. We stayed there for a few hours and then had coffee near the Palais Royal.

—*Letter to my parents from Paris, fall 1963*

One exception to not baking at home, though, was challah—or, as the French wrote it, *chola*. In those days, if you wanted to buy twisted challah, you would have to go to the Marais district, also called the Pletzl, a dark, dingy area that was traditionally the immigrant Ashkenazic Jewish quarter of the city. It was filled during this postwar period with "everything in Hebrew—the notices, the pastry-shops, the meat, the secret meeting places, the sounds and smells," wrote the author of *The Paris We Love,* a book published in 1950.

But if you were Jewish and lived in the Sixteenth Arrondissement during the 1960s, as I did, you usually bought a baguette, and you would say the Friday-night prayers over that. I found that rarely did a walk to buy a baguette end up with the bread intact. It was just too much fun to break off the crackly end and nibble on it after breathing in the aroma emanating from the bakery. Most people never return home without eating at least one huge hunk of the bread. Bertrand used to say that he would buy two baguettes so that one would be good for Friday night and one for him.

In the early 1960s, Paris was just getting out of its dreariness from World War II. You could tell by the buildings that were cleaned up in the Sixteenth Arrondissement, for example, but not in the Latin Quarter, which was still gray and grimy.

Less than twenty years after the war, I could also see the insecurity of Jews in the city that they loved, but that had abandoned them during the war. Monsieur Cerf, for example, was the only Jewish person in a management level at his large company. The Cerfs never talked about where they had been hidden during the war. Paris was Paris, this was my junior year abroad, I was there to make my own discoveries, and I was too young to understand and too timid even to ask.

Almost forty years later, in 2001, we brought my mother-in-law, Paula, to Paris. All she wanted was to visit the Pletzl. It was there that many Polish Jews living in Paris had told each other that they would meet after the war. And Paula promised herself that if she survived the war she would one day visit the Pletzl. Allan and I took her there for her eightieth birthday. Interestingly, when we visited, we found that most of the Jewish shopkeepers, such as the Finkelsztajns and the Gold-enbergs, still came from places like Łódź, Poland.

Pletzlach, like bagels and challah, were made uniquely in Jewish bakeries in Poland. Everybody liked these delicious rolls with onions and poppy seeds. While I was writing this book, my son, David, was visiting a small town outside Zamość, Poland, and sent me a picture of the pletzl that he bought from a bakery every morning; the bread was still made there, all these years after the last Jews left during the Holocaust. And pletzlach are still to be found at 19 rue des Écouffes, at Florence Kahn's in Paris, where they've morphed into bread for sandwiches stuffed with pastrami, pickles, hummus, spicy tomatoes, and more—like a falafel-stuffed pita, but with Polish roots.

Pletzl remains one of my favorite breads to make. I like it so much that I've included different renditions in several of my books. Here is one I have adapted from Florence Kahn in Paris and saw in a recent visit to Warsaw, where pletzlach have regained a little popularity and are known as "Białystoker pletzl kuchen." Bialys was a term used across the ocean in New York before the First World War.

Pletzlach
(Białystok Onion Poppy-seed Rolls)

1. Pour 1 cup (236 ml) lukewarm water into a large bowl. Stir in the yeast and the sugar until dissolved. Add 4 cups (500 grams) of the flour, the eggs, ¼ cup (60 ml) of the oil, and the salt. Mix well, and knead for about 10 minutes, or until smooth, adding more flour if necessary. You can also use a stand mixer fitted with a dough hook. Transfer the dough to a greased bowl and let it rise, covered, for 1 hour.

2. Meanwhile, heat 1 tablespoon of oil in a medium skillet set over medium-high heat. Add the onions and cook, stirring often, until they begin to soften. Reduce the heat to medium-low and continue cooking until lightly caramelized, 20 to 30 minutes.

3. Preheat the oven to 375 degrees, and cover two baking sheets with parchment paper.

4. Divide the dough into twelve balls, and roll or flatten them out into rounds about 6 inches in diameter. Put the rounds on the baking sheets, and use your thumbs to press down the center of each, leaving an inch border. Brush the dough with water, and divide the onions equally among the indentations. Then brush the rounds with the remaining vegetable oil, and sprinkle the poppy seeds on top. Let the rolls sit for 15 minutes, uncovered.

5. Bake for 20 minutes. Then, if you like, slip the pletzlach under the broiler for a minute to brown the onions. Serve lukewarm as is, or slice and make a big pletzl sandwich, using your imagination for the fillings and toppings.

Makes 12 pletzlach

1 scant tablespoon active
   dry yeast
¼ cup (50 grams) sugar
4 to 5 cups (500 to 625 grams)
   unbleached all-purpose
   flour
2 large eggs
¼ cup (60 ml) plus
   3 tablespoons vegetable oil
2 teaspoons kosher salt
2 cups diced onion
   (from about 2 medium
   onions)
3 to 4 tablespoons poppy
   seeds

In 2008 I met a young American chef named Daniel Rose at his restaurant, Spring, in Paris (he now has restaurants in New York, Chicago, and Los Angeles). He kept telling me what a Jewish city Paris was, something I never saw in the early 1960s; it was a period still too raw, and some people still hid that they were Jewish. The hundreds of thousands of Jews who were just beginning to arrive from the French-speaking Maghreb—Egypt, and a little later Algeria, Tunisia, and Morocco—were not subject to mass deportations, and thus were less fearful of living overtly Jewish lives, although they suffered, too, during World War II. In the years to come, they would become the majority of French Jews.

Nanou, who was studying law when I spent my junior year in France, introduced me to all her friends and took us both out on her father's franc (credit cards would come later, in 1965) to what she thought of as exotic restaurants. I remember one dinner at a fancy Russian restaurant on a side street off the Champs-Élysées, where we ate caviar and buckwheat blini for the first time, exotic foods even for the French in the early 1960s.

Another time, we went with her grandmother to Normandy, supposedly to study for our exams, stopping in local restaurants and visiting abbeys along the way. We had a grand time and ate very well, trying all the brie, Pont l'Évêque, and Camembert we could get our hands on and (my favorite dessert to this day) delicious tarte Tatin—but we barely passed our exams. In France, exams mean everything for your grade at the university.

Nanou's family was not the only French family I met. My father's sister Trudel, who throughout my life continued to introduce me to a huge

cadre of people, insisted that I meet Renée Dreyfus and her husband, Camille, who was Charles de Gaulle's personal physician. Periodically, the Dreyfuses would invite me to their grand apartment on Avenue Foch, filled with no fewer than twenty-one original Chagalls (Camille was Chagall's doctor as well, and probably bartered doctor's visits for paintings). Besides being a distinguished physician, the doctor was a gifted painter, and I enjoy one of his watercolors in my home.

It would usually be the three of us at a table with a beautiful centerpiece. I often had trouble seeing over the flowers and was a bit shaky on the proper French etiquette, which became a problem when they served asparagus. In Paris, in those days, there was a special way of handling the spears. You were allowed to use your fingers, and for that purpose the butler set a bowl in front of me filled with water. Since I couldn't see what the Dreyfuses were doing, the butler coached me gently; I didn't know the water was there for dipping before and after I was supposed to pick up the asparagus spears gingerly with my fingers.

But usually, when I dined with students, we would eat either at self-service places or at the even cheaper restaurants for students called *"resto u,"* slang for *restaurant universitaire*, where I was introduced to such homey and regional dishes as choucroute garnie. For a flat fee of a couple of francs, you could get a *plat principal*, plus cheese or dessert, though you would pay extra for wine. Or, at self-service places, you could get a steak, frites, a piece of bread, and a carafe of everyday wine for practically nothing.

Restaurants in the Latin Quarter, like a Greek

one we often frequented, were cheap and more often than not served immigrant food. As America would a few years later, after the 1965 Immigration and Naturalization Act, France saw a great influx of immigrants from the Indo-China War, as well as those from Tunisia and Morocco and later Algeria, following the independence of these North African countries. The Vietnamese, Algerians, Tunisians, and Moroccans brought delicious food with them that slowly got integrated into French cuisine.

There was so much to see and experience in Paris. I loved my very large lecture classes at the Sorbonne, led by some of the great teachers of the world, including Marcel Duverger, who taught political science. My seventeenth-century literature class was so crowded that I often had to sit on the floor behind the teacher. But we also had smaller classes, like our *cours pratiques*, where we worked on the structure of the language and were able to meet other students, often working in tandem.

As students, we were also able to get cheap tickets for museums, the Comédie Française, the Opéra, and the Théâtre de la Huchette in the Latin Quarter, where I first saw Eugène Ionesco's *Rhinoceros* and Samuel Beckett's *Waiting for Godot*. The French love film, and I went with them to the tiny cinemas on rue Champollion that played movies all day long. And, of course, in between classes, we studied at cafés. Somehow, everything was so new and exciting that I just drank it all in.

Just after exams in the spring, Seth Shulman, a friend from the United States, asked if I wanted to accompany him in a Citroën Deux Chevaux to the Loire Valley, with a Frenchman named Henri, who was an architecture student at les Beaux-Arts and usually did not like Americans. Despite misgivings, my college roommate Barbara Schwartz

(later known as the photographer Barbara Ess), who was in Paris at the time, Seth, Henri, and I all piled into this tiny car and set off.

Not only were the châteaux romantically beautiful, especially my two favorites, Saumur and Chenonceau, but I fell madly in love with Henri, who gave me an introduction to the buildings of Paris. He lived just outside the Place des Vosges, the oldest planned square in Paris, built under Henri IV between 1605 and 1612. It is still the square I must return to whenever I am in Paris. Henri also introduced me to courtyards, staircases, and beautiful buildings during our walks through the Marais district, as well as to so many workers' restaurants in Les Halles, the early morning wholesale market, where we had late-night soupe à l'oignon. Alas, Les Halles no longer exists, though that is still the name of the area and a Métro stop. The wholesale market is now outside Paris, in Rungis.

A favorite restaurant that Henri and I frequented, as did all the plumbers of the capital, at 1 rue du Pont Louis-Philippe, was fittingly called La Plombière (the wife of the plumber). Its slightly grubby but beautiful painted ceiling harked back to its previous incarnation as a bread bakery in the nineteenth century. Twenty years later, after the market had moved to the suburbs, I ate with the *New York Times* Paris bureau chief, Richard Eder, at an upscale chic bistro called Chez Julien that seemed very familiar to me. I felt I knew this restaurant, and finally recognized it by its Art Deco ceiling, now cleaned up for a more elegant clientele.

Henri also invited me to a château about fifty miles from Paris to attend the Bal des Beaux-Arts, a romantic ending to my year. The theme of the *bal* that year was La Belle et la Bête, taken from Jacques Cocteau's 1946 film. Along with many of the other students and their dates, I took a chartered bus that dropped us off in the middle of a wooded property. (Henri would join me after racing his 1908 Renault from Paris to Rouen.) As I remember, it was pitch dark, with candles and crosses indicating the way. When we reached the eighteenth-century château, there was a grand procession of girls dressed in gowns of the epoch of Louis XIV, and boys dressed as beasts. Music from the seventeenth century added to the atmosphere. On the lawn of the illuminated château was a dinner served à la *Tom Jones,* a popular bawdy movie of the period that won the Academy Award as best movie of the year, which meant that in our finery we ate like lower-class Englishmen. I remember thinking Henri's arm was around me but instead finding that it was a huge drumstick that he was eating. Afterward, we danced until dawn, and all slept in dorms in the château overnight. The next morning, we drove in Henri's Renault to a barbecue near Paris. As we rode by in our antique convertible, people waved with such pleasure that I felt as if we were rendering humanity a favor!

Tarte des Demoiselles Tatin (Apple Tart)

If I had to choose one recipe to remind me of my year abroad, it would be tarte Tatin. Like so many others who spent their junior year in Paris, I later turned to Julia Child for my first recipe. But recently, after failing dismally when making my own caramel at home, I asked Gregory Lloyd of Le Diplomate in Washington—whose tarte Tatin is so good that the apples, with a syrupy gloss on top, melt in your mouth and the crust just crackles on your tongue—to show me how to poach the apple quarters and make a caramel. Though Greg makes a dry caramel in his restaurant, I found it easier to make a wet one, dissolving the sugar in water first to avoid ending up with crystallized sugar. Although it dirties another dish, you must make the caramel in a pot and then pour it into your baking skillet to avoid burning the caramel from residual heat.

After baking, when the crust is golden and the apples cooked through, I remove the pie, set a plate on top, say a small prayer, and flip. Or I make it all in the morning and reheat it for a few minutes before flipping it in front of my guests. It is worth the fuss, and with these chefs' tricks, it is so much easier than it ever was before.

---

1. **To make the crust** Pulse the butter and sugar in a food processor fitted with a steel blade until the butter is in pebble-sized pieces; then add the flour, salt, egg yolk, and 2 tablespoons ice water. Pulse until a dough comes together, adding another tablespoon of water if needed. The dough should clump together when pinched, but it might not form into a mass around the blade.

To make the crust by hand Whisk the flour and salt in a large bowl. Beat the egg yolk and 2 tablespoons ice water in a small bowl with a fork. Using the wide holes of a hand grater, grate the frozen butter quickly into the flour, and toss with your fingertips to combine. Using your fingers, mix in the sugar and egg until a mass is formed.

2. Scrape the dough onto a piece of parchment paper, and use your hands to smush it together; wrap it in the paper, and refrigerate for at least an hour. Then lightly flour a work surface and roll out the crust so it's ⅛-inch thick and ½ inch wider than a 9- or 10-inch ovenproof nonstick or stainless-steel skillet or copper tarte Tatin pan. Prick the crust a →

Serves 8 to 10

For the Crust
6 tablespoons (85 grams) unsalted butter, frozen in 1 piece
2 tablespoons sugar
About 1½ cups (190 grams) unbleached all-purpose flour, plus more for dusting
Good pinch of kosher salt
1 large egg yolk

For the Filling
2 cups (400 grams) sugar or vanilla sugar (see note, page 47)
1½ sticks (12 tablespoons/ 170 grams) unsalted butter
1 vanilla bean
7 to 8 Granny Smith, Gala, or Fuji apples, peeled, quartered, and cored (about 3 pounds/ 1⅓ kg)
2 tablespoons Calvados or rum (optional)
Whipped cream or vanilla or rum raisin ice cream, for serving

few times with a fork, then refrigerate it until you're ready to bake. (You can also do this ahead and freeze it until you're ready to use it.)

3. **To make the filling** Mix 2 cups of water with ½ cup (100 grams) of the granulated sugar and the unsalted butter in a large, wide saucepan, and bring this to a slow boil. Add the vanilla bean, and the apple quarters; the liquid should almost cover them. Don't overcrowd the pot or the apples may cook unevenly—do this in batches if necessary. Poach the apples for 10 to 15 minutes, or until they're fork-tender, taking care that pieces don't turn to mush. Remove the fruit with a slotted spoon, reserving the liquid, and cool the apples on a parchment-lined tray. Some of the butter may cling to the apples; leave it there.

4. While the apples are cooling, make the caramel. Have the skillet or copper tarte Tatin pan ready.

5. Whisk the remaining 1½ cups sugar with ½ cup water in the pan over medium-high heat. Stir until the sugar dissolves, then let it bubble without stirring until the caramel turns a deep golden brown. Swirl the pan every once in a while, so the caramel browns evenly. This will take about 13 minutes. Remove from heat, then quickly and carefully pour the caramel into another skillet, unless you are using a copper tarte Tatin pan; let it cool until it hardens.

6. When the apples are cool, preheat the oven to 350 degrees and arrange them in concentric circles, sitting on their sides, on top of the caramel. Fit as many apple slices as you can in a single layer. If you have any left over, eat them with ice cream or yogurt. Drizzle the Calvados or rum on top.

7. Gently set the rolled-out pastry on top of the apples, tucking in the overhanging dough around the apples.

8. Set a baking sheet on the rack below to catch any drips, and bake for 20 minutes. Then increase the temperature to 400 degrees and bake for another 20 minutes, and then back to 350 degrees for 20 more minutes. The pastry will be quite brown—better to overbake slightly than to underbake. Let it cool for an hour or so.

9. While the tarte is cooling, reduce the apple cooking liquid over medium-high heat until it's thick and syrupy, about 20 minutes. Keep this for drizzling over ice cream or yogurt, or stirring into whiskey. →

10. When you're ready to serve, reheat the tarte on the stove over low heat for 5 minutes. Then carefully work a knife blade around the edges, flip the tarte onto a plate, and serve it with whipped cream or à la mode with vanilla or rum raisin ice cream.

Note Tarte Tatin is also delicious made with quinces, pears, peaches, or even rhubarb. If you're making this with rhubarb, cut the stalks into small pieces and arrange them in two or three layers of concentric circles. When you flip the tarte over, it will be beautiful.

8.

Graduation, a Taste of New York, and Graduate School

Hamantaschen   107

Hamantaschen *(continued)*

Poppy-seed, Date,
and Nut Filling
(Makes about 2 cups)
½ cup (72 grams) poppy
  seeds
½ cup (118 ml) milk
½ cup (100 grams) sugar
10 dates or figs, pitted
¼ cup (40 grams) raisins
¼ cup (25 grams) walnuts
¼ cup (30 grams) ground
  almonds
Grated zest of 1 lemon
1 large egg yolk

roughly, then add the poppy seeds and milk, and pulse just until every-thing is combined. Refrigerate until the batter is chilled.

4. When you're ready to bake, preheat the oven to 375 degrees, and line two baking sheets with silicone mats or parchment paper. Lightly flour your work surface.

5. Remove the dough from the refrigerator and, working one piece at a time and flouring as needed, roll out to about ⅛-inch thick; then cut them into 3-inch circles. Gather the scraps, shape them into a disc, and roll and cut again; repeat, to use all the dough. Put a heaping teaspoon of filling into the center of each circle. To shape the hamantaschen: First brush water around the rim of each circle with your finger. Pull the edges of the dough up to form a triangle around the filling and pinch the three corners together, leaving a tiny triangular opening in the center. Transfer them to the baking sheets, separating the cookies by ½ inch, and bake for 12 to 17 minutes on the middle and bottom racks, swapping the sheets halfway through, until the tops are light golden.

9.

New York, New York: Stepping into the Real World

men were beginning to cook and wine was starting to take off in America, the magazine would be called the *International Review of Food and Wine*. I, who, in my twenties, tried to make every centerfold menu from *Gourmet* magazine and constantly clipped recipes by Craig Claiborne in *The New York Times*, was intrigued.

Eventually, Hugh Hefner from *Playboy* became the major backer of the magazine, and its name was shortened to *Food & Wine*. The Batterberrys, as the editors in chief, set up shop in their small apartment on upper Madison Avenue. From there they moved to the *Playboy* offices and eventually their own. When the first issue of the magazine appeared in 1978, Michael asked me to pitch some ideas. The excitement of writing for a new magazine was exhilarating, with the Batterberrys so appreciative and excited by ideas. In one of the first issues, I wrote an article on the charming Chanticleer restaurant in Siasconset on Nantucket Island, a place I visit often because my brother Alan has a house there, and later another about goose served at Hanukkah.

Those early years were great fun because of the Batterberrys' energy, excitement, and creative ideas. But it was short-lived, because American Express bought the magazine in 1980. Eight years after the sale, in 1988, the Batterberrys started *Food Arts*, a magazine for chefs, which made its own mark at a time when chefs were beginning to become superstars.

Most of the time, through the years, I would see the Batterberrys either at Bill's, in their various offices, or at tiny ethnic neighborhood restaurants where we would explore new foods and ideas. In the late 1980s, when I was already working on *Jewish Cooking in America*, Michael coined the phrase "newish Jewish" and had me write an article on one of those chefs, Lenard Rubin, who dared change the face of traditional Jewish food with his Southwestern chicken-and-lime matzo-ball soup, blackened and braised brisket of beef, tzimmes stuffed into chiles, and noodle kugel with cilantro and corn. One of the columns I loved to write for them, "Front Burner," consisted of short takes about food around the country, something that fit in with my life in the eighties with one, then two, then three children.

Michael also introduced me to bigos, a Polish stew that he made for us one time around Christmas, an easily expandable dish with sausages that he bought from Schaller & Weber. Making bigos is a three-day affair, because it cooks in stages, with its layers of slightly sweet and slightly sour flavors of cabbage and sauerkraut, as well as tomatoes to make the dish red. It is slightly reminiscent of choucroute garnie, another winter favorite, in my *Quiches, Kugels, and Couscous*.

The Batterberrys were great listeners and magnificent storytellers who could talk about anything. It was like they breathed oxygen into the air. I still miss Michael, who died of cancer in 2010.

Bigos (Polish Sauerkraut and Sausage Stew)

The recipe for bigos, the national stew of Poland, is so forgiving, with different cooks changing ingredients to suit their diets and the ingredients they have on hand. The key is to create layers of flavor that balance sour and sweet. I found an old Jewish version with short ribs or brisket, tomatoes, and sauerkraut with cinnamon. Instead of starting with ham, as many bigos recipes do, I started with brisket. Then I added cabbage and kosher kielbasa, which lent a bit of savory smokiness, and rounded out the dish with sauerkraut and prunes.

The whole process takes three days from start to finish, but don't let that scare you. It takes that long to really develop the flavor, making it the perfect do-ahead stew to serve at a dinner party. You can use all pork (shoulder or ham, for example), as in the original recipe, or do as I do with beef and kosher kielbasa sausage.

3½ pounds (1.6 kg) short ribs of beef or 5 pounds (2.27 kg) brisket of beef

6 cloves garlic, crushed

1½ teaspoons sea salt, or to taste

½ teaspoon freshly ground black pepper, or to taste

1 teaspoon ground cinnamon

2 tablespoons olive oil

3 large onions, sliced into rounds

1 ounce (28 grams) dried porcini mushrooms

3 bay leaves

2 teaspoons dried marjoram

1½ teaspoons smoked paprika

8 allspice berries, or ½ teaspoon ground allspice

6 juniper berries

6 large tomatoes, halved, or one 28-ounce (793-gram) can whole tomatoes

1 medium green or red cabbage, thinly sliced

One 25-ounce (708-gram) jar of sauerkraut (about 4 cups), such as Bubbie's brand →

Day 1

Rinse the short ribs or brisket with cold water and pat dry. Rub on all sides with the crushed garlic, then sprinkle with some of the salt and pepper, and the cinnamon. Heat a tablespoon or so of oil in a large (8-quart/7½-liter) heavy-bottomed pot set over medium-high heat, and brown the meat slightly on all sides. Remove the meat, and add the onions. Cook covered for 5 minutes, then uncover and cook another 5 to 10 minutes, stirring often, until the onions are soft and translucent. Return the meat and any juices to the pot, add 3 to 4 cups (709 to 946 ml) water, or to just cover, and cook, partially covered, over medium-low heat (to maintain a steady simmer) for 2 hours. Let everything cool completely, then cover the pot and refrigerate it overnight, or for at least 8 hours.

Day 2

Soak the dried mushrooms in 2 cups (473 ml) hot water for 15 minutes. Take the pot from the refrigerator, and use a spoon to remove the fat that has accumulated on top of the meat. (Save the fat for another use, if you like.) Set the pot over medium-high heat, and add ½ teaspoon salt and pepper, the bay leaves, marjoram, smoked paprika, allspice, and juniper berries. Strain the dried mushrooms to remove any grit, saving the →

Bigos (Polish Sauerkraut and Sausage Stew) *(continued)*

1 to 2 cups prunes, roughly
     chopped, or to taste
12 to 14 ounces
     (340 to 397 grams) fresh
     mushrooms, cut into
     bite-sized chunks
2 to 3 pounds (907 grams
     to 1⅓ kg) kielbasa, such
     as Grow & Behold kosher
     kielbasa sausage, sliced into
     thick rounds
Crusty bread, for serving

cooking liquid, and add the mushrooms and their soaking liquid, along with the tomatoes and cabbage. Bring the liquid to a boil, then stir, reduce the heat to maintain a simmer, and cook, uncovered, until the cabbage is tender, 1 to 1½ hours, stirring every so often. Add a little water if it seems to be getting too thick, but aim for a stewy consistency rather than soupy. Remove from the heat, cool, and return the pot to the refrigerator overnight (or for at least 8 hours).

Day 3

About 45 minutes before serving, set the pot back on the stove. Rinse and drain the sauerkraut, then add it to the pot, along with the prunes, fresh mushrooms, and sausage. Bring to a boil over medium-high heat, then reduce the heat to maintain a steady simmer and cook, uncovered, for about 30 minutes, or until the stew is warmed through. Serve with hearty, crusty bread to soak up the juices.

10.

Jerusalem—Learning About Living and the Meaning of a Meal

I have thought this over very carefully and am still thinking it over. I won't commit myself to anything until November 15 at which time if I decide to go, I will give notice at my office. I have made preliminary plans with the Jewish Agency to enroll me in Ulpan Etzion in Jerusalem which begins January 15 for a five-month period. I will try to get in as a full pension and board student $125 for the entire time and if two to three to a room proves unbearable, I will move out. Anyway, this gives me a chance to appraise the situation. Hopefully, I will also be able to audit or take a course in Biblical Studies at the Hebrew University and do some writing for U.S. magazines about Israel to make some money while I am there—more about that after I have made some inquiries here.

What are my reasons for going? They are many—and all positive. Frankly, if I were going to run away from something I wouldn't go but I promise you I'll take my problems with me!

—Letter to my parents, September 1969

———————

I am busy but I also am learning what moderation is. I can see from people like Kollek that all this work doesn't get you anywhere. Don't worry, I spend lots of leisure with dates and playing tennis and making date nut cakes (Dr. Silver sampled one). Now that I have exhausted every recipe in several cookbooks—have also brandied dates, I have decided to start with oranges, now that they are in season. You see, what I do is peel oranges or dates when I am on the phone, quickly make cakes, freeze them and then when guests drop in, I always have something homemade to serve—it is quite fun. Golda does it too, maybe she doesn't peel dates on the phone though—it is quite difficult.

—Letter home, 1970

Thursday last went on a super trip to the desert with some people from my office—visited convents built on cliffs, drove in jeeps with an army escort, went along wadis to the Dead Sea, ate in an Arab restaurant in Jericho (you know I think I am the only Jew who immigrates to Israel and is more familiar with East Jerusalem merchants than West Jerusalem) and returned through some other magnificent country. Quite unbelievable to behold—you'll see it this summer.

—*Letter home, 1971*

When I turned twenty-six, there were two things I knew: I wanted to fall in love, but more than that, I wanted to have an interesting life. All my mother wanted me to do was get married, but I knew that there was more to explore before I settled down.

The place I was least interested in exploring was Israel, because my German-born father was a Zionist, and at that point in my life, whatever my parents were into, I wanted to do the opposite.

Then I sat next to a returning Peace Corps volunteer on a plane who told me that Israel was the most fascinating place he had ever visited. So I went there in the summer of 1969, landing the same day Neil Armstrong landed on the moon. And that very day, I met the son of my father's friend, with whom I later thought I was in love.

On that first quick trip, to my great surprise, I had an immediate affinity with the wildness and frontier feeling of the country. I felt at home there. I spent two weeks volunteering on Kibbutz Yifat in the Jezreel Valley, near Nazareth and Afula, where I saw firsthand the now famous kibbutz breakfasts of cucumbers, peppers, tomatoes, and whatever had been picked that day. The kibbutzniks cut up the vegetables at the table, turning them into their own salads. I also had coffee every afternoon after work at kibbutz

homes, with a homemade cake baked on a German contraption called a *Wundertopf,* something like today's Instant Pot. This tube-shaped cooker, with a hole in the middle, sat on top of a propane stove and miraculously baked delicious Bundt cakes.

I visited Jerusalem and vowed to return as soon as I could.

When I came back to the States after my short stay, my Israeli boyfriend's father offered me a job if I moved to Haifa and learned some Hebrew. So I started studying Hebrew at the Herzl Insti-

On the rooftop of my office at the Jerusalem Municipality, 1971

tute in New York and six months later, in January 1970, I flew back to Israel. I couldn't wait to see my boyfriend. And there he was, picking me up at the airport. Unfortunately, his Israeli girlfriend was right beside him. I quickly realized that what I thought was love was my own infatuation, and that I was no longer interested in working for his father.

What to do? I went to Jerusalem to immerse myself in Hebrew at Ulpan Etzion and it was there that I fell in love, not with a person but with a place. I would walk the old, cobbled streets and put my hands on the walls of Jerusalem stone. I felt in sync with this city, a calmness coming over me. I remember once, when I was escorting the great Elie Wiesel around Jerusalem, he asked me what I did to ward off depression. I told him that I just tried a new walk in this city. When I asked him the same question, he replied, "With me it is not so easy."

When I wasn't studying Hebrew at the ulpan, I was discovering the aromas and tastes of new foods. Few had heard of falafel and hummus in the States in those days, and I relished the new-to-me spices like cumin and coriander, as I watched the cooks in tiny restaurants and stands throughout the city. I discovered Moroccan Jew-ish slowly cooked stuffed vegetables, Kurdish Aramaic soup with kubbeh (meat-filled dumplings) made from bulgur or semolina at Morduch, a tiny restaurant in the Mahane Yehuda neighbor-hood, where the recipes have not changed in fifty years, and a coconut Cointreau torte at a Friday-evening get-together at a friend's house. Later, when I included that torte in *The Flavor of Jerusalem,* my first cookbook, someone said that it tasted so good it was better than sex.

To my surprise and delight, while living in Jerusalem I was introduced to and beguiled by cuisines representing cultures from around the world. I was particularly attracted to the subtle flavorings of Moroccan food and couldn't get enough of Armenian specialties like stuffed grape leaves, lahmajoun, and tahinli, a spectacu-lar bread made by spreading dough with tahini and sugar, rolling it up like a jelly roll, then coil-ing it into a circle. And I savored Kurdish soups made from recipes that may have dated back to Biblical times.

I soon developed a love for eggplant in all its manifestations: eggplant-and-pepper kugels, egg-plant soufflés, and salads of either roasted or fried eggplant. I began to think of Jerusalem as the epi-center of eggplant preparation.

Eggplant Rounds Topped with Tahini, Yogurt, and Pomegranates

Many years after my first visit, when my husband, Allan, and I returned to Israel for his seventy-fourth birthday, we visited Mitzpe Ramon with its huge crater, once on a trade route for perfumes and spices to Africa. At night we ate at Hahavit, a simple restaurant filled with young men and women serving their time in the army, where we shared delicious eggplant rounds with tahini and a pile of vegetables on top. Of all the eggplant dishes I ate in Israel during that trip, this simple rendition was the best. It inspired me to try this preparation at home.

I have learned, through years of cooking eggplant, that salting, waiting, and then patting the slices dry removes some of the liquid, thus preventing the slices from absorbing too much oil, and also concentrates the flavor. (Fresh eggplants aren't bitter at all—it's old or overripe ones that ruin the fruit's reputation.)

This is my favorite new eggplant appetizer, beautiful to look at and amazingly delicious to eat. I call it an either/or dish: choose some of the toppings or none. Use cilantro or parsley, pomegranates or dried cherries, pomegranate syrup or date honey, tahini or yogurt. Or do it all, and make it rich. You can't go wrong.

---

1. Cut the eggplant into ¾-inch-thick rounds. Sprinkle with salt, and let them rest for about an hour. Run cold water over the rounds, then blot them dry. Warm ½ inch of oil in a skillet set over medium-high heat, then add the eggplant slices, and fry until they're golden on both sides. (Do this in batches if necessary.) Let the rounds drain on paper towels until you're ready to serve.

2. Stir two cloves of garlic into the yogurt in a small bowl; season with salt and pepper. In a separate bowl, mix the tahini, remaining garlic, lemon juice, and more salt and pepper, adding more lemon juice and/or water to thin the mixture as needed (the sauce should be smooth).

3. When you're ready to serve, preheat the oven to 350 degrees and warm the rounds in it for a few minutes. Treat this as a salad, with greens on the bottom, then eggplant, yogurt, and on top a smattering of the →

Makes about 12 rounds; serves 6 or fewer

1 large eggplant
  (about 1 pound/453 grams)
Kosher salt, to taste, and
  freshly ground black pepper
Olive oil, for frying
4 cloves garlic, minced
½ cup (120 grams)
  Greek yogurt
½ cup (118 ml) tahini
Juice of ½ lemon
Handful of torn spring greens,
  like arugula, variegated
  sorrel, or watercress
Drizzle of pomegranate syrup
  or date honey
Handful of pomegranate
  seeds, or dried cranberries
  or cherries
Small handful of roasted
  almonds, slightly crushed
2 tablespoons chopped fresh
  Italian parsley or cilantro

tahini mixture, pomegranate syrup or date honey, pomegranate seeds, and nuts. Or eat the slices as an appetizer, with a swath of yogurt and tahini on top, a drizzle of pomegranate syrup or honey, then a few pomegranate seeds and nuts. Top in either case with a few greens and parsley or cilantro.

Note You can also roast the whole eggplant in a 450-degree oven, pricking it first with a fork; then spread it with the toppings and serve lukewarm.

One day at the ulpan, I was talking with Uzi Benziman, a journalist from *Haaretz*, who was writing an article on olim (new immigrants), about my desire to remain in Jerusalem to work after I learned more Hebrew. He immediately said, "I know a great job in Mayor Teddy Kollek's office. . . ." He described it vaguely as taking foreign journalists around Jerusalem and, it was hoped, helping them find something to write about that wasn't war-related.

I'll never forget my interview for the job as foreign press attaché. The press spokesman and his secretary interviewed me together. At that point, I spoke excellent French, and some Italian and German, but I was still learning Hebrew, which I thought should disqualify me. For some reason, they didn't think speaking Hebrew was too important. I got the job; months later, I found out that the spokesman and his secretary were having an affair, so they were happy to hire someone who didn't understand all the nuances of what they were saying to each other.

On the job with Teddy Kollek, the mayor of Jerusalem

Working as the foreign press attaché for Teddy, as he was called by everyone, was an extraordinary experience for me, in which I learned firsthand about a very divided city, a new culture, and what it meant to be a post–World War II Jew living in Israel.

What a job it was! I had to know Jerusalem cold. If you were a foreign celebrity or journalist, I would take you around the city, tell you about its history and its present, and keep you fed and entertained.

I don't remember the details of showing Barbra Streisand around, but I'll never forget my first assignment: spending several days with the legendary David Ben-Gurion, then eighty-four years old. Teddy, as gently as a son would, introduced me to the great man and first prime minister of the State of Israel. My instructions were to translate for the French television crew doing a documentary about him. As we stood on Mount Scopus, this tiny lion of Israel told us how he wanted to really integrate the city and tear down the walls of Jerusalem, because walls separate communities. He wanted more trees all over, and told us to be patient: the then stark area around Mount Scopus would be beautiful in maybe twenty years. He told the crew that he had spoken Hebrew from the age of three in Russia, but few people spoke Hebrew in Jerusalem when he came there at age twenty, in 1906, although they spoke many other languages. The most important Zionists, as far as he was concerned, were the French who came in 1871 with Baron Edmond de Rothschild, the one man he considered most responsible for Israel's wine and silk culture.

But I most remember his carefully chosen words. When asked if he was a Zionist, he said:

"I am a Jew, an Israeli Jew, not a Zionist, not a socialist. I am a Jew who wants to live in a world where there is peace among all nations and where there is no exploitation but mutual help among human beings. Between peace and all the territories, I would choose peace with two exceptions: Jerusalem and the Golan Heights." And then he said, "I don't believe one person can make change. People make change. I never guide them. I guide myself." Two years later, in 1973, this wise and beloved leader passed away.

While Teddy was the mayor of Jerusalem, Golda Meir was one of the prime ministers of Israel. As a young person from America, I arrived with the image of Golda as the kindly grandmother who wielded a big stick and charmed the world to help Israel. Teddy and the rest of the Ben-Gurion clan—like Moshe Dayan, who came to the office occasionally—didn't talk about her in such kindly terms. Today I would interpret it as sexism, but she, like Margaret Thatcher, was a tough, inflexible leader, who got ahead by hard work and a good work ethic. Women at that time who wanted to be effective in high places believed that that was the way that all women could succeed. There were few strong women leaders in those days, and chauvinistic men didn't know how to handle them.

In late 1970, when I heard Golda speak at the Jerusalem Municipality, I wrote in my diary how she talked about her emotions at the Western Wall in 1967, on the Friday after reunification (following the Six-Day War), when a young paratrooper wept in her arms. I sat with members of the Knesset, judges, and old-time leaders as we listened to her describe the wonder of the creation of Israel. Most of them were Ashkenazic, but there were a few token Sephardim, like the minister of police, and some city guards and policemen. Meanwhile,

down the street, groups of poor youth, egged on by the police, caused a riot, purportedly at the outset to protest the inequality of the conditions toward Sephardic and Middle Eastern Jewry in Israel at that time. This movement became known as the Israeli Black Panthers. One or two Arabs and Druze also sat in the audience that day, listening and perhaps wondering if any of their people could ever become "honored citizens" of Jerusalem.

Although I never met Golda Meir, I tasted her matzo balls. They were very hard and inflexible, like her foreign policy; I featured the recipe in my book *The Flavor of Jerusalem*.

Everyone came to meet Teddy, the greatest builder of Jerusalem since Herod. He was quite a character! Charismatic, but quick-tempered: If he got mad, he'd throw a book at you or call you at one in the morning to let you know he was upset. He would yell, but then he would be sweet to make up for it. Today, in the current work climate, we might see this behavior differently, but I accepted it at the time. Of any boss I have had in my lifetime I learned the most from Teddy, especially about the ethics of hard work and how to make things happen in a bureaucracy.

Teddy also had this odd habit of taking power naps inside the elevator. He'd close his eyes when he got on, and by the time he reached the fourth floor, he'd snap open his eyes and claim to be fully rested.

And he loved to eat. Not only what was on his plate, but on everybody else's plate, too. He also had the politician's gift of being able to make just the right joke at just the right moment to lighten the tension so often sparked by politics.

While breaking bread with Teddy in the homes of Orthodox Jews in Mea She'arim, White Russians at their churches, and Palestinians in far-flung villages, I saw how he made connections with people who otherwise would not agree with him in any way. Through the common bond of food, we had relationships that in a more politicized context would never make sense.

One day, Teddy asked me to join him and his deputy mayor, Meron Benvenisti, for a visit to an Arab village halfway between Jerusalem and Bethlehem. Teddy explained that the villagers wanted a road, but that it wasn't going to happen, because it would be too expensive. Still, we had to go hear their petition face-to-face, and he wanted me to come along so I could learn.

We drove to the village on a long, dusty, and bumpy dirt road between bucolic fields filled with sheep. Teddy complained the whole way. When we arrived, we were greeted by the village's mukhtar, or leader, and a few elders. I was the only woman, and I was feeling a little out of my element.

Immediately, they brought out coffee—delicious Turkish coffee infused with whole cardamom pods. Once the chitchat was over, the mukhtar explained why they needed a paved road, and Teddy responded, "Yes, yes, I know you need a road, but we really can't afford it."

The mukhtar nodded and invited us to stay for lunch. We sat down at low tables, and then the mezze started arriving: olives; Bedouin cheese; baba ghanouj, made from eggplant and tahini; warm hummus drizzled with olive oil from the village; and deep-fried torpedo-shaped kubbeh filled with pine nuts and ground meat. I was

intrigued by the just-from-the-oven pita bread baked on what looked like an inverted wok.

Then the mukhtar poured some arak, made from anise—no wine at this Muslim feast—and said that he noticed his neighbors got a new road. Teddy explained again that, yes, they did get a new road, but the road they needed was much shorter than the road that the mukhtar needed, which would be ten times more expensive.

Undaunted, the mukhtar nodded again, and out came the main dish. It was something I had never seen before: a platter of chicken pieces that had been roasted with cumin, cinnamon, and pine nuts, with tons of sautéed onions colored pink by sumac. All this was cooked and served on a large pita bread soaked in olive oil while being warmed in the oven. The dish was called mousakhan, and what I didn't know then was that I was about to eat one of the great Palestinian dishes from the city of Nablus.

As we feasted, something remarkable happened: We forgot to be uncomfortable. I forgot that I was the only woman, and that I didn't know why I was there. Teddy forgot that he was there to say no to a road. By the time we had eaten our fill of the chicken and were sipping our mint tea, everyone had gotten what they wanted: The mayor got fed probably one of the finest meals of his life. The village? They got their road. And me? Well, I got a lifelong career. That meal showed me how food can break down barriers and bring people together. I understood then that food is not ornamental—it is central, and worthy of study—and that I could explore the world through food. I also got my favorite chicken dish.

Mousakhan
(Chicken with Sumac, Pine Nuts, and Onions)

I learned to make this dish years later, from Adnan Abu Odeh, the minister of culture of Jordan and later a member of the senate, whom I met in graduate school at Harvard in 1975. When I told him of my love for this luscious Palestinian dish, he said, "Invite me to your house. I'll make it for you." And he did, thus beginning a lifelong friendship. Allan, who was writing his dissertation at the time about the military occupation of the West Bank, was thrilled. The two talked while I learned how to make what became my favorite chicken dish.

What I like about it is the many red onions, flavored with sumac and other spices, that permeate the chicken. The texture of the pine nuts adds depth, and baking it on a huge pita with lots of good olive oil makes you want to tear it apart and eat it all with your fingers—which is exactly what you should do.

Serves 8

½ cup (118 ml) olive oil
5 medium red onions,
    sliced into thin half-moons
Kosher salt and freshly
    ground black pepper,
    to taste
8 bone-in, skin-on chicken
    thighs
4 to 5 tablespoons ground
    red sumac
1 teaspoon ground allspice
¼ teaspoon ground cloves
4 rounds pocketless pita,
    or 1 large lavash
    (about 450 grams)
¾ cup (100 grams) toasted
    pine nuts

1. Heat the olive oil in a large sauté pan. Add the onions, and sauté for 20 minutes, or until golden, stirring occasionally. After 5 minutes, add salt to taste.

2. Preheat the oven to 450 degrees. Season the chicken with salt and pepper and put on a sheet pan. Scatter with 1 cup of the onions. Bake, uncovered, for 5 minutes, reduce oven to 375 degrees, and bake for 20 minutes.

3. Meanwhile, drain and reserve the oil from the remaining onions. Stir the sumac, allspice, and cloves into these onions.

4. Remove the chicken from the oven, and add the onions, placing them over and around the chicken. Sprinkle with ½ teaspoon more salt. Bake for 30 minutes or until the chicken is done. Before the chicken is finished, soak the bread in some of the reserved oil, and drape it over the chicken, so the bread warms through and crisps a bit.

5. To serve Arrange the bread on an ovenproof platter, scatter some of the spiced onions on top, then add the chicken and top that with more onions and the pine nuts. Return the pan to the oven and bake a few more minutes before serving, just to warm everything through.

Today I walked around the walls of the old city—what an interesting experience. There is a huge field at one corner of the Moslem quarter where a farmer plants his vegetables and fruit including Jerusalem artichoke! I am sure he has no concept of how expensive his property is.

—Letter to my parents, December 4, 1971

Throughout my two and a half years in Israel, I met so many interesting people and discovered so many wonderful places to eat. Henry Kissinger famously remarked about the food in Jerusalem, "Why can't a country of two and a half million Jewish mothers have better food?" But there was good food: in people's homes. Today the food has come out of the homes, with the sons and daughters of the next generation who studied to become chefs. During the Intifadas of the 1990s, when Israel was isolated, chefs started looking inward instead of outward, and they updated the food of their mothers and grandmothers. The appetites and attitudes of the next generation (as well as their pocketbooks) have all fueled the development of their food.

Although the dietary laws have not changed for three thousand years, the idea of adapting ingredients to make food kosher has. Today there's no reason to suffer when keeping kosher. Good olive oil, small-batch cheese made with vegetable rennet, meat recipes made with coconut or soy milk, and kosher varietal wines have transformed kosher tables.

What Teddy didn't tell me (and I learned much later) was that, when the state was created, Ben-Gurion made an agreement—called the status quo—with the religious leaders. One of the many issues to be resolved in this new Jewish country was the official position on the dietary laws. Ben-Gurion decided to maintain rabbinical supervision of kashrut in all government organizations, military service, schools, hospitals, and hotels affiliated with the Ministry of Tourism. In the 1950s, these hotels served boiled chicken, gefilte fish—typical tired Ashkenazic food. Today these hotels offer delicious kosher food prepared by some of Israel's best chefs. And Israeli restaurants like Zahav in Philadelphia, Mishiguene in Buenos Aires, and Balagan in Paris are now some of the hottest restaurants in the world. I often say that Israeli food trumps politics; everyone loves Israeli food.

My best friend at the time was Genia Horvitz, the director of Ulpan Etzion, a beautiful, mysterious young woman with bright green-hazel eyes. Her mother was descended from the Romanovs, and her father was Russian Jewish. When he decided to emigrate from the Soviet Union in the 1960s, before the USSR stopped diplomatic relations with Israel after the Six-Day War in 1967, she chose to accompany him on aliyah to Israel.

One of our favorite places to stop in those days was a coffee shop that we called Rails, right inside the old city. I suppose it got that name because we rested our feet on the iron rails while sipping coffee and eating freshly baked sesame bagele. Located across from David's Tower, the café was a great and delicious perch from which to watch a hurried procession of Jerusalemites going by. It was there that I first understood Teddy's description of the city as a mosaic of peoples. From one boyfriend of the moment, I also learned that you had to watch closely—if a shoe shiner or peddler was sitting right outside one of the gates of the Old City, wearing an expensive watch, you could bet that he was an informer for the Israeli government.

We always bought the bagele, floppy rolls with a hole strung on a stick. I later learned that similar sticks were used by bagel vendors in Poland before the war. These rolls were like Russian bagels, called obvarinok (baked only), and thus softer than the typically boiled and baked bagel. They were sold with a spice mixture of salt and za'atar in a tiny piece of newspaper and sprinkled on the still-warm bread. Today you can still find the same bagele at the same corner, with the same spices.

During that time, Genia and I spent a day together that would change both our lives. It was late December 1970, near the Western Wall. Genia was organizing a protest for the Soviet dissidents on trial who had tried to hijack a plane to go to Israel. At first, they tried to charter an aircraft, telling people—too many, as it turned out—that they were going to a wedding in Armenia. When that story was found out, a core group of activists switched tactics and decided to board a smaller plane with a route along the Finnish-Russian border. At the stopover they would overpower the pilot and fly the plane out of the Soviet Union and, presumably, to freedom. They were arrested on the tarmac before they could even carry out their plan. After a trial that gained the world's attention, the two leaders, Edward Kuznetsov and Mark Dymshits, were sentenced to death and the others to many years in prison.

Although there had been much dissension within the Soviet Union before, somehow this "First Leningrad Trial," as it was known then, brought attention to human-rights violations in the USSR, with such international attention that the Soviet regime commuted the death sentences and began, over time, to loosen emigration restrictions, culminating in a grand exodus of Soviet Jews by the 1990s.

Genia needed my help in organizing the protest. We arrived at the designated place, about fifty feet from the Western Wall. Soon a tall, imposing blond man arrived, who I later learned was a member of the Israeli Ministry of Justice, who was sent to the protest to try to seduce a woman the Israeli government thought was a spy. Another good-looking Russian scientist, a geologist, was also one of the protesters. The

In my kitchen in Jerusalem, 1971

upshot of that day was that I fell in love with and later married the tall blond man, Allan Gerson, and Genia married the geologist. Coincidentally, neither Genia nor I started going out with our future husbands for a few years. For me, it was only when I finally returned from Israel to New York in 1972 that Allan and I reconnected.

During all this time, I lived first at the ulpan, then at various places until I stumbled on an apartment on the top floor of an old house with a large, circular rooftop porch looking over Bethlehem on one side and the Old City on the other. It had a big bedroom and huge living room with a gallery-bar-type kitchen attached. The rent was about $110 per month. I loved it.

At about the time that I moved to this apartment, I had an idea: why not write a book about all the people in Jerusalem, using food to tell their stories? "Did I tell you that a friend and I are working on a future best seller?" I wrote to my parents. "We are writing a cookbook on Jerusalem—getting recipes from all the ethnic backgrounds in this city." Thus began my cookbook writing career, with Judy Stacey Goldman, a colleague and later a guide in Israel. Our idea

in the beginning was to invite the foreign press and their wives for cooking lessons in homes throughout Jerusalem, so they could get to know people through their recipes. We did this as a lark, and it turned into a profession for me. I watched home cooks make hummus, stuff vegetables for ancient Kurdish and Moroccan delicacies, and so much more, learning their techniques and tricks. That's how I have learned to cook through all these years—not by professional training—and I still bring each person into the kitchen with me every time I make their recipes.

If you are writing a first cookbook, I recommend working with another person. It is so helpful to have someone to push you, and the project is not so lonely. Although, in retrospect, I admit that if you have great editors, as I have had, and a good assistant to help hone your words, you do not feel so alone during the process anyway.

Because we both knew so many Jews, Christians, and Muslims in the city from working in Teddy's office, eating in their homes, and just living in Jerusalem, we decided to include headnotes to the recipes about the communities from which the cooks came.

Am presently in Caesarea with friends in a lovely home overlooking a Roman aqueduct. Have been relaxing away from the turmoil of Jerusalem for a few days working on the book and interspersing my writing with horseback riding and tennis with an occasional plunge into the sea. This kind of life is becoming dangerously appealing to me—so much so that the idea of returning to New York City has less than any appeal whatsoever.

—*Letter to a friend, July 1, 1972*

When I came back from Caesarea, Judy and I had enough material for me to show to Teddy. Knowing that he relaxed and read *Time* magazine at home on Friday nights—I have no idea how I knew that!—I put our manuscript on the pile of papers he would take home to read. Two days later, he tossed the manuscript on my desk, saying, "It is charming. I will do anything I can to help you." He wrote the foreword to the book.

That same year, Cornell Capa, a member of the collective Magnum Photos, was in Israel, working with colleagues like Marc Riboud, David Rubinger, and Ernest Haas on a book that would become *Jerusalem: City of Mankind*. Cornell laughingly told me that if ever I got a publisher for our book, he would provide the photographs. When Little, Brown eventually agreed to publish *The Flavor of Jerusalem*, he stuck to his word.

Later that summer, with some friends from Jerusalem, I took a jeep trip to the Sinai. After climbing the mountain where Moses had received the Ten Commandments, I felt that I had been carried back thousands of years. There was nothing then in the Sinai but multitudes of different kinds of rock formations—pinks, blues, and grays—an occasional miniature Grand Canyon, an oasis here and there with flowers sprouting up in surprising places, Bedouins with their ibexes, and, once in a while, a bus or car. After a day or two, time seemed so unimportant and I felt so insignificant.

Ever since my trip to the Sinai, I have played a little game with myself. When I think of Jewish food—and all food, really—I think about being in the desert where the most basic food is found. I look at a filled plate and think about what people ate once and what travel and civilization have brought to the palate. Today, when we are going through climate change, this game has special significance, because it seems to me that we are returning to the very basics of civilization: to dishes like hummus, falafel, and simple flatbread that can be cooked quickly over a fire. Chickpeas, the protein of the poor in the past, which require little water to grow, have already become the protein of the future.

Ancient Yet So Modern "Risotto"

Serves 6 to 8

1 cup freekeh

1 cup #3 (coarse) bulgur

1 cup wheat berries

4 scallions, thinly sliced

2 cloves garlic, minced

3 tablespoons olive oil

1 cup yellow, red, or orange
   lentils

4 to 5 cups (946 ml) vegetable
   broth

Kosher salt and freshly
   ground black pepper,
   to taste

1 teaspoon ground cumin

1 cup diced fresh tomatoes

½ cup chopped fresh Italian
   parsley

2 tablespoons lemon juice

2 tablespoons butter
   (optional)

Za'atar, for sprinkling

When I returned to Israel in 2022, I started my visit in the bucolic village of Ein Kerem, outside of Jerusalem. Poppies and anemones (Allan's favorite flowers) were starting to bloom in the fields, and my host, Ezra Kedem, one of the first of the new Israeli chefs with his high-end restaurant, Arkadia, set chairs down right in the middle of the ancient field in the Jerusalem Hills. I felt I was back at the time of the Romans in this birthplace of Saint John the Baptist and so close to the Convent of the Sisters of Zion. Nearby were cardoons, which Ezra Kedem's Kurdish mother used in stews for him while he was growing up in Jerusalem, and wild artichokes similar to those eaten in Rome in 400 B.C.E., according to Aristotle. Mentioned with other thistles in the Talmud, they have been immortalized in Rome as carciofi alla giudia.

Here, too, grew emmer wheat—the mother of wheat—and lentils, wild greens that we in America call weeds (such as mallow, known in Arabic as khubeiza), and cultivated lettuce. Thyme, rosemary, and mint grew wild here, with mint used in the tea offered to me while we were chatting. I felt so at peace in this field that I didn't want to leave. It was as if time stood still. Then Ezra took me to his kitchen and made for me a simple, delicious dish that he thinks was the precursor of risotto. After gathering freekeh, bulgur, wheat berries, and various lentils—some from the garden, some from the market—he sautéed spring onions and lots of garlic, and added vegetable stock made from the wild "weeds." Then he added a variety of ancient legumes, some soaked first in water, stirred as he would a risotto, and added a little local olive oil and a bit of butter. It was delicious and nutritious. At home, I top it with za'atar to recall the wild herbs of antiquity.

1. Bring a medium pot of water to a boil over high heat, then add the freekeh, bulgur, and wheat berries, blanch for 2 minutes, and drain.

2. In the same pot, sauté the scallions and garlic in 2 tablespoons of olive oil for a few minutes. Then add the lentils, and cover with about 2 cups of the broth. Sprinkle with salt, pepper, and cumin, stir in half the tomatoes and parsley, and bring the liquid to a boil over medium-high heat. Cook, stirring often, for about 10 minutes, or until most of the liquid has been absorbed.

3. Gradually add the remaining broth, and cook, stirring, until the wheat berries and freekeh are cooked and the liquid is mostly absorbed. Then add the remaining tomatoes and parsley, the lemon juice, and the last tablespoon of the olive oil. Stir in some butter, if using, taste, and adjust the seasonings. Sprinkle with za'atar, and serve immediately.

Note You can also cook the risotto ahead and then put it into a well-greased nonstick frying pan to reheat for about 20 minutes, forming a crusty bottom. Then flip it when it's done, sprinkle with za'atar, and serve immediately as a pilav with a crusty top.

When I returned from the Sinai, and during my remaining time in Israel, something else came over me. I realized how small the country was, and, for me, it became slightly claustrophobic. I missed my family and the English language. It was 1972, and I was excited about the McGovern campaign. I realized, too, that until I was finished with this exciting job with Teddy, I would never have a personal life. So I decided to return home.

When I moved to Israel, I thought it would be for one year; I ended up staying two and a half. And I made my mother happy because I did meet my husband there. Even after I returned to the States, Israel never left me. There's a saying that you don't have to live in Israel, but that Israel teaches you how to live. Each time I taste eggplant, Kurdish kubbeh, hummus, or any of the other great dishes I learned from people in Jerusalem, I remember the many lessons Israel taught me. And I also carried a manuscript back with me that would become my first cookbook, *The Flavor of Jerusalem*.

My experiences in Jerusalem in the early 1970s, often centering on people and food, taught me so much about myself as a Jew, but also about other human beings, and the role food plays in all our lives. Since then, although still not kosher, I have not served shellfish or pork in my house, and I have spent a lifetime trying to find the old recipes from around the world that have come back to Jerusalem.

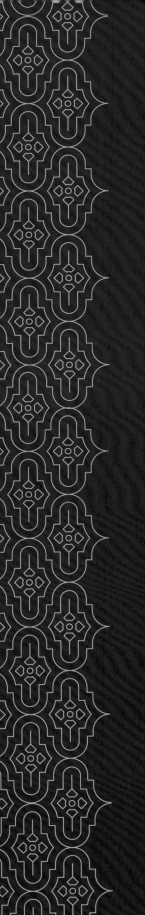

11.

A Short Sojourn in Africa

Mango Poached in a Vanilla Syrup

Serves 6 to 8

6 mangoes, ripe but not too
   ripe (preferably Ataúlfo
   mangoes)
1 cup (200 grams) sugar
1 tablespoon lemon juice
1 vanilla bean
1 cinnamon stick

When I visited Madagascar's highland city of Antsirabe, one of the most gorgeous French colonial cities I have ever seen, we stayed at a Frenchman's home right in the middle of a rice field. One day, I noticed a glass jar of ripe mangoes in sugar water with a scraped vanilla pod, which sat in the sun for several days. The sun's warmth infused the vanilla into the syrup, perfuming the mangoes. It was delicious in its simplicity. When I make it now, I give the mangoes and vanilla a little push with heat from the stove.

I love using vanilla bean in syrups, and it's even better with cinnamon added. Serve this dish alone with some fresh mint, or better yet, with vanilla ice cream.

1. Since the mango and its pit have a flattened shape, you have to follow the natural contours of the fruit when cutting. Hold the mango flat, with the stem side in the palm of your hand. Using a sharp knife, slice along the flat side from the stem end down over the pit. Open the mango up, score one half carefully crosswise into six or seven strips, and pull the peel back, releasing the strips so they fall into a bowl (discard the peel). You might need your knife to help scrape the flesh from the pit. Repeat with the second half. Do the same with the remaining mangoes. Set them aside in a large bowl.

2. Add the sugar and lemon juice to about 3 cups of water in a saucepan. Bring it to a boil, skimming off any foam that may accumulate, and boil for about 10 minutes, stirring occasionally, until the liquid thickens ever so slightly. Then add the mango pieces, and simmer for about 5 minutes.

3. Remove the mangoes from the stove and scrape the vanilla bean to release the tiny flecks of seeds, and sprinkle these, with the pods and the cinnamon stick, over the mangoes. Let this mixture sit until you're ready to serve. Serve alone or, better yet, with a scoop of vanilla ice cream. This will keep for a few weeks in the fridge.

12.

Planting the Seeds for a Writing Career

When I came back from Israel, in the early fall of 1972, I first tried to become a freelance writer and to find a publisher for our cookbook. To my surprise—as a novice at this game—freelancing was a difficult and solitary business.

Trying to get a publisher was also not so easy. I tried sixteen before I found one that was willing to accept our manuscript. Judy and I were so young that we insisted the book be exactly as we had written it. Soon it became clear that it was being rejected by so many because we had decided that, since Jerusalem was a mosaic of people, with some following the Jewish dietary laws and some not, we would show the city as it really was—a mixture of Jews, Christians, and Muslims, all with their own dietary laws. Finally, Little, Brown clinched the deal, through the help of Blaine Littell, then Jerusalem correspondent for *Time* magazine, whose parent company, Time Life, was Little, Brown's owner at the time. Then we still had to wait for months for the contract to be signed, and yet another year for the book to be published.

When *The Flavor of Jerusalem* finally came out, in 1975, and received excellent reviews, Little, Brown's publicity department had the not-so-brilliant idea of putting a shrimp sukiyaki recipe in a promotional brochure they made announcing I would be willing to speak at Hadassah groups all over the country. The shrimp recipe—shellfish and therefore not kosher—was like serving pork to Muslims. Not great publicity.

It was during this time that, while accompanying a mutual friend from Jerusalem to speak at Yale, I met Allan Gerson again. At the time, Allan was studying for his doctorate in law. Allan and I started dating right away. Our first official date was accompanying his parents to Radio City Music Hall, a treat Allan was giving them on their retirement from running a dry-cleaning store. I thought that was so sweet.

Somehow, I have always been attracted to men who were born abroad and were dreamers. When I was in France with Henri, I wrote in my diary,

"Yesterday I realized that I never wanted to reach the point where a boy meant my entire life. I never want to be dependent on another for my happiness. Perhaps someone can help me find happiness, but it is too helpless a feeling to totally depend on another. I am too strong for that to happen, I hope." Allan may have been a different kind of dreamer than Henri was, but throughout our forty-five years together, he supported me in having my own career, and even reveled in it.

And, unlike so many of my boyfriends through the years, Allan slowly fit like a comfortable glove. But he was also someone with whom I wanted to spend a lifetime—whose values I admired, who was unafraid of a strong woman, and who made me laugh, something I so appreciated throughout my life.

As Allan and I got to know each other, I learned more and more about cooking. I was testing my own recipes and trying Craig Claiborne's and Julia Child's. The 1970s only increased the options: Madeleine Kamman's *The Making of a Cook* was published in 1971, Diana Kennedy's *Cuisines of Mexico* in 1972, then Marcella Hazan's *Classic Italian Cook Book* and Madhur Jaffrey's *Invitation to Indian Cooking*, both in 1973, the year after I came back from Israel. I spent my time cooking at home, honing my skills, saving money, and reading my favorite cookbooks, especially Claudia Roden's *Book of Middle Eastern Food* (1968), because I was so impressed with the archival and hands-on roots research she had done into the origins of Middle Eastern food.

At about that time, with the publication of Julia Child's second volume of *Mastering the Art of French Cooking* in 1970, a young publicist who had chutzpah, Jane Friedman, created the notion of the author's tour with television, radio, and print interviews as well as cooking demonstrations in department stores. Jane, who later became the CEO of HarperCollins and then founder of Open Road Media, wasn't sure what would happen, but she set up this tour for Julia, who was already known from her *French Chef* series on PBS. "I looked out the window in Minneapolis," Jane told me. "It faced Dayton's Department Store,

With Allan when we were courting

and I was amazed by a line of mainly women that wound around the block, waiting for the store to open so that they could get a good seat to watch Julia. And they all bought books."

The rest is history.

When I realized that I needed more money to live on, I went to Tom Morgan, Mayor John Lindsay's press secretary, whom Teddy had suggested might want to help me. As luck would have it, Tom's favorite mayor in the world was Teddy, so he found me a job doing public relations for the New York City Mayor's Office of Midtown Planning and Development.

When I got back to New York, I stayed at a friend's on West End Avenue until I could find my footing and a place of my own. With the financial security of a job, I asked Allan to help me find my next apartment. We found a great one on the East Side, right on the top of a 1925 prewar building at 108 East Eighty-sixth Street, between Lexington and Park Avenues. From the fourteenth floor, you walked up to the roof from the elevator (when it was working), where there was a little house with a bedroom, a living room, and a tiny kitchen. Although I loved it, I thought it was too expensive. But Allan encouraged me to rent the apartment, and I never regretted it.

Shortly after I started working, I got a call from Charles Guggenheim, an Academy Award–winning documentary filmmaker who had made his career at the 1968 Chicago Democratic Convention with the eulogy film *Robert Kennedy Remembered*. "You want to go back to 'Jeru' for four months?" he asked. Charles wanted me to be his assistant on one of the films he was making for the Israeli Ministry of Foreign Affairs. I had met him and his family when he was scouting two movies in Jerusalem.

Since I had just started my job with the may-

or's office, I was reluctant to request a leave of absence, but I did anyway. It helped that Allan was also going to Jerusalem, to work on the dissertation for his J.S.D. for Yale, about the legal aspects of the military occupation of the West Bank; it was published later as *Israel, the West Bank & International Law*. So we went together in mid-August 1973, and stayed with the crew at the American Colony Hotel.

Before Charles and his team came, I accompanied Allan on his interview of the mayor of Nablus, Mazoz Masri. They talked about politics for at least two hours. By one-forty-five, I was hungry and a little bored. So I interrupted, asking a question of the mayor: "Is it true that the best knafeh in the Middle East is in Nablus?" Not missing a beat, the mayor looked at his watch and said, "The best is in my house. Have you had lunch yet?" And off we went, for a wonderful meal, including Middle Eastern mezze, rice, chicken, and, for dessert, a large tray of knafeh, a dessert made from kataifi—crisp spun pastry—soaked in a sugar syrup and layered with sheep's cheese, which I am sure that, at such short notice, the mayor ordered from a local pastry shop. The whole tenor of the two men's conversation changed during that meal. Not only were we all more relaxed, but certain barriers were broken.

Most of that trip, I was working with Charles on his documentary film (*Jerusalem Lives*), doing advance and production work. The film was to be a contemporary profile of the city of Jerusalem, seen through the eyes of a Jew, a Catholic, a Protestant, and a Muslim, narrated by Meron Benvenisti, Jerusalem's deputy mayor in charge of East Jerusalem, whom *Time* magazine called the prophet of Israel. The film profiled this fractured city by illustrating its subjects' common love of Jerusalem, the city where they all lived, despite their different perspectives. Charles chose Meron, fondly calling him the Bear, because Meron, whose family had lived in Jerusalem for generations, was deeply rooted in the land of Israel, with all its beauty, history, and contradictions.

On the morning of Yom Kippur, October 6, 1973, Meron arrived in the courtyard of the American Colony, where Charles and I were sitting, and told us, "Golda Meir just announced that the Syrians have attacked the Golan Heights. We are at war." I thought Charles's eyes would pop out of his head. "What? I have a family. I am the father of three children. I must leave." We got him on a plane back to Washington as soon as we could, but Allan and I stayed. Allan's parents were living in Netanya at the time, and we both thought the war wouldn't last long, so I was to finish up loose ends of the film. After all, the Six-Day War only lasted six days.

That same day, I got a phone call from Charlie Mohr, the *New York Times* war correspondent, whom I knew from my days with Teddy. He urged me to come up to the front in the north. Allan thought I was crazy, but we both wanted to volunteer in the hospitals, so we took Charles's van and hightailed it up north through the Jordan Valley for a day or two. Strangely enough, when we were up near the Golan Heights, we felt less nervous than we felt farther from the war, in Jerusalem. We stayed a couple of days, but no hospitals needed volunteers. I remember watching planes playing chicken in the air. When we got back, the news got worse and worse. This would be no Six-Day War.

A few days later, Allan went to see his parents, and I flew home to give speeches to Americans, asking for help. Eventually, the war stopped, and Golda Meir lost her position as prime minister. Our film was edited in the States, but unfortunately never shown.

Starting the Ninth Avenue Festival

Ninth Avenue is a marvelous gastronomic melting pot of—we are told—
22 ethnic groups. It is a vibrant, colorful, serious, knockabout, hodgepodge
of good things to see and feast from 36th to 53rd Streets. And that
monumental 17-block marketplace will celebrate its existence with a two-day
carnival on May 11, and 12—a festival that will offer music, prizes, free food
and wines, dancing in the streets, and joy in general.

—*Craig Claiborne,* The New York Times, *May 8, 1974*

Almost fifty years after its founding, the Ninth Avenue International Food Festival is touted as the largest and oldest continuous street food festival in New York City, attracting each year hundreds of thousands of food lovers from around the world.

But in the late winter of 1973, when John Phillips, who also worked in my office, and I had the idea of creating a festival along that corridor bustling with mom-and-pop businesses, international grocery stores, and a diverse immigrant population, the only street festival in New York was the Feast of San Gennaro.

When I returned from Israel and resumed working at the Mayor's Office of Midtown Planning and Development, I met John, an urban planner (and avid cook) in the office located on Forty-second Street near the porn shops that were to be cleaned up (another part of the office's job!). When the Ninth Avenue Association approached us one day, asking how they could raise the neighborhood's visibility, John and I suggested a festival highlighting the ethnic and culinary diversity of the area. Although some of the merchants in the Ninth Avenue Association loved the idea, they couldn't budge the other

small shopowners. Our idea had no budget and no financial support.

But that didn't stop us.

First, we convinced Sid Frigand, the press secretary to the new mayor, Abraham Beame, that we wanted to reserve the city's mobile park units and bandstands for the festival on the second weekend of May 1974, and that we wanted the mayor's office to cooperate with us. Ultimately, with their backing, we forged ahead.

Then we formed a committee of merchants and lovers of Ninth Avenue. Lili Fable from Poseidon Bakery, Maria Gardini from Alps Drugstore, and our team started by walking up and down the long avenue, from Thirty-seventh to Fifty-third Street, going into the stores, trying to convince the owners how nice it would be for them to participate in a festival to take place in May. That was the hardest part; many of them were just trying to survive, despite rising real-estate prices. Even convincing the owners to put flags outside their stores proved difficult.

We next visited James Beard at his home on Patchin Place, a block from today's James Beard House. A few days later, after taking a short stroll with John and me down Ninth Avenue, James was sold on the project. With him on board, we met with Craig Claiborne, George Lang, Madhur Jaffrey, and Tom Morgan (then the managing editor of *New York* magazine) and asked them to be on our planning committee. Since at that time everyone in New York—before food had achieved the star status it has today—had a soft spot in their hearts for Ninth Avenue, they all cooperated.

Each time someone new agreed to participate, we were so excited. In order to get a better idea of what we were doing, the group planned to meet at Wolf's paint store (Stephen Wolf was then president of the Ninth Avenue Association) at Fifty-second Street and walk down to have lunch at Giordano's, the now long-gone Triestine restaurant on Thirty-ninth Street. A few days before the meeting, we learned that James had a bad foot and could not walk down the avenue. We decided to find a golf cart for him. (Unfortunately, he wound up in the hospital and couldn't come.)

At the luncheon, we laid out our plans, which included asking cookbook authors to stand outside stores, demonstrating recipes and selling their books. We also wanted to engage people from local communities, like the Croatian church, to grill meats outside and have food demonstrations in front of stores, such as making phyllo dough outside Poseidon Bakery. The second year, the bakery sold five thousand tastes of spanakopita, giving New Yorkers a broad introduction to a dish that had been known primarily within the Greek community.

Lili Fable, her baker son Paul, and his family still live and work in the building that her husband's father bought on Ninth Avenue in 1950. He found it after being displaced by the Port Authority from his original bakery, on Fortieth Street off Ninth Avenue, which, as an immigrant from Greece, he had found years before, literally walking off a boat from Epirus. "By saving and buying this building," Lili told me, "he secured our future. That is the American dream."

Poseidon's Spanakopita
(Greek Spinach Pie)

Craig Claiborne introduced non-Greek New Yorkers to Greek spanako-pita in 1961, when he ran a recipe for a spinach-feta strudel from Mr. and Mrs. Leon Lianides in the Appetizers section of his *New York Times Cookbook*. He called their Coach House Restaurant "one of the city's best 'American' restaurants." Nine years later, he talked about "an incredibly good spinach pie baked in layers of leafy thin phyllo pastry" for Greek Easter.

Although this is Lili Fable's classic recipe, which you can still watch people in the family making in their store, feel free to include Swiss chard, kale, or broccoli with the spinach, or leeks or shallots for the scallions, as I am sure the ancients did. This recipe is so good that you can vary it quite a bit and still end up with a winner for your family.

---

1. In a large (10-inch) ovenproof skillet, warm the olive oil over medium heat, then add the spinach. Cook until it's wilted, about 3 minutes. Remove it and drain it in a colander. Wipe the skillet clean, then add the ¼ cup of butter, and sauté the onions and leek or scallions until they're golden, about 10 minutes.

2. Put the cooked onion mixture into a large bowl, then add the feta, dill, parsley, eggs, and egg yolk, and mix well. Add the spinach, and mix to incorporate it.

3. Preheat the oven to 400 degrees, and wipe the skillet clean. Brush the bottom and sides of the skillet with some of the ¾ cup of melted butter, then brush a little on your work surface.

4. Quickly brush some butter on a phyllo sheet, and lay it, buttered side up, on the skillet so that plenty hangs over the edge. (Keep the yet-to-be-buttered phyllo covered with a damp cloth as you work.) Press to get rid of any large air bubbles between the phyllo and the pan, then continue buttering, laying, and pressing as you add each phyllo sheet, rotating the pan so that the bottom is completely covered and the overhang goes all the way around the skillet. →

Serves 8 to 10 as
a main course

3 tablespoons olive oil
2 pounds (907 grams) fresh
   spinach, washed, drained,
   and chopped, or two
   10-ounce (284-gram)
   boxes frozen spinach
   (substitute or mix with
   Swiss chard, kale, or beet
   greens if you like)
¼ cup (½ stick/56 grams)
   unsalted butter, plus
   ¾ cup (1½ sticks/168 grams)
   melted unsalted butter
2 large onions, minced
   (about 3 cups)
1 large leek or 2 bunches
   scallions, finely chopped
1½ cups (8 ounces/226 grams)
   crumbled feta cheese
½ cup chopped fresh dill
¼ cup chopped fresh Italian
   parsley
2 large eggs, plus 1 large egg
   yolk
Eight 9-by-14-inch
   phyllo sheets, at room
   temperature

5. Add the spinach mixture in an even layer to the skillet. One at a time, lift the overhanging phyllo sheets over the spinach mixture and toward the center, crinkling the dough as you go. You'll end up with a circle of uncovered spinach in the middle, surrounded by a ring of phyllo.

6. Cook over medium heat on the stovetop for about 5 minutes, to crisp the bottom crust. Transfer the pan to the middle rack of the oven, and bake until the phyllo is golden and the filling is warmed, 20 to 25 minutes.

We gathered quite a group, including Diana Kennedy, who stood outside Alps Drugstore demonstrating guacamole on a table, and other giants, like Edna Lewis, and George Lang, one of my intellectual heroes, a Renaissance man. His *The Cuisine of Hungary* has so much more than recipes in it, and reflects the culture and history of his time. After the festival, I visited his apartment, near his restaurant Café des Artistes, and was so impressed with his Traulsen refrigerator that I promised myself to have one just like it when I had my own house—minus the see-through windows that would reveal my, let us say, more casual or hurried way of organizing food. When Allan and I finished building our house in 1987, I got that refrigerator.

Among the many ideas going through our heads for the festival was to have an artist design a food float. The mayor's office agreed to the float but insisted that it be smaller than the horse-drawn carriage of tiny Abe Beame, his wife, and Steve Wolf, who was representing the Ninth Avenue Association merchants, so we enlisted the help of the Hilton Hotel on nearby Sixth Avenue, which provided space for an artist, Tony Miranda, to build a sculpture out of two thousand pounds of dyed rice and pasta, decorated with colorful vegetables and fruits and brightly dyed bread, on a flatbed truck, to go down the avenue pulled by a horse-drawn cart. That wastefulness would (or should) never pass muster now.

Up until a few days before the two-day festival, not all the shop owners had agreed to open for the weekend. Then a small miracle happened, despite our zero-publicity budget—an unexpected burst of publicity on Tuesday and Wednesday—and they all wanted in, decorating their stores with colorful flags. Craig Claiborne devoted almost an entire page to Ninth Avenue on the Wednesday before the festival. And *New York* magazine published a pull-out section with a map and photograph of the avenue on shiny paper that could stand alone. Both Craig and Tom were furious with us. Each wanted exclusivity. When they both complained, John and I realized we were quite naïve about the press.

As a result of this advance publicity, at a time when most food-interested people in New York read either *The New York Times* or *New York* magazine or both, we had great local TV and radio press. Still, the night before the festival, I called John—no texting or email in those years. I was not sure if anyone would show up. To our delighted astonishment, more than a hundred thousand people came, and everyone, politicians included, wanted to participate. The festival opened with Mayor Beame, seated in his horse-drawn carriage, followed by the lower food float on a flatbed truck going down the avenue, ending up at Forty-second Street at one of the mobile units set up for the occasion, where the mayor would cut the ribbon to open the event. I remember that as he and his political cronies walked onto the stage, Bella Abzug, the feminist congresswoman who wore her wide straw hat as always, came up to John and me and said, "If I'm not up there on the stage, I'll have your job." She got onstage.

One part of the festival that warmed my heart was the spaghetti-eating contest, in which participants dug into large bowls of tomato-dressed pasta, with their hands tied behind their backs. Allan entered and came in second, behind a hefty opera singer. Every time we ate spaghetti after that, we heard the messy, tomatoey story, with

Allan's usual hilarious embellishment, as only he could do. A few weeks after the festival, while relaxing on the beach in Bermuda, we relived the experience when we read about it in a *New Yorker* Talk of the Town piece on the event.

The neighborhood, despite the Ninth Avenue Association's wish, has changed drastically, caught in the real-estate tidal wave. But the Ninth Avenue Festival has continued every year since (except during COVID), and attendance has grown to a half-million people. Though it may not be as homespun as that first year, it still proclaims the love of good food that overflows in New York. And, fortunately, Lili Fable's Poseidon Bakery continues making homemade phyllo, one of the few places in America still to do so.

This was, in a way, a sort of template that I would continue to use throughout my life: putting together people, food, and culture, whether it be in a fair, a cookbook, or a dinner party. And John Phillips, who wrote two *Ninth Avenue Cookbooks*, is still cooking one of my favorite chicken dishes, with the pungent flavor of curry and ginger combined with the sweetness of orange juice, a dish that I also cook to this day.

Orange Ginger Chicken

1. Dredge the chicken breasts in the flour seasoned with salt and pepper and put on a plate.

2. Heat the oil in a skillet until it bubbles slightly. Stir in the curry powder and ground or fresh ginger, and cook for about 15 seconds. Add the chicken breasts to the skillet, skin side down, and cook for about 5 minutes, until they're golden brown on one side. Turn them over, and cook for about 2 minutes on the other side. Remove the chicken from the skillet to a plate.

3. To the skillet add the wine, chicken broth, and orange juice. Scrape the bottom of the skillet to dislodge any stuck-on bits. Bring the liquid to a boil, return the breasts to the skillet, skin side up, add the orange sections, and spoon the sauce over them. Dot the chicken with the crystallized ginger, and simmer, covered, for about 10 minutes, or until the chicken is done. Serve with rice.

Serves 4 to 6

4 to 6 boneless, skin-on
   chicken breasts
1 cup unbleached all-purpose
   flour or matzo meal,
   for dredging
Kosher salt and freshly
   ground black pepper,
   for dredging
⅓ cup (80 ml) extra-virgin
   olive oil
1 teaspoon curry powder
2 teaspoons ground ginger,
   or 1½ tablespoons freshly
   grated ginger
½ cup (120 ml) white wine
1 cup (240 ml) chicken broth
1½ cups (360 ml) orange juice
1 orange, cut into sections
½ cup (60 grams) crystallized
   ginger, finely chopped
Cooked rice, for serving

Allan and me a week before our wedding

13.

Love, Marriage, and a New Beginning

One of Allan's favorite stories was that when he arrived in Manhattan Harbor from Europe, as a five-year-old child in 1950, he put his hand up in the air and covered the Statue of Liberty with his fingers. "See, it is not so big," he said in Yiddish to his parents, who were standing with him on the deck. Liberty and patriotism were hallmarks of his life from that day on. He wrote about that, believed in it, and tried to live his life by it.

The Gersons arrived here with the help of HIAS, the Hebrew Immigrant Aid Society, from the Föhrenwald displaced-person camp outside Munich after the war. His parents, Morton and Paula Gerson, were originally from Zamość, Poland—a beautiful late-Renaissance town, built in 1580 and modeled after Siena with its wide piazza. Jewish people had lived there since the

Allan (far right) with his parents, Morton and Paula, and his younger brother, Sam, on the way from the DP camp to the U.S.

sixteenth century when they were invited from Italy by the nobleman Jan Zamoyski. In the fall of 1939 Morton and Paula fled to Soviet-occupied territory but they were deported in June 1940, to Siberia. After the United States entered the war in the summer of 1941, they were released from forced labor in the gulag and then worked their way down to Samarkand, Uzbekistan, where Allan was born in 1945. Although the Gersons initially wanted to go to Palestine, they changed their route, for many reasons—one being that they had lost a baby during the war and knew life was difficult in Palestine with children—and went to Germany and the Föhrenwald DP camp, eventually assuming the papers of the Blumstein family, who went to France. As the Blumsteins, they later entered the States, where they lived in Brooklyn, then the Bronx, fearing every day that they would be discovered and sent back to Europe. It was only when Allan, as he was about to turn thir-teen, wondered why his parents weren't preparing a Bar Mitzvah for him that he learned of his real identity and age . . . eleven. He would have to wait another year and a half for his Bar Mitzvah.

Despite the secrets of their lives, and the difficulties of starting a dry-cleaning store with no money, his mother—who had lost almost her entire family at the Belzec concentration camp, only a few train stops from Zamość—still had a love for her early life in Poland and always, despite the horrors of her wartime experience, maintained a strong sense of pride in herself and her family. Paula had an amazing memory of the fraises du bois and farmer's cheese that she had found in the farmers' markets in the springtime in Zamość. She was a marvelous cook, and introduced me to homemade gefilte fish, kreplach, and so many other Eastern European Jewish foods with which I had not grown up.

Caramelized and Spiced "Jewish" Apple Cake

7 medium apples
   (such as Honeycrisp,
   Granny Smith, Jonathan,
   Gala, Stayman, or any that
   are flavorful and will hold
   their shape), cored, peeled,
   and cut into eighths about
   ½-inch thick (about 8 cups)
Grated zest and juice of
   1 lemon
4 large eggs
1 cup (236 ml) vegetable oil,
   plus more for greasing pan
2 cups (400 grams) sugar
1 tablespoon vanilla extract
½ cup apple cider
3 cups (405 grams)
   unbleached all-purpose
   flour, plus more for the pan
1 tablespoon baking powder
½ teaspoon salt
1 tablespoon ground
   cinnamon (divided)
½ teaspoon ground
   nutmeg (divided)
1 teaspoon ground
   cardamon (divided)
1 teaspoon ground
   ginger (divided)
2 tablespoons diced
   crystallized ginger

I am a fruit-dessert person and love to make apple pies, crisps, and cakes throughout the winter.

Years ago, I stumbled on a recipe for "Jewish" Apple Cake in *Mrs. Kitching's Smith Island Cookbook* (1981). When I asked Frances Kitching, who ran a boardinghouse on this remote island in the Chesapeake Bay—population about 550—where the recipe originated, she said she got it from her grandmother, who had lived on Smith Island all her life. When I baked it at home, my husband was thrilled. It tasted, he said, just like his mother's Polish apple cake, which she made in a beaten-up rectangular baking pan.

Around the year 1981, I found the recipe in other local cookbooks. Since then, I have learned that it is also called Philadelphia Jewish Apple Cake, some people thinking it originated with the Pennsylvania Dutch. I suspect that someone, years ago, got the recipe from an immigrant Jewish woman in Baltimore or Philadelphia who used vegetable oil or Crisco rather than lard or butter in the batter, thus making it parve. For many Gentile cooks it became Jewish Apple Cake.

Just recently, I returned to the old dessert and gave it a facelift, caramelizing the top layer of apples.

---

1. Preheat the oven to 350 degrees. Line the bottom and sides of a 9-inch springform pan with parchment paper.

2. In a large bowl, toss the apples with the lemon zest and juice, and add ½ cup sugar, 1½ teaspoon cinnamon, ¼ teaspoon nutmeg, ½ teaspoon cardamon, and ½ teaspoon ginger. Set them aside.

3. In the bowl of a standing mixer beat the eggs until foamy. Then add the vegetable oil, the remaining 1¼ cups of the sugar, the vanilla, and the apple cider and continue beating until mixed.

4. Stir the flour, baking powder, and salt into the wet ingredients and stir until well blended.

5. Remove a third of the apples and set aside in a bowl to use later. Spoon one third of the batter into the prepared pan and cover with half of the remaining apples. Then spoon on a second third of the batter, then the rest of these apples. Top with the remaining batter.

6. Add the reserved apples and the juices from the bowl to a medium skillet. Cook them until they soften very slightly and the sugar starts to caramelize, about 10 minutes. Be careful not to crowd the apples lest they steam and create too much moisture. Then cool slightly and place them on top of the cake, either in concentric circles or haphazardly. Sprinkle the crystalized ginger on top.

7. Bake for one hour and 15 minutes, or until a toothpick comes out clean. Let the cake sit a few minutes to cool, run a knife gently around the sides, and remove the springform. Serve the cake slightly warm or at room temperature.

Allan's father, Morton, had a strong sense of Judaism, even though his sympathies were with the Misnagdim, a movement like the Enlightenment that resisted the rise of Hasidism in the eighteenth and nineteenth centuries in Eastern Europe. He was also very active in the Workmen's Circle. When Allan and his younger brother, Sam, were growing up, the only people his parents socialized with were the like-minded Yiddish-speaking family and friends with whom they had been during the war. Allan listened to the stories they told, and spent hours staring at the photographs in the drawer of the coffee table of a world that was no more—photographs his mother's cousin Raya Eskin had found scattered on the floor of a train platform after Allan's parents had fled to Siberia. According to Raya, who took the following train, they were some of the personal belongings that the travelers were forced to leave behind. When no one was looking, Raya searched for more family photos and scooped them up, keeping them throughout the war until the family that survived were reunited in New York. Perhaps that is why, as long as I knew Allan, he always had a camera in his hand, and would beautifully capture natural wonders. I believe that this close-knit extended family group gave strength to a young child. And this was the group to whom I was introduced when we were dating, on our first Passover at the Gerson apartment in the Bronx.

Allan's family Seder was a profound shift from the gastro-cultural events of my own childhood. The story was the same and the matzot were still square—until an ultra-Orthodox friend started sending us round shmura matzo—but that about sums up the similarities. And I was fascinated by the differences, and the Gersons' ability to speak and read Yiddish. I could listen to the two of them for hours as Paula remembered stories and the food of her childhood.

As we entered Allan's parents' small apartment, we were welcomed by the aroma of chicken soup and a barrage of introductions for me to his entire family. The tiny living room was crammed with borrowed tables and chairs, to seat about forty. Morton conducted the Seder in perfect Hebrew and Yiddish and halting English. The men listened; the women hovered. Paula, secretly delighted, moaned over the number of relatives attending, all from the same town in Poland. For weeks she had been preparing the house and foods including the gefilte fish (although Aunts Ruchsha and Chuma insisted behind her back that Paula's lacked the right amount of ground almonds and salt).

No one would miss the Seder. Morton had learned how to conduct the service from his father, and Allan learned by watching and listening to him. Morton made his annual heartfelt speech in hesitant English, reminding us of the Warsaw Ghetto Uprising as an analogy to the flight to freedom long ago in Egypt. He desperately wanted his children to remember their Jewish roots and the horrors that had befallen his family before they migrated to the United States.

At my family's Seder, the meal began with two light matzo balls in a clear chicken broth and a sprig of parsley. Thank goodness, Allan approved of light matzo balls as well. Some Jews prefer matzo balls that plummet to the belly's floor like cannonballs, and marriages have shattered over less. At the Gerson Seder, the gefilte fish and matzo-ball soup were preceded by hard-boiled eggs in salted water, a custom unknown to me.

They also did not consider the kosher Israeli dry Cabernet Sauvignon a substitute for Manischewitz sweet. (To the Gersons, wine was not wine if it was not sweet.)

But I was so glad that Allan and the Gersons became part of my life. I often have thought that it was destiny that brought us together, so that Morton could translate tractates from YIVO, like Hirsz Abramowicz's now-translated chapter "The Diet of Lithuanian Jews," from *Profiles of a Lost World,* and so that Paula, a handsome woman with white hair, could nostalgically share with me her memories of Jewish food when she was growing up in a community that was mostly annihilated during the war.

As much as I enjoyed them, life was not always easy with my in-laws. They would sometimes stay for weeks, even visiting us just after we got married, when we were adjusting to living together. And, unlike my parents, they needed us to take care of them. My parents always took care of me.

Our wedding, in the fall of 1974, was a great party, with friends and family from afar, at Temple Beth-El in Providence, Rhode Island—no destination weddings in those days.

A few months before, my mother-in-law and I headed to Henri Bendel's in New York to look at wedding dresses. Paula, a dressmaker who had saved her and her family's lives by making shirts for soldiers during the war in Siberia, had a pad and pencil with her. As soon as the salesperson left the fitting room, she took notes. Then we headed to the Lower East Side, and she bought *peau de soie* fabric and duplicated the dress.

Although Allan and I planned the food, it was, as the custom was then, essentially my mother's party, with many of her and my in-laws' friends

At our wedding in the dress that Allan's mother made for me

attending. I remember a friend of my mother's taking me out to lunch and saying not to fight it. I didn't. After all, my parents were paying.

Since the meal was kosher, out of deference to a few of the Gerson guests, my mother hired a kosher caterer from nearby Massachusetts. Allan and I wanted food from Israel, so we told the caterer about hummus, something he had never heard of, as well as an orange chicken recipe I had eaten in Israel, and the American Colony's chocolate cake for dessert. Before it was popular on the East Side of Providence, we danced the hora, and Allan and I were put on chairs, as were our parents. Guests from Providence said that Temple Beth-El would never be the same again; my parents' proper friends had so much fun dancing the hora, and appreciated the chuppa, the de rigueur marriage canopy at so many Jewish and non-Jewish weddings today.

After the wedding, Allan and I drove to the Grafton Inn in Vermont for a short honeymoon.

What I remember most about our honeymoon is Allan's feet sticking out of our four-poster canopied bed. Allan was almost six foot four—beds never fit him lengthwise—and to make it worse, this bed was only full-sized. Fortunately, throughout our forty-five-year marriage, having cold toes peeking out beneath the covers never bothered him. When we inquired if we could change beds, the innkeeper said that, because it was at the height of the fall leaf colors, they were sorry, but the hotel was full. So Allan just automatically pulled the sheets out and slept on his back in his kingly pose with his feet sticking out. We had a lovely but not very romantic time in Vermont, our favorite state, hiking and tasting delicious food.

When we returned to Cambridge to meet the movers, Allan went back to work at the New England School of Law, where he was already teaching while working on his J.S.D. for Yale University. I spent the day unpacking in our apartment in a turn-of-the-century building, a short walk from Harvard Square. Allan, always the absentminded dreamy professor type and always the joker, came home thinking the six-room apartment would be readied and the table would be set for a candlelit meal for the first dinner in our new home. All he found was boxes, their contents yet to be put away, and, as he always liked to say in future years, sandwiches made of bologna that was on special at the supermarket. I can't

remember the bologna or much else about the condition of the apartment that day except that I loved it, as I loved all the places we lived throughout our long marriage.

A month later, I wrote a letter to a friend in Israel saying that if I had known how much I would enjoy married life I would not have been so hesitant to get married. What made our marriage work from the beginning was that Allan and I were two independent souls, both respecting each other. Although we rarely agreed politically, we had similar values and liked each other, good company, good food, and good conversation. It wasn't always easy for two strong-willed people to live together, but it was totally worth it! And he was certainly my touchstone, and I miss him terribly.

As we settled into married life, I discovered local ethnic markets. When I lived in Jerusalem, I was fascinated by the Armenian community who lived in their own quarter just inside Jaffa Gate. Like many others, I had grown up with "you have to finish your meal because the starving Armenians have so little food," and the events of the Armenian genocide certainly struck home in my family. One of my favorite dishes was lahmajoun, a flatbread covered with meat, spices, and herbs, which I had tasted while in Jerusalem and discovered again in Watertown's Armenian community. I soon befriended Rose Sanasarian, a sewing machine operator at a local dress factory, who taught me some of the secrets of Armenian food, especially her superb stuffed grape leaves. I feel that Armenian food is so rich because Armenians were merchants who, like the Jews and so many Arabs, explored the culinary landscape as they looked for new products to eat and to sell the world over.

Yalanchi Sarma
(Armenian Stuffed Grape Leaves)

Throughout my career, I have tried countless stuffed-grape-leaf recipes. But none equals the taste of those from Rose Sanasarian, who was born in Turkey. We were introduced by Rose's next-door neighbor in Watertown, Sheryl Julien, later the food editor for *The Boston Globe* for many years. The story about Rose and her fellow members of the St. James Armenian Apostolic Church Ladies Auxiliary that I wrote for the *Globe* was one of my favorites; I really got to know them and dove into their culture.

I can't pinpoint exactly what makes this recipe so special, but I suspect the slow cooking of the flavorful sauce has something to do with it. Whenever I'm having a large party, I serve it, and it's always a star.

---

1. Warm the oil in a large, heavy pot (such as a Dutch oven) over medium-high heat. Sauté the onions, nuts, and currants in the oil until the onions are soft but not taking on much color, 10 to 15 minutes. Add the parsley, dill, cinnamon, salt, pepper, rice, sugar, tomatoes, and ½ cup (118 ml) water. Simmer, covered, for about 15 minutes, or until the rice is almost cooked. Uncover, and squeeze juice of half the lemon over the mixture. Continue cooking, covered, 5 more minutes. Remove the pot from the heat, and scrape the filling into a bowl to cool. Rinse the pot.

2. Remove the grape leaves from the jar to drain, snip away any long stems, and line the bottom of the pot with ten leaves, dull side up. Put another leaf, dull side up, on a flat surface with the stem end facing away from you. Put 1 tablespoon of the filling on the leaf, near the stem, and flatten the filling into a rectangle about 2½ inches long. Fold the stem end over the filling, then tuck in the sides and roll from the top, away from you, to make a fairly tight cylinder. Repeat with the remaining leaves and filling, using more or less filling depending on the size of the leaf. (To go more quickly, make an assembly line: lay out as many grape leaves as you can, then add the filling, shape the filling, and roll.) →

Makes 60 to 70 grape leaves

¾ cup (178 ml) vegetable oil

6 cups diced onions
(about 2 medium onions)

⅓ cup (45 grams) pine nuts
or roughly chopped
blanched almonds, toasted

⅓ cup (48 grams) currants
or golden raisins

¾ cup chopped fresh Italian
parsley (about 1 bunch)

¼ cup snipped fresh dill
(about ½ bunch)

½ teaspoon ground cinnamon

1 tablespoon kosher salt,
or to taste

½ teaspoon freshly ground
black pepper

1 cup (200 grams) long-grain
rice

1 tablespoon sugar

1½ cups chopped tomatoes
(1 to 2 medium tomatoes)

1 lemon

80 grape leaves
(from a 1-pound jar)

3. Arrange the stuffed grape leaves in two or three rows in the lined pot. Add 1 cup (236 ml) water. Place a small plate on top to press the leaves down, then cover the pot with a lid. Bring the water to a boil, and reduce the heat to maintain a simmer. Cook for 20 minutes. Remove the covers, and squeeze the remaining half-lemon over the leaves. Replace the plate and lid, and simmer for 10 minutes more. Allow the leaves to cool in the pot, then chill them.

4. Serve them as a cold appetizer or a side dish. These don't freeze well, but will keep in the refrigerator for 1 week.

Given the richness of Armenian, Italian, and other local foods, I started the tradition of testing recipes for Friday-night dinner and dinner parties. Two of our first guests in our early married life were Jim and Jay Feron, whom I had known in Jerusalem, where Jim was the *New York Times* correspondent. I can still see us all sitting on the floor, trying to unfurl the recipes on a long scroll-like sheaf of papers, the galleys for *The Flavor of Jerusalem,* which came out in 1975.

One day, while I was getting my hair cut at Le Pli Salon in Cambridge, Sidney Moss, the hairdresser, was telling me how stratified Cambridge social life was because of Harvard. He added that there was one couple, State Supreme Court Justice Benjamin Kaplan and his wife, Felicia Lamport, a writer, who were not like the others. The next time I came for a haircut, I told him that Allan was invited to speak at a conference of international lawyers in Jerusalem and there were two other people from Cambridge going, one a Justice Kaplan. I asked if that could be the Kaplan he was talking about. He said no, they went to Martha's Vineyard in the summer, and he really doubted that they would go to Jerusalem.

The first evening at the conference, we went to an opening reception at Beit Belgia at the Hebrew University, only to meet the Kaplans. As soon as I mentioned Sidney's name, Felicia imperiously said to me, "Sit down." We became instant friends, and I listened to her marvelous stories for years after. It turns out that the Kaplans lived around the corner from us in Cambridge, and I tested recipes on them that winter for my second book, which became *The Jewish Holiday Kitchen*. Felicia and Ben, who knew everyone in Cambridge, became quasi-parents to both of us. Ben,

who seemed so severe to the lawyers who faced him when he was a Supreme Court justice, loved the Jewish food of his childhood, and shared with me his recipe for schav, sorrel soup. "I didn't know Judge Kaplan even ate," one stunned lawyer told me.

Felicia had written a marvelous memoir of growing up in New York called *Mink on Weekdays (Ermine on Sunday)*. In it, she talks about her Bat Mitzvah. Samuel Lamport, her father, had helped fund the conservative synagogue of Rabbi Mordecai Kaplan, who later founded the Reconstruction movement. Because he had four daughters, the rabbi instituted the first Bat Mitzvahs in 1922, starting with his oldest daughter, Judith. In the second, Felicia was Bat Mitzvahed along with the rabbi's daughter Naomi.

Felicia was clever and witty, and became known for her weekly limericks in *The Boston Globe*. In 1981, when Jeane Kirkpatrick became ambassador to the United Nations and Allan started working for her as a senior counsel, Felicia said she would not use her poison pen against her because, she said, Jeane couldn't be that bad if Allan was working for her.

I also learned so much about cooking from Felicia. She figured out, for example, how first to put hard-boiled eggs through a garlic press to make them look like faux crabmeat, then to mix them with celery, cocktail sauce, and mayonnaise, and finally to spoon them into cream puffs to be served as appetizers. While stuffing cream puffs, I would listen to Felicia's great gossip (some people call it sociology) about people like Lillian Hellman and other Vineyard luminaries of the period. She had such a dry sense of humor, and I adored being with her. Ben, on the other hand, was very quiet unless he was talking with Allan in Yiddish—about life and law, but mostly about the Nuremberg Trials, which Ben had worked on as a young man. And while Felicia and Allan would be playing poker, Ben and I would be discussing anything from the schav of his childhood to nineteenth-century classics such as *Daniel Deronda,* a novel that we both liked. To many, Felicia was the Perle Mesta of Cambridge. After we spent time with them in Israel, she invited us to their party following the Harvard-Yale football game. We arrived only to see a who's who of Cambridge, from the economist John Kenneth Galbraith and the mathematician and songwriter Tom Lehrer to Julia Child with her husband, Paul. Julia could not have been nicer to me, urging me to come visit.

Cambridge was Julia's town, and after we saw her at Felicia's we met several times. The first was when Diana Kennedy came from New York to publicize *The Tortilla Book* in 1975. I knew Diana from the Ninth Avenue Festival, and she asked me to fetch her from Julia's house, where she was staying, and take her to a local television station. When I picked Diana up, Julia came out to greet me and gave me a signed copy of *The French Chef Cookbook* from 1968.

When we were alone, Diana was fuming. Julia had told her that at their ages (Diana was fifty-two and Julia sixty-three) they must wear makeup if they were on television. Diana disagreed totally.

First of all, she was younger than Julia, and, besides, it was none of Julia's business. And that was that.

While Allan was teaching at the New England School of Law, I studied for a year at the Kennedy School of Government at Harvard, having received a scholarship for their mid-career program because I'd worked for two mayors. It was a wonderful year; I took courses at Harvard and MIT on food and sociocultural systems, including Nathan Glazer's classes, Oscar Handlin's History of the City, and Daniel Patrick Moynihan's Ethnicity and Politics.

When it came time to write a paper, I wanted to do something on food, not politics. I made an appointment to see Professor Moynihan and asked him if I could, telling him that I had a crazy idea; he said he was game for crazy ideas. When I told him that I wanted to write about ethnicity and food in the city of Jerusalem, he agreed. When he finished grading my paper, "Food Traits: An Overlooked Component of Ethnic Identity," he wrote on the first page that, unlike George McGovern, who ate a corned-beef sandwich with a glass of milk (which contributed to his loss in New York State), he would not make that mistake in his run for the Senate. Who knows? Maybe avoiding the taboo of mixing milk and meat in one meal did help him win. He held the Senate seat until 2001, when Hillary Clinton took it over.

14.

Learning to Be a Food Writer

In 1976, shortly after my year at the Kennedy School was over, I got up the courage to write a letter to the legendary, beloved restaurant critic Anthony (Tony) Spinazzola at *The Boston Globe*, who was also the editor of the newspaper's *New England Sunday Magazine*. At our interview, I showed him a copy of my cookbook, *The Flavor of Jerusalem,* which had just come out, and told him I would love to write portraits of Boston's ethnic groups, because I thought I would like to get a Ph.D. in sociology or cultural anthropology. He called me after the interview and asked me to write a column instead, about ethnic food in the Boston area. My work was to appear in the magazine once a month; my column would be alternating with columns by, among others, Madeleine Kamman, whose restaurant I enjoyed so much.

Food writing was not something I had ever thought I would do, but, luckily, I learned on the job, with an editor who took a leap of faith in hiring me. Given the lack of staff who really knew how to edit recipes in those days, and my lack of professional background in the discipline of writing, this job was my baptism by fire. I had a ball talking with cooks, learning their stories, and writing it all down—until my first few articles came out.

One early article was given a two-page spread with a huge picture of luscious shortbread from the Scottish Highlands that everyone wanted to make. I was so excited to see it in print, with a full-page photograph! But then I received a few polite handwritten letters from readers. Evidently, I had written "½ cup or 4 ounces flour" instead of "1 cup or 4 ounces flour." *And* I forgot to include the cornstarch in one step. One reader wrote that the shortbread was a complete disaster. "It tasted good but it was more like a thin piece of peanut brittle!" Words no food writer wants to hear.

A few months later, in September 1976, probably just before Rosh Hashanah, another article appeared, this one about an extraordinary woman who, despite terrible arthritis in her hands, still made challah every week at the age of eighty-one. Ada Baum Lipsitz, who was, and still is in spirit, an inspiration for me, said that her hands came alive when she kneaded bread. Her challah became the cornerstone for my own challah in years to come.

I was so excited when the article came out that I called her right away. Ada, however, was not very happy. Apparently, her sister was so angry that I hadn't written about her, too, that she was furious. This experience taught me that there may be unforeseen consquences in having attention drawn to you. Ada knew I was writing about her but she didn't know how her sister would react. People don't always like it . . . at the beginning. When they are used to the limelight, then they love it. Lesson learned.

Then I got what I thought was a fan letter. "Nathan," it read. "I assume you're very young—you must feel terribly liberated (I assume that too.) and you're a pretty fair columnist. But of one thing I'm positive—you have very bad manners. How could you possibly be so lacking in grace—in respect—for a lovely lady like Ada Lipsitz—as to keep referring to her as 'Lipsitz?' Thanks for publishing those great recipes—but, Nathan, try to learn a little deference for the real women of this world." The letter was signed "Sincerely, (Mrs. Harold) Doris F. Levy." (It seems the *Globe* stopped using honorifics for women in the early 1970s, when the title "Ms." began appearing elsewhere.)

Another reader, Pat Pellows, wrote to Tony to complain about the challah recipe. "There was a marvelous picture of Ada Baum Lipsitz and her challah breads," she wrote. "In fact, the picture was so enticing, I had to try the recipe. It was a great idea, but the bread didn't rise. You should know that after 33 years in the kitchen I am reputed to be an excellent cook, and I'm not accustomed to failures. Now my self-esteem has been restored—it was not my error, but the fault of the recipe!"

I checked the recipe, and it worked just fine.

Tony wrote her back. We thought that would be the end of the matter, but then Ms. Pellows wrote to me again. She had tried the recipe once more.

"I did try the challah again and it did work! One of my friends said it was better than cake and didn't even need butter spread on it. I certainly owe you an apology and I hope I'm forgiven. I think my problem was in mixing the yeast. The second time I mixed it in water instead of with the sugar in the 'well.'"

Despite the criticism, which I have always taken seriously from my readers, when I think back about those days I feel it was a perfect first writing job for me. In the mid-1970s, Boston was a mosaic of ethnic pockets filled with unsung culinary heroes, my favorite subject to this day. For a writer like me who loves learning about the history of an area through its people, the early days were heaven.

The only thing I dreaded was retyping an entire page on my typewriter, even for just one tiny mistake. In a letter—almost like a performance review—Tony once kindly told me they were having a "bit of trouble with my copy." At first, I was very defensive about his advice, but it has stuck with me for the rest of my life.

He also told me that, though he didn't want to minimize the importance of the ethnic nature of my articles, "ethnicity" should relate in a direct way to the food. I have always loved tangents when speaking or when writing—as everyone who knows me can attest—though sometimes people can't follow my train of thought. I learned to write more tightly and, when following tangents, to circle back to the overall story . . . or at least try to.

Additionally, Tony explained to me how important deadlines really are and what depends on them. Finally, he encouraged me to fact-check, so that I'd avoid small but significant errors, like the weight of a cup of flour.

Seasonal Challah

Ever since Ada Baum Lipsitz showed me how to make challah so many years ago in Boston, I have tried to bake it almost every week. The days of using margarine instead of butter are over, as are those of baking the bread in a tin. And as I have watched other bakers throughout the world who shared tips with me, my own loaf has evolved, varying the flavor elements of seeds and herbs to match the season. I like rosemary and basil from my garden in the summer, and fennel and anise seeds in the cooler months. Sometimes I add emmer wheat or rye, depending on my mood. Part of the fun is that my challah never comes out the same, but it always tastes good.

As for braiding, ever since I visited Laupheim, Germany, the ancestral town of the Nathan clan, I have varied braiding from including six braids to braiding my challah in the German way (see page 15 for this method). And like so many Jewish women the world over, inspired by TikTok and other challah influencers, I sometimes make mine with many balls, like a pull-apart monkey bread.

For the blessings over the bread, symbolic of the manna distributed in the desert on Friday, but more so of the comfort of family, faith, and community, we all join in, holding the challah or touching someone holding it, to make an unbroken chain connecting us to the food that comes from the earth. Then we tear it apart to share and to eat. For that minute when we are holding the fresh bread with its wonderful aroma, we are all united. Friends are family. To this day, I try my hardest to celebrate Friday night with my family or friends, whether we tear the bread together in person or virtually, through a video call.

⌐═◆╼

Makes 2 challahs

⌐═◆╼

1½ tablespoons active dry yeast

1 tablespoon plus ⅓ cup (66 grams) sugar, divided

⅓ cup (79 ml) vegetable oil, plus more for drizzling

3 large eggs

1 tablespoon kosher salt

1 tablespoon anise seeds

3 tablespoons chopped fresh herbs, like basil, rosemary, tarragon, dill, or whatever you have in your garden or farmers' market (optional)

7 to 8 cups (875 grams to 1 kg) unbleached all-purpose flour, plus more as needed, or use 3 cups (339 grams) emmer or einkorn flour and all-purpose flour for the rest

Poppy, sesame, or nigella seeds, for sprinkling

---

1. In the bowl of a stand mixer, whisk the yeast and 1 tablespoon sugar in 1½ cups (355 ml) lukewarm water.

2. Whisk the oil into the yeast mixture, then add 2 eggs, one at a time, the remaining sugar, salt, anise seeds, and 2 tablespoons of the fresh herbs, if using. Attach the dough hook, turn the mixer to its lowest setting, and gradually add 7 cups of flour. Increase the speed to medium-low (4 on a KitchenAid), and let the machine knead the dough for about 5 minutes, adding more all-purpose flour as needed to make it slightly sticky, smooth, and elastic. You may need more flour, depending on the humidity and how much liquid the flour absorbs. →

3. In the bowl of the mixer, scrape the sides of the dough down, then drizzle it with a little oil, and turn to coat the dough. Cover the bowl with a kitchen towel, and let the dough rise in a warm place for 1 hour, or refrigerate for up to 8 hours.

4. When the dough has almost doubled, punch it down, remove it to a lightly floured counter, knead it briefly until it's smooth, and divide it in half.

5. To make a challah with six braids Divide one half of the dough into six pieces, then roll each into a strand about 12 inches long. Put the strands in a row, parallel to one another, then pinch the tops of the strands together. Move the outside right strand over two strands, then take the second strand from the left and move it to the far right. Take the outside left strand and move it over two, then move the second strand from the right over to the far left. Continue this until all strands are braided, then tuck the ends under the braided loaf. Position the challah on the baking sheet, repeat the process with the second half of dough, and separate them on the baking sheet by at least 4 inches.

6. Beat the remaining egg, and brush about half of it onto the loaves, reserving the rest. Let the dough rise, uncovered, for another ½ hour at room temperature, or overnight in the refrigerator.

7. If the dough has been refrigerated, bring it to room temperature. Heat the oven to 350 degrees. Brush the loaves with the remaining egg, then sprinkle with the poppy, sesame, or nigella seeds and the remaining 2 tablespoons of herbs.

8. Bake for 35 to 40 minutes, or until the loaves are golden and firm when tapped with a spatula. Cool them on a rack.

Hanging out with Daniela

daughters to the day care for a few years, to give me free time to do my writing and cooking in the mornings.

When Daniela was about a year old, I also joined a neighborhood babysitting cooperative where we all shared the babysitting duties. I was not such a fan of the co-op as I have never been a great joiner, but sometimes it came in very handy. One night, I answered a phone call when I was finishing up *The Jewish Holiday Kitchen*. "My name is Cathy Sulzberger," said the person on the other end of the line. "My husband and I have tickets for the Bob Dylan concert. Could you possibly babysit?" I heard the desperation in her voice, but stopped at the name Sulzberger and asked if

Me holding Daniela

she was Iphigene Sulzberger's granddaughter. A silence at the other end of the line. "Yes, why?" I explained to her that I had taken her grandmother, Cathy's sister Karen, and their cousin Susan Dryfoos around Jerusalem when I worked for Teddy Kollek. I asked her if her son, David, was likely to sleep while I was babysitting. Yes, she said, then I agreed.

When I met Cathy, we formed an instant friendship. I recalled having read her wedding announcement the year before in *The New York Times*. Her husband, Joe Perpich's parents were emigrants from Croatia, as my husband's were from Poland. I had thought when reading it that Allan and I would like this couple. Now I can't even remember any time before the Sulzberger-Perpiches. We have celebrated more than forty-two Seders together, we have traveled together, gone through life-cycle events together, both the good and the bad.

A few months after I met Cathy, I called the Israeli Embassy to see if they knew any Yemenite Jews for a story I was writing. They told me to call an artist named Carol Brown Goldberg, because Benjamin Levy, a Yemenite Israeli artist, was staying with her the next week. I called Carol and biked over to her house to meet her. We talked for hours. When I got home, I told Cathy that I had met someone I thought she would love. The three of us have been friends ever since.

My mother told me early in my life that female friendships are very important, in some ways more important to us for support than our husbands. Her best friends her whole life were from Raquette Lake Girls Camp. I have lots of acquaintances, as we all do. But my mother was so right. My strong friendships have lasted a lifetime.

A birthday party

16.

My Kitchen Is My Laboratory

One of the pluses of being a food writer is that your kitchen is your laboratory, and your friends and family are your guinea pigs. As soon as we were married, I was testing recipes for books or for articles by opening our home, and cooking for guests was a happy part of our forty-five-year marriage. If a recipe works at the dining-room table, you receive accolades; if not, well, the blame lies with the recipe. And guests feel that it gives a certain cachet to be invited to a food writer's home for dinner, if only to see the kitchen.

We built our dream house in the mid-1980s, abutting Rock Creek Park, a twenty-minute drive to the White House. In the process, I visited thirteen kitchens, asking everybody what they liked best and what they wouldn't do, to learn how I would make mine. Lessons learned: Put drinking glasses in a drawer, reachable by children. There are never enough thin, vertical cabinets for baking sheets and muffin tins. Deep double sinks hide messiness, but only if not in the center island. I had originally put the sink plumbing into the island, but one day, when the British cookbook author Anne Willan was visiting, she ordered me to switch the sink to the wall side of the counter, saying that if I ever wanted to teach or do TV from my house, I would need a central cooking island. A few weeks later, Barbara Kafka, another blunt cookbook writer, was in town during the construction; she told me to have a marble counter with bins beneath for flour and all the other ingredients and implements for baking. She also said that my pots and pans should be on the wall, but with that I disagreed—I'm too messy to make it work.

Since then, I typically spend one or two days testing recipes during the week. If I am lucky, Maria Hernandez, my longtime cleaning woman, works on the testing day, so she can either assist me in prep or clean up. Kara Elder, who helps me with cookbooks, and friends who like to test also come over to help. We divide up the five or six recipes of the day, marking up sheets of paper and talking to one another. At lunchtime, we always take a civilized break for some variation of a tuna or feta cheese salad.

Lunch Salad with My Vinaigrette

I always have salad ingredients on hand, whether they be crunchy heads of lettuce, like romaine, or a selection of mixed greens from the farmers' market. Whoever is helping me with recipe testing that day, whether friends or assistants, will look at whatever is available in the fridge. Each person makes it so differently, but it's always a mix of chopped vegetables, red onion for sharpness, and good canned tuna or salty feta. Use whatever you have—leftover roasted eggplant, string beans, tomatoes in the summer, citrus segments in the winter, anything goes. Pickled onions (page 68) are a hit. We toss it lightly with a vinaigrette that I learned to make when I lived in France, or we'll simply salt the vegetables and dress them in good oil and the juice of half a lemon. It's easy to scale up if there are more people around; I use one head of lettuce per two to three people.

I serve it with crackers or bread, or perhaps the leftovers of whatever recipe I'm testing, which sometimes get tossed right into the salad. I always set the table with place mats, fork on the left, knife on the right, napkins (preferably cotton or linen), and a glass of water for everyone. Then we sit down and eat together, pausing for a few minutes to enjoy this fresh and light lunchtime ritual, something I much prefer to going out to lunch.

I. Add everything to a large salad bowl as you prep it: Cut or tear the lettuce into bite-sized pieces. Chop the bell pepper. Thinly slice the fennel bulb. Peel and chop the kohlrabi. Mince the onion. Peel and chop the avocado, if using. Toss in however many olives you'd like, and flake the tuna on top, if using, or cubes of as much feta as you like. Dress lightly with the vinaigrette, toss gently, and serve.

2. To make the vinaigrette Put the garlic into a small bowl. Add the vinegar, mustard, salt, honey or sugar, and onion or shallot; stir with a fork. Gradually stir in the olive oil, until the mix is emulsified.

⌖

Serves 2 to 4

⌖

1 head of crunchy lettuce,
    such as romaine or gem,
    or tender butter lettuce,
    or several big handfuls
    of mixed greens
½ bell pepper (any color)
1 small fennel bulb
1 small kohlrabi bulb
¼ to ½ small red onion
1 avocado (optional)
Olives or capers
1 can tuna packed in oil
    (optional)
Feta (optional)

For the Vinaigrette
(Makes about ½ cup, enough
to dress several large salads)
2 cloves garlic, pressed
    or minced
2 tablespoons red-wine
    or balsamic vinegar
1 teaspoon Dijon mustard
Pinch of salt
1 teaspoon honey or sugar
2 slices red onion, diced,
    or 1 shallot lobe, diced
3 to 4 tablespoons
    (45 to 60 ml) extra-virgin
    olive oil

Living in an exciting place like Washington, I'm often asked to, and sometimes offer to, throw parties for friends, especially if they've written a book or had a significant birthday. One of my favorites was in 2006, a party for the journalist Jeffrey Goldberg, to celebrate his book *Prisoners: A Muslim and a Jew Across the Middle East Divide*. I made a point of preparing finger food from warring countries in the Middle East, what Allan used to call the Muddle East—Iranian stuffed grape leaves, Syrian mahammar (page 317), and Iraqi kubbeh, to name a few.

Another party that was very memorable was for David Cicilline, a dear friend of my mother's, who was the mayor of Providence and had his own legendary annual tradition of asking guests to bring turkeys for the needy to his home each year just before Thanksgiving.

When David was running for Congress from Rhode Island, I promised to give him a small dinner party if he was elected. On January 6, 2011, just after David was sworn in, Allan and I assembled some of our friends and acquaintances whom we thought he would like to meet. As we sat down at our long, narrow farm table, Wolf Blitzer suggested that each of us write down for David some advice for surviving in Washington. Since David kept the paper and framed it, he shared this well-thought-out advice. Wolf started with "Honesty is the best policy." Lynn Blitzer said, "Recognize you are in the minority; go with it. Happy to offer shopping advice." Trish Vradenburg: "Read newspapers about yourself. Read the bad and the good." George Vradenburg: "Republicans are people too." Bob Woodward: "Straight talk. Develop a plan for representing your constituents. Discount personal experience." David

Brooks: "Go to the House gym. Make an area of specialty." Cathy Sulzberger: "Find someone you don't agree with but respect." Elsa Walsh: "Have a personal life and fall in love." Allan: "Don't underestimate the role of incompetence." And I added, "Try to laugh a little and keep your old friends." Perhaps in part thanks to this advice, he was a congressman for twelve years, giving it up to head the Rhode Island Foundation. We had a follow-up party where he told us that the most important thing he had learned was to listen to and befriend a Republican because getting anything done in Congress required bipartisan support.

Ever since our children went off to college, and then moved away for good, the cast of characters at Friday-night dinners, and other meals throughout the week, has of course changed. Not only do we discuss current events, but I ask my guests for comments about the dishes we are all eating. Even now that Allan is gone, I still continue this tradition, though I do host fewer people than before.

I particularly enjoy cooking "dress up" food—the harder recipes we find, those that test our skills, and recipes that many of us are hesitant to try out on guests, such as updating very ancient dishes like cholent. These dishes, and traditional recipes for holidays that tell us where we come from, are what I make for Friday-night meals. I rarely repeat myself, unless I am testing the recipe for the second or third time. These recipes excite me, especially if I feel I am finding something new and interesting for my family or my readers. And, believe it or not, after almost fifty years of testing, I still enjoy discovering new recipes from far-flung communities around the world.

The only trouble with testing recipes is that if I like something, like a baked good—sticky buns, for example—I taste it, and even if the recipe is not to my liking yet, I keep tasting it, hoping that maybe this time it will be good and I won't have to test it again. On the other hand, if it is good, I keep trying it because it's so good. I can't win either way!

Despite the excess calories, this type of cooking and entertaining fit well into the life I created for myself and my family. To me the process is logical: I get feedback on my recipes, I meet interesting people, and I feed family and friends. My son, David, in one of his college entrance essays, bemoaned the fact that the food eaten at our house was not the same as at his friends' homes—no Oreo cookies, no Kraft Mac & Cheese, no boxed brownies, only start-from-scratch food that I was testing. Even if our food was "weirder" than that of his friends, life growing up was not really so bad. And although he got accepted at that college he chose not to go there. My cooking wasn't always new and exciting. At the beginning of each week, I, like so many of us, would make meal plans, with soups, stews, pasta, hummus, and so on. This is everyday food, meals that we sometimes find repetitive, meals that our kids don't always like, but food to get us through the week.

Making gefilte fish in my kitchen at Passover

Pasta with Almond Pesto, Green Beans, Eggplant, and Cherry Tomatoes

Many foods that were novelties only a decade ago are taken for granted now. Consider, for example, greens like arugula, radicchio and lamb's lettuce or herbs like fresh coriander, chervil, ginger and basil, which I first encountered 20 years ago in a restaurant in Manhattan's Little Italy. My lunchtime host recommended that I sample fettuccine with a basil-based sauce called pesto; it was love at first taste. For many Americans basil and other condiments entered the lexicon only recently—but with a vengeance signaling a major shift in culinary tastes from the provincial to the cosmopolitan.

> —Craig Claiborne, "Culinary America: Food Fascination Sweeps the Nation," The New York Times, January 1, 1986

This major shift in "culinary tastes" owes much to the Cuisinart and other food processors, which became essential kitchen products for pie crusts, hummus, and pesto in the 1970s. A great line in the late Nora Ephron's 1989 movie, *When Harry Met Sally,* was: "Pesto is the quiche of the eighties." And during this same period, when my children were young, Larry David and Jerry Seinfeld wrote "The Busboy," a *Seinfeld* episode that aired June 26, 1991. George says, "Everybody likes pesto. You walk into a restaurant, that's all you hear—pesto, pesto, pesto." To which Jerry responds, "I don't like pesto." George has the last line: "Where was pesto ten years ago?"

When asked what their favorite recipe was while they were growing up, my children, now in their thirties and forties, invariably say pasta with pesto and string beans. I used to think they simply liked the alliteration of "p's." Nuts, basil, garlic, and pasta are just a great combination, one invented by the Genovese and made with gusto at home by Americans, in their food processors. (Most Americans would never have had the patience to use a mortar and pestle to grind the ingredients!) But a few years ago, when I tasted Pino Maggiore's pasta with pesto at his restaurant Cantina Siciliana in Trapani, Sicily, I truly understood why it tastes so good. Pino, as he ground his pesto with a mortar and pestle into a chunky pasta sauce, dismissed the food processor, saying that it chopped too quickly, and provided no pleasure for the cook in the act of grinding. As a mother who knew her kids loved pasta but wanted →

Serves 4 to 6

- 1½ teaspoons kosher salt, plus 2 tablespoons for the pasta pot
- 1 pound (453 grams) Japanese eggplant, sliced into ½-inch rounds
- 4 cloves garlic
- Leaves and tender stems from 1 bunch fresh basil (about 2 cups)
- 1 cup (140 grams) blanched almonds
- 1 cup (236 ml) extra-virgin olive oil, plus more if needed
- ½ cup (50 grams) grated Pecorino, Romano, or Parmesan cheese
- Freshly ground black pepper, to taste
- 12 ounces (340 grams) busiate, or other pasta of your choice
- 8 ounces (227 grams) string beans, broccoli, and/or zucchini, cut into 1-inch pieces
- 1 cup fresh cherry tomatoes, halved

to steer clear of macaroni and cheese for every meal, I found pesto a quick alternative. With the addition of green beans, I must admit it was and still is absolutely delicious. I now follow Pino's addition of cherry tomatoes and fried Asian eggplant, and his substitution of almonds for the Sicilian pine nuts, which makes the dish much more affordable.

Try walnuts, almonds, pecans, pistachios, or pumpkin seeds instead of the pine nuts, or use dandelion greens or even nettles (blanched first to remove their sting) for the basil. My mom used to make a large batch and divide it among ice-cube trays, which she froze for future meals. A woman after my own heart.

---

1. Sprinkle about ½ teaspoon of the salt over the eggplant slices, and let them sit in a single layer on a paper towel for about an hour.

2. To make the pesto Put the garlic, all but a few leaves of basil, all but 2 tablespoons of the almonds, and 1 teaspoon of salt in a mortar or food processor. Slowly add ¾ cup (176 ml) of the olive oil and all but a table-spoon of the cheese. Pulse just a few times in the food processor, or work the mortar with a pestle, to grind until the sauce is rich and crunchy, yet spreadable, and the nuts are grainy in texture and still slightly crunchy; add a little more oil if desired. Adjust seasonings to taste.

3. Blot the eggplant dry. Put the remaining ¼ cup (60 ml) of the olive oil into a frying pan, and warm it over medium-high heat. Add the egg-plant rounds, and cook until they're golden on both sides. Drain them on paper towels, and sprinkle them with pepper to taste. Fry the remaining almonds until they're golden; then drain them.

4. Bring a large pot of water to a boil, add the pasta with 2 tablespoons of salt, stir, and cook until al dente, stirring occasionally. When the pasta has been cooking for a minute or so, add the snipped beans, broccoli, and/or zucchini and cook until done, or steam the vegetables in a colan-der over the pasta and cook until they are both al dente.

5. Strain the vegetables and pasta, and transfer them to a bowl. Gen-tly stir the pesto into the pasta and vegetables until everything is thor-oughly combined. Sprinkle with the remaining tablespoon grated cheese, the remaining basil leaves, and the fried almonds. Decorate with the eggplant rounds and halved cherry tomatoes. Serve warm or at room temperature.

17.

A Gastronomical Awakening in Washington

Jean-Louis's Brioche   195

When I left Boston in 1977, Gail Perrin, the food editor from *The Boston Globe*, wrote to Bill Rice and Marian Burros, the co-editors of the Food section at *The Washington Post*, to tell them that I was moving to the Washington area and loved writing about ethnic food. I met the two in their office that fall, after I turned in the manuscript for *The Jewish Holiday Kitchen*. Bill was very quiet and gentlemanly; Marian embodied the tough journalist, always seeking the truth. They were both down to earth, great writers each in their own way, and became mentors whom I looked up to through the years.

Bill asked me if I wanted to write a weekly column on food. As soon as he suggested this, I stiffened. At thirty-four years old, ancient in those days to have just had a first child, I thought that I would hate the pressure of a weekly column, along with the pressures at home taking care of my daughter, a husband, and cooking. I said no but told them I would love to write for them when I wanted. They were surprised—although the Food section was its own sort of domain, it was still *The Washington Post*, which had investigated Watergate earlier that decade—but they accepted the arrangement. Through the years, I often wondered if I made the right decision. If I had been born one generation later, I would have jumped at the chance of writing weekly, with the security afforded me of eventually writing full-time for a newspaper. But then I didn't think I could handle the extra pressure and besides, I also had the stability of a husband who was working.

Washington at that time was still a sleepy, stodgy city. As much as we enjoyed the embassy dinner invitations, once Allan worked for the government (because in those days your husband, not you, merited these invitations), dinners were more frequently long, formal, boring affairs, and the food was not very exciting, because the food wasn't the point. One small dinner at the French Embassy for Nina Hyde, fashion editor for *The Washington Post*, stands out. The tables were white, the flowers were white, and everything was beautiful—but even there, in my opinion the Ambassador's residence where you could hope to dine the best, the dinner was classically delicious, but predictable.

But a scent of change was in the air. Civil war in El Salvador would result in the largest ever concentration of emigrants from the country, eventually making pupuserias as common here as steakhouses. Vietnamese, Ethiopian, and other restaurants were on the rise, too, started by refugees and former embassy chefs. Nixon's opening of trade and his trip to China whetted the appetite for Americans to eat Szechuan and then Hunan cuisine. At the same time, there was a new recognition of American regional food, starting with Southern soul food—coming from the pride of the Black Panthers—and, because of Leah Chase and Paul Prudhomme in New Orleans, a new interest in Creole and Cajun cooking. Food in restaurants was becoming more interesting, and I was eager to start writing about the growing multiethnicity of American cuisine.

The tap-tap-tap of the typewriters at *The Boston Globe* gave way to pure silence at *The Washington Post*. This was the beginning of writing with a new device called a computer; Bill and Marian told me that I could write in the newsroom if I liked, to learn more about word processors. I loved the collegiality of the Food section and the magazine staff, where I would occasionally bump into Ben Bradlee, who would strut throughout the newsroom saying hello to everyone, including this lowly freelancer. Thus began a wonderful arrangement that lasted until 1987.

My first book and early articles were all typewritten, so I bought my first IBM PC to write my second book and all subsequent articles. I remember going into the newsroom one Saturday, when no one was around, with my then toddler, Daniela. I was writing a long piece on Thomas Jef-

ferson and his love of food. Daniela was playing with the machine—as children now do with their iPhones and laptops—and she deleted the entire article. I've never been particularly proficient with computers, and I had no idea how to get it back. So I rewrote the entire article the next day; this time, I left her at home with Allan.

It was during this period that I really learned to write, from William MacKaye, who edited my copy. He made me look at the importance of strong verbs and simple phrases, like using "she said," to let my interview subjects shine in their own words. I am so grateful to him for showing me how to write and what to look for when interviewing.

My first article, in 1979, was about a cooking class that Paula Wolfert taught at the home of Barbara Aledort, a marvelous cook who owned Chanterelle Catering and lived in Chevy Chase, Maryland. Paula's majestic book *Couscous and Other Good Things: Food from Morocco*—establishing her as America's doyenne of Moroccan cooking—appeared in 1973, and Barbara, who came from a Lebanese background via North Carolina, loved the book. I had met Paula at Diana Kennedy's apartment in New York on one of my trips there in the mid-1970s, and we struck up a friendship, so I was delighted to connect Barbara and Paula and to participate in the class. Paula's enthusiasm for her subject spilled over to us all. I took notes and suggested a piece to *The Washington Post*. Now, in hindsight, I realize that through the years I have always liked writing that way—finding inspiration in the moment—rather than going on assignments to do something. If I say so myself, the article reads very well, even today.

The week when Paula was visiting Washington, Jean-Louis Palladin, a thirty-three-year-old chef from Condom, in southwestern France, had literally just arrived to open a restaurant in the basement of the Watergate Hotel, made infamous by Nixon. Paula knew Jean-Louis from just gathering recipes for her book *The Cooking of Southwest France,* and asked me if Allan—who was just starting a new job, prosecuting Nazi war criminals at the Department of Justice's Office of Special Investigations—and I would like to dine with her at the restaurant the week it opened.

The tiny space, located in the same building as the famous break-in at the Democratic National Committee, had thin, square, orange-tinted silk-paneled curtains fluttering over the walls, with tiny lights glowing behind them, creating the impression you were in someone's cozy dining room. Nicolas M. Salgo, the Hungarian head of the Watergate Complex, had discovered Jean-Louis at his two-star restaurant in France and lured him across the ocean. As soon as we sat down, Jean-Louis, a lanky, appealing man with a mustache and a gravelly voice, brought out his ethereal rectangular brioche, to be spread with anchovy butter.

That same night, acting like a mother hen, Paula kept running into the kitchen, cautioning Jean-Louis to cut down on salt for his new American clientele, who like their food less salty than the French. I was totally dazzled by Jean-Louis. This was a time when my proficiency in French helped, because he spoke very little English. We got along immediately, and I invited him to come with me the next day: I was working on an article for *The Washington Post* on a Black storefront church supper. I thought this would be interesting for a chef who had just told me how much he loved American corn and crabmeat. He asked if he could bring his friend Francis Layrle, who at the time was the chef at the residence of the French ambassador. The two charmed the children at the supper, who immediately started crawling over them, and Jean-Louis pronounced the Jiffy corn muffins and sweet-potato pie *génial*!

Jean-Louis's Brioche

I can still remember watching Jean-Louis meticulously make his profound stocks and this light-as-a-feather brioche. Watching him work made me realize how many years the French labor to become chefs, starting their work in restaurants as young teenagers.

I stood in Jean-Louis's tiny kitchen to learn how to make this bread. It's easy—your stand mixer does all the heavy work. But, like all bread, it takes time, as you slowly wait for the dough to rise. This brioche is well worth the wait. Serve it with anchovy fillets puréed with ½ cup unsalted butter.

☞
Makes 2 loaves
☞

1⅓ tablespoons active dry yeast

6 cups (750 grams) unbleached all-purpose flour, plus more for sprinkling

½ cup (100 grams) sugar

1 tablespoon kosher salt

7 large eggs

1½ cups (3 sticks/339 grams) unsalted butter, softened, plus more for greasing

---

1. Dissolve the yeast in ¾ cup (178 ml) warm water. Put the flour into the bowl of a mixer fitted with the dough hook, add the sugar and salt, and begin mixing at low speed, gradually adding the dissolved yeast.

2. Whisk one egg in a small bowl, then pour all but 2 tablespoons of it into the stand mixer (keep the small remaining amount refrigerated until the next day, for an egg wash). Add the remaining eggs one by one, continuing to mix at low speed for about 10 minutes. This seems long, but it takes that long for the eggs to mix with the flour and achieve a smooth, shiny texture. Let the machine rest briefly if it begins to overheat. Add the butter, little by little, mixing until it is totally absorbed, or the dough is smooth, 3 to 4 minutes after all the butter is added. You may need to use a spatula to push the butter down into the dough a few times.

3. Remove the dough from the mixer to a greased bowl, cover the bowl with a towel, and let the dough rise for 6 hours at room temperature. Then punch it down and let it rise, covered, in the refrigerator overnight.

4. The next day, grease two 9-inch loaf pans and form the dough into two long cylinders. Using a dough cutter, divide them into plum-sized pieces, weighing about 2 ounces each. Roll the pieces into logs 3 inches long, and fit them crosswise, in two layers, into the pans. You should have seven or eight logs per row.

5. Let the dough rise, covered, for about 3 hours in a very warm room or in the oven with a pilot light, until it almost reaches the top of the pans.

6. Preheat the oven to 350 degrees, brush the dough with the reserved egg, and bake for about 35 minutes, or until the brioche is golden brown on top.

I bought a Halston silk blue skirt at Loehmann's and wore it to Jean-Louis'
Monday night. Jean-Louis made us proud—4 kinds of wine, 8 courses—
monkfish with truffle butter, pigeons with truffles, strawberry soufflés—
divine. He even prepared a special menu with a poem by Allan on one side.
Then we all went dancing until 1:00 a.m.

—Letter to my parents, 1981

Jean-Louis came to Washington at just the right moment. People were becoming more adventurous with their palates. This youngest French chef ever to receive two Michelin stars—at twenty-eight—started to wake up the stiff, stodgy American capital, at the same time that Americans were discovering their own regional ingredients, acting as a model for the next generation of chefs by integating American regional food such as corn, crab, and V8 juice into his dishes.

Very quickly, his reputation for cooking, especially goose or duck liver, spread across the nation. The way he paired rhubarb, peaches, and apples with foie gras to complement the richness of the meat was reason enough for food professionals and any lover of good food to visit his restaurant.

In 1980, a year after Jean-Louis arrived, Daniel Boulud, another talented young Frenchman, became the chef at the Delegation of the European Union in D.C. but was soon stolen from us by New York City, where he has had a stellar career. As soon as he arrived in Washington, Daniel headed to Jean-Louis at the Watergate. He had just tasted his food in France and wanted more.

Similarly, Ariane Daguin, the daughter of André Daguin, the foie gras king of France, visited Jean-Louis whenever she came to Washington. Later, she would be the prime person behind D'Artagnan, an organic, antibiotic- and hormone-free meat purveyor that started out selling foie gras.

Pierre Chambrin, the French chef at Maison Blanche restaurant, who later became chef at the White House for George H. W. Bush, told me that in the late 1980s and early 1990s the White House kitchen was using dried herbs in their recipes and only serving food from "safe" places. Jean-Louis, on the other hand, was discovering farmers everywhere who would make pilgrimages to his kitchen door bearing fresh, edible gifts, which he would in turn serve to his patrons.

I will never forget those early years. Jean-Louis and his wife, Régine, also had young children, and even though Allan spoke little French, we all got along beautifully. For years, we celebrated every life-cycle event at Jean-Louis's restaurant, sometimes with a child being nursed on the banquette, and I still have the signed menus as mementos.

18.

A Mentor for the Two of Us

In the summer of 1981, Allan and I went to Israel. While there, he received a call from the lawyer Max Kampelman, a Washington insider, telling us that Jeane J. Kirkpatrick, the newly appointed first woman ambassador to the United Nations, was looking for an international lawyer to be her legal adviser. He thought Allan would be perfect. As soon as we returned home, Allan met Jeane and immediately started working in New York. Since I was pregnant with Merissa, and we didn't know how long Allan would be in New York, we thought it better for him to commute than for us all to move.

Shortly before Merissa was born, in February 1982, I met Jeane. She reminded me of Margaret Thatcher as portrayed in *The Crown:* she was

With Jeane Kirkpatrick in the South of France

brusque and smart, and I did not think she was very warm at all. "So—you are the pregnant wife," she said, and I felt judged. But I was so wrong about her. Jeane and I spoke a common language, sharing a love of cooking, motherhood, France, writing, and so many other things. We became fast friends. And, most important for all of us, Allan was indispensable to her in international politics.

Most of my memories of Jeane are very personal, much different from Allan's, who lauded her tough stance during the Reagan administration on so many issues. Although I have always been a staunch Democrat and Allan a voting maverick, not liking to peg himself into any one hole, he became enamored of Reagan and Kirkpatrick, though not necessarily the neoconservatives. And, for the record, through the years, he mostly voted Democratic, although he did vote for Reagan.

One time, we attended a dinner at Jeane's residence in the Towers of the Waldorf-Astoria for the members of the Security Council. As the permanent representative of Russia to the United Nations, Oleg Troyanovsky, tried to cut his quail, the meat of choice prepared by her chef, a piece flew off his plate and landed on someone's lap. Not missing a beat, he looked straight at Jeane and said, "This quail is as tough as your foreign policy."

Before Christmas for many years, our children would go to Jeane's house, in nearby Bethesda, Maryland, to trim her tree; they loved all the stories she told of how each decoration came to be part of her family's history. Since her three sons were grown up and no longer present to help decorate the tree, inviting my children to do so made Jeane feel that she was "contributing ecumenicism" to our Jewish family. The last task to finish the tree was for one of the children to climb on a ladder and carefully put the angel on top. After that, we'd eat a variety of Christmas cookies I made for a neighborhood cookie swap when we were living in Chevy Chase. Although I varied what I made each year I always included this favorite.

Double Ginger Molasses Chewies

Makes about 26 cookies

¼ cup (85 grams) molasses

¾ cup unsalted butter
  (1½ sticks/168 grams),
  melted

½ cup (100 grams) plus ⅓ cup
  (66 grams) sugar

1 large egg

1 teaspoon baking soda

½ teaspoon kosher salt

1 tablespoon ground
  cinnamon

2 teaspoons ground ginger

½ teaspoon ground cloves

½ teaspoon freshly grated
  nutmeg

2 cups (250 grams)
  unbleached all-purpose
  flour

2 tablespoons finely diced
  crystallized ginger

My daughter Daniela has always loved two things: York Peppermint Patties and ginger cookies, probably because Betsy Hague, the mother of her childhood friend Aimee, made them. I, too, have always liked chewy ginger cookies, which were also made during my childhood by a friend of my mother's. This beloved cookie dates from the Revolutionary period, having come to America with French, English, and Dutch immigrants. My recipe is adapted from Betsy and from my mother's friend Ellen Driscoll, who I assume got the recipe from *The Fannie Farmer Cookbook*. I add even more ground ginger to my version, as well as a touch of crystallized ginger at the end.

---

1. In a food processor equipped with the steel blade, mix the molasses, butter, and ½ cup of sugar, with the egg. Then add the baking soda, salt, cinnamon, ground ginger, cloves, nutmeg, and flour. Process until everything is well blended. (You can also do this by hand, with a large fork and bowl; in that case, sift the baking soda, salt, and spices into the flour first.) The dough will be stiff. Refrigerate it for a few hours or overnight.

2. Preheat the oven to 350 degrees, and line a baking sheet with parchment paper. Stir the crystallized ginger with the ⅓ cup of sugar in a bowl. Take about a teaspoon of dough—use two spoons or a cookie scoop—and roll it into a ball. Repeat with all the dough. Roll the balls in the ginger sugar, and then transfer them to the parchment-lined baking sheet, leaving about 2 inches between the balls. You should get twenty-four to twenty-eight, depending on how large your scoops are.

3. Bake for 25 minutes. Remove the baking sheet from the oven, and let the cookies cool on the pan.

Since Jeane and I both loved good food, we often cooked for each other and went to restaurants in D.C. But Allan's and my relationship with the Kirkpatricks was cemented during our two summer visits to them in France. The day before I left for our first trip, in 1983, leaving my parents in charge of our two little girls, I got a big surprise: I was pregnant with not one but two children. Allan had left for Europe first, so I told him the news as soon as I landed in Nice. We had several days to get used to the idea of being the parents of four little girls.

Before we left the States, Jeane had told us not to be late for our visit in Saint-Rémy because she was having a local cook make a surprise for me. When we arrived, we had a meal I shall never forget. A local chef made us Provençal eggplant with roasted lamb that had fed on and then been dressed with herbes de Provence. Although Allan had thought he was allergic to lamb his whole life (because he must have tasted mutton in Uzbekistan as a child), Jeane and I told him it was beef, and he adored it. Like this meal, each one at the Kirkpatrick home was a gastronomic adventure.

Besides the delicious meals on that trip, Jeane gave me some advice. As the mother of three sons, each a year apart, she told me, while we were swimming together in her pool, to take time out for the children. She said I would not be able to work full-time with four little ones, but I should keep my fingers in the food world with an article or two, so I could go back to it when the children were in kindergarten. As a freelancer, it would be easier for me to schedule my own time.

When we weren't cooking our meals, the Kirkpatricks, who liked to splurge on good food, insisted we go to the Michelin three-star L'Oustau de Baumanière for one meal; they enjoyed watching as Allan and I tasted each dish for the first time. I don't recall everything we ate, but I do remember the glorious setting, surrounded by Alpine rocks, and the divine dessert, a chocolate-mint soufflé, which I have played around with through the years. Luckily, pastry chef Sherry Yard—who told me on one of our walks, years later in Los Angeles, that she had also been to Les Baux—not only remembered the same chocolate-mint soufflé, but actually made it for years at Spago, where she was pastry chef, and she helped me simplify this beautiful recipe.

Chocolate Mint Soufflé

I have always thought of soufflés as intimidating for a home cook. And I am not wild about last-minute potchkeying, as my mother would say. But Sherry changed my mind. If you have the ingredients prepped in advance, all you must do is excuse yourself for a few minutes to beat the egg whites, fold them into the egg-chocolate mixture, and bake, and—voilà—you have a stunning dessert. And if you overcook the souf-flé, relax: it will become the flourless molten chocolate cake that we all dearly love.

---

1. Warm the milk to a simmer, then remove it from the heat, scrape the vanilla bean into it, and add the chopped mint. Turn off the heat, and infuse the mixture overnight, refrigerated.

2. The next day, generously butter a 10-ounce soufflé mold, and chill it in the refrigerator until you are ready to fill it and bake.

3. Remove the vanilla bean, and strain out the mint, pressing firmly to release the milk into a medium bowl. Add the granulated sugar and cocoa powder, and whisk until the cocoa is incorporated. Melt the choc-olate briefly in a microwave or in a double boiler, and fold it into the milk mixture, whisking well to blend. Then add the egg yolks, again whisking well. You can do this several hours ahead of time.

4. A half hour before serving, preheat the oven to 400 degrees.

5. Beat the egg whites until stiff peaks form. Carefully fold the chocolate mixture into the whites, until incorporated; then quickly pour the mix-ture into the cold soufflé mold, smooth the top with a spatula, and put it directly into the oven. Bake for 15 minutes—not a minute more. Serve, sprinkled with the confectioners' sugar and with sprigs of fresh mint for garnish.

Serves 6

½ cup (118 ml) milk

1 vanilla bean, split and scraped (set the pods aside and put them in your sugar bowl to make vanilla sugar)

Handful of fresh mint leaves, finely chopped, plus a few sprigs for garnish

10 tablespoons (125 grams) granulated sugar

5 tablespoons good-quality unsweetened cocoa powder

6 ounces (170 grams) 70% chocolate

5 large eggs, separated, at room temperature

Confectioners' sugar, for sprinkling

My First Real Encounter with Sadness

When we got back from that idyllic vacation, I kept gaining weight, but was eating practically nothing. At first the doctor thought that I was pregnant with conjoined twins because there was so much amniotic fluid, but then he changed his diagnosis. He told me I had developed something called acute polyhydramnios, an excess of amniotic fluid. I was put on bed rest, and Allan, clearly not knowing what to do, went to a medical library (in those days, there was no Internet in which to look up the condition) and read about the hopeless outcome. Eventually, the twin girls were born early, one a stillborn, the other alive and as beautiful as my other two girls, so tiny and perfect. But the doctor at Georgetown University Hospital told us that he would advise letting her go: she weighed so little, would require countless operations, and ultimately would be unlikely to survive. It was all the more striking and serious for us that he was advising us to let our baby go because the hospital was affiliated with the Catholic Church. Today this condition can be monitored, but at the time there was nothing to be done. Allan and I discussed it at length and felt that this was the right thing to do. He immediately brought photographs of our daughters to me in the hospital, which was exactly the medicine I needed. But I also thought about other women I knew who were having trouble getting pregnant for the first time.

Of course, I remained sad about my lost twins, but, given the business of motherhood, I could not spend too much time feeling sorrow for what could not have been helped or sorry for myself when I had so much in my life. I also did not want to ruin my children's lives. After all, I had two healthy children.

A few months later, when we were at a dinner in D.C. with PBS's sorely missed Cokie Roberts and her husband, Steve, Cokie told me that she was born after her mother, Congresswoman Lindy Boggs of Louisiana, had a miscarriage. Her mother told Cokie, who was the youngest of four, that she was conceived because Lindy wanted her children to think of pregnancy as a positive, not a negative, experience. I wanted to instill in my own daughters the same strength and positive thoughts.

And so, a year later, without even trying, we were surprised and thrilled when I found myself in a healthy pregnancy; the outcome would be a healthy little boy we called David. It was during this period of my life that I really began to believe in some sort of a godly spirit, who sometimes tests us. A woman told me that when her brother was injured in a diving accident, and her family were all at the hospital waiting to see if he would survive, her father said to the family, "You can't tell God how to run his business." It is how you react to misfortune that is most important. Being strong is sometimes almost impossible, as is setting an example when your insides are so broken you can hardly bear it.

A generation later, when Daniela and Talia were pregnant with twins, I was so happy for them—surprisingly, in retrospect—never dwelling on my own very painful experience. What a joy Alma and Aviv have been for all of us.

19.

Our Life in Washington and on the Road as a Food Writer

Jean-Louis may have been the reason food lovers started making pilgrimages to Washington in those years, but Julia Child and, in a lesser way, Madeleine Kamman were magnets to Boston, the city where we'd recently lived. As fine a cook as Madeleine was, she was always very controversial in a town where Julia, with her relaxed personality, was the queen of French cuisine. I heard Julia call Madeleine "that woman in Newton," and Madeleine dismissed Julia as an American who capitalized on French cuisine. Their competition got so bad that Madeleine, who refused to be in the same room with Julia, often pointed out that Julia was neither French nor a "chef," but was merely an American cooking teacher. According to Madeleine, as cited in an article in *The New York Times*, "When you try to teach a cuisine that is not your own, there is always one dimension missing." In my opinion, they were both great: that woman in Newton was a fabulous and creative French cook, and that woman in Cambridge demystified French cooking for Americans. They both had their places, and I have put their books together on the same shelf in my kitchen with the hope that in heaven they are friends, toasting each other with a fine glass of Chateau Lafite Rothschild 82!

Madeleine was born in Paris but came to the Savoyard Alpine children's village in October 1939 to escape the war-torn French capital. After the war, when she married, she and her husband moved to Philadelphia and in the late 1960s came to Newton, where she founded a highly successful professional school and restaurant called Chez la Mère Madeleine in 1969. But in 1980, when French cuisine was still "the" cuisine in America, Madeleine moved back to France to fulfill a lifelong dream of opening what would become a very short-lived French cooking school.

Since we really enjoyed the food at Chez la Mère Madeleine—where the prix fixe dinners were praised like those downstairs at Chez Panisse in Berkeley, which opened in 1971, but were more strictly French—I was thrilled when Madeleine invited me to attend a food editors' seminar in Annecy for six journalists, including former students like Jimmy Schmidt, who would become chef of the Rattlesnake Club in Detroit, and Gary Danko, whose eponymous restaurant was in San Francisco.

I had hardly traveled anywhere other than one- or two-day trips since Daniela was born. But because Annecy was where some of my French relatives lived, Allan encouraged me to take the trip. My parents came from Providence to help him during the day with Daniela. I still have the three-page list of instructions I assembled for the week to help them.

As soon as I got off the plane in Paris, I called Allan. I told him I wanted to get right back on the plane and come home to Daniela and him. I thought my trip was a terrible mistake. Separation has always been difficult for me at first, but by the time I was on the train to Annecy, I was fine, and ultimately I had a great learning experience with Madeleine.

On the train to Annecy, I met Robert Finigan, one of the well-known wine experts of the day. He was at the height of his career, having helped his friend Steven Spurrier—an Englishman who had a wine shop in Paris, the Académie du Vin—select wines for the famous 1976 blind tasting of American wines in France. This meeting of the most prestigious French vinophiles was eventually immortalized in the movie *Bottle Shock*. Bob told me how he selected the wines from, at that time, largely untested Napa Valley vintners to pit New World wines against revered vintages from the Old in what became known as "the Judgment of Paris." Results from the tasting rocked the wine world to its core: the upstart wines were declared superior to their venerable French counterparts. With his help, I later learned, the long-held hierarchy had shifted.

Bob and I had a good time talking as one only does on that kind of trip, when you don't think you will see someone ever again. During the time we spent together, he told me how he went to California, where he played the stock market, starting at 6:00 a.m. West Coast time, working on his investments; after that, he would play with his real love, wine. Eventually he started a very successful wine newsletter, called *Robert Finigan's Private Guide to Wines*, an early and influential monthly guide to both domestic and European vintages.

In Annecy, we spent three days learning the complex history of the region and then toured the nearby mountain areas, including one visit to the Chartreuse factory that produced alcoholic beverages. There were other trips—to the local marketplace at 7:30 a.m. to find just the right wild mushrooms for a fricassée des champignons; to a modern Reblochon cheese factory; to a local Alpine farm where cheese is made twice a day; and to a mountain restaurant with a pool from which the chef fished out the local trout for our lunch.

The high point of the trip was the demonstration and tasting of Madeleine's food. Taking ancient dishes, she added new techniques and her own creativity and also put each dish within its contextual history. One of the dishes I make to this day is her baked polenta with cheese and wild mushrooms.

Polenta with Cheese and a Fricassée of Wild Mushrooms

½ cup (1 stick/113 grams)
plus 1 tablespoon unsalted
butter

2 medium onions,
finely chopped

1½ cups (205 grams) coarse
cornmeal

4 to 5 cups (946 to 1,182 ml)
vegetable broth or water

Kosher salt and freshly
ground black pepper
to taste

½ cup (118 ml) heavy cream

1 cup (100 grams) grated
Swiss cheese, like Gruyère
or Emmental

*Fricassée des Champignons
(Sautéed Mushrooms)*

3 tablespoons unsalted butter

8 ounces (227 grams) or more
fresh mushrooms of your
choice, cleaned and cut into
½-by-1-inch pieces

Kosher salt and freshly
ground black pepper
to taste

1 large clove garlic, minced

2 tablespoons minced fresh
Italian parsley

The polenta in Savoie, France, is made like a pilaf, as opposed to the Italian style, which is prepared by slurrying the cornmeal into cold liquid before adding it to the bulk of the boiling liquid. At the time of the Roman occupation of Romania in the rich Danube Valley, most people ate a flour gruel as their breakfast. With the Columbian exchange in the sixteenth and seventeenth centuries, flint corn replaced flour, cut as thick as grits. In the 1980s, this dish was unusual. Today it is more everyday, since we can find wild mushrooms and good polenta or grits everywhere.

---

1. Melt the ½ cup butter in a large frying pan set over medium heat. Add the onions, and cook until they're translucent, about 5 minutes. Stir in the cornmeal, then pour in 4 cups (946 ml) of the broth or water and bring it to a boil.

2. Turn the heat down, and let the mixture cook for 5 to 6 minutes, stirring often to fluff up the cornmeal so there won't be any lumps, until it becomes the consistency of porridge; add more broth if necessary. Season well with salt and pepper, and remove the pan from the heat.

3. Preheat the oven to 350 degrees. Butter a 9-by-13-inch baking dish with the remaining tablespoon of butter. Add the polenta in spoonfuls. Cover with the heavy cream, season with salt and pepper to taste, and sprinkle with a thin layer of grated cheese. Bake for about 25 minutes, or until it's golden and bubbly.

4. Meanwhile, make the fricassée Heat the butter in a large skillet set over medium heat. Add the mushrooms, stir to coat them in butter, then season with salt and pepper to taste, cover, and let the mushrooms' water release. Uncover, increase the heat to medium-high, add the garlic and parsley, and cook, stirring, until all the water evaporates. Serve sprinkled on top of or as a side dish to accompany the polenta.

Back in America, the women's movement was in full swing. Carol Brock, a food writer who in 1976 founded Les Dames d'Escoffier in New York, came to Washington to talk about starting a second chapter, which we did in 1981. (In 2015 I was honored to be chosen as a Grande Dame with such luminaries as Alice Waters, Edna Lewis, and Marcella Hazan.) In the eighties, after Barbara Aledort, along with some friends, started a "woman's catering company" called Chanterelle in Georgetown, we did a Dames event in their new space. We invited Paul Prudhomme, for whom we borrowed a chair large enough to fit him from the Jefferson Hotel. We also invited Frances Kitching, from Smith Island, who had just written her cookbook, first published in 1981, who talked spicily about local folk and food.

Once, Anne Crutcher, the first president of our local Les Dames chapter and *The Washington Star*'s food and editorial columnist, invited a few of us food writers, including Bill Rice (then my editor at *The Washington Post*), for lunch after *The Star* folded. Anne, well known for her neighborhood soup dinners on Capitol Hill, where she lived, had never invited me to her home before. When I got there, she and Bill were working hard in her big, light-filled kitchen, pounding almonds and garlic with Anne's mortar and pestle to make a white gazpacho.

I knew the Andalusian red gazpacho, with tomatoes and green peppers, from my mother, who made a great one—often with leftover salad thrown into her blender, which I still do all summer long—but white gazpacho? How exotic for me, who had hitchhiked throughout Spain during my junior year abroad, but during the wrong season to taste this soup. I have never forgotten that day, or how the tart mélange of garlic, wine vinegar, olive oil, and bread contrasted with the sweetness of the peeled grapes and ground almonds. But at the time, I dismissed the preparation as too difficult: the recipe instructed us to peel fresh grapes, blanch the almonds, grind all the ingredients with a brass mortar and pestle, and then put everything through a sieve to avoid graininess, before serving it with carefully sliced whole grapes.

White Gazpacho with Almonds and Grapes

Two 7-inch pita rounds,
  plus more if needed

½ cup (118 ml) white-wine
  vinegar

2 cups (280 grams) blanched
  almonds, plus more if
  needed

2 medium cloves garlic, peeled

⅔ cup (158 ml) extra-virgin
  olive oil

1½ teaspoons kosher salt,
  or to taste

1 bunch or 24 white grapes,
  sliced in half lengthwise

Recently, Anne's daughters gave me a recipe (perhaps even the one that Anne used) from *The Spanish Cookbook* by Barbara Norman, first published in 1966. Almond soup is clearly a much older recipe than red gazpacho, because tomatoes and peppers came from the New World and were not eaten in Spain until the seventeenth century. The so-called white gazpacho dates back at least to the tenth century, as I learned from the Iraqi scholar and cookbook author Nawal Nasrallah, who shared with me a similar recipe that she found in Ibn Sayyār al-Warrāq's tenth-century Baghdadi cookbook, which she translated and published in 2007 as *Annals of the Caliphs' Kitchens*.

Today, with blanched almonds readily available, with our modern powerful blenders, and with no prejudice against eating the outer skin of grapes, the soup takes minutes to prepare. Top it with green grapes or, if you like, chopped apples, Bing cherries, or melon balls. Whatever you do, the fruit should be sweet to contrast with the tangy, delicious soup.

---

1. Shred the pitas, and dip each piece of bread into a bowl of the vinegar, coating it well; then squeeze out the vinegar. Put the bread into a powerful blender or food processor, with the almonds and garlic, and grind until the mixture is pulverized. Then stir in 2 cups (473 ml) ice water, gradually add ½ cup (118 ml) of the olive oil, and blend again; add salt to your taste. Depending on the flavor, you might need to adjust: add ¼ cup more almonds, or another half-pita, or up to a cup more water. Refrigerate the soup until you're ready to serve; you will want it to be very cold.

2. Serve the gazpacho with five to seven grape halves in each individual soup bowl, drizzled with the remaining olive oil.

Note To blanch almonds: Bring water to boil in a sauté pan. Add the almonds, and boil for a minute or two. Let them sit in the water until they are cool enough to handle. Then simply pinch the almonds, and they will come out of their skin.

In the late 1970s and early 1980s, if you wanted fresh fruits and vegetables, you joined a food co-op. While I was schlepping down to my neighborhood co-op, two friends, Anne Luzzatto and Eleanor Dunn, sourced their produce from the wholesale market to sell at their Corner Market, a bright-red van with a big window and a scale, along with a boom box playing Italian opera arias. "We were one of the first D.C. vendors to be able to park in the street and sell from the sidewalk," Anne told me. "But we got chased away before we were able to establish our right to be situated there."

Wearing red-and-white-checked aprons, the two soon introduced baby artichokes, fennel, and radicchio, delivering them in chicly done-up wooden bushel baskets with old copies of *Le Monde* as linings. "We went to the markets every morning at five and loaded up with new and exotic things, like blood oranges, tiny Japanese eggplants, radicchio, and good olive oil," Anne said. "We always had a fabulous baguette sticking out of each basket. We never made a profit, but did we have fun!"

Another person had more lasting success in Washington. Mark Furstenberg, whom I met when we lived in Cambridge, had told me of a dream when we were visiting the Italian North End together. He wanted to open a neighborhood market. "I was very much taken with a store in Cambridge called Jardin. A guy had opened a store with beautiful fruit and vegetables sitting in bins. It was something I had never seen in this country. I thought, 'I could do this.'"

When Mark moved to Washington in 1982, the year of our second daughter Merissa's birth, he followed his dream. By 1984, his sister Carla Cohen had opened Politics and Prose, a beloved independent neighborhood bookstore.

His brother Frank was a sociologist at the University of Pennsylvania. "I put the arm on him to design a questionnaire, asking the neighborhood what it wanted," Mark told me. "My sons and I handed it out while people were raking their leaves." The responses showed that people wanted good bread in Washington. "It was obvious. But though I had always baked bread and baked pizza, I was too dumb even to know that I didn't know how to bake professionally," he told me later. So he apprenticed at Nancy Silverton's La Brea Bakery and other places around the country to hone his baking skills.

In July 1990, down the street from Politics and Prose, Mark opened Marvelous Market. At the beginning it was so popular that the lines wound around the block. Unfortunately, it only lasted for a few years; in 1994, it was taken away from him by investors.

Then, in 2014, lucky for us Washingtonians, Mark opened a neighborhood artisan bakery called Bread Furst, about a mile away from our house. One of my favorite walks is to make my way through Rock Creek Park and up to the bakery, where I am rewarded with an ethereal croissant and a fine cappuccino.

Though the shop is located on a difficult site, right next to a car wash, Mark made the space work for the consumer. You can watch the bread bakers shaping baguettes and braiding challah, or smell the pastry baking near the back door while the pastry team are icing cakes or making brownies.

"I had a fantasy that parents would come in with little children," Mark told me recently. "It worked like a dream being realized. I wanted everyone to see everything." Bread Furst is truly a neighborhood place and a comfortable gem in this city.

My Favorite Brisket

Serves 8 to 10

3 onions, cut into chunks
One 5-pound (2.6 kilogram)
 brisket of beef, shoulder
 roast of beef, or chuck roast
2 teaspoons kosher salt
Freshly ground black pepper
 to taste
2 cloves garlic, peeled
One 15-ounce (425-gram) can
 diced or crushed tomatoes
2 cups (473 ml) dry red wine
2 stalks celery with leaves,
 chopped
1 bay leaf
1 sprig fresh thyme
1 sprig fresh rosemary
¼ cup chopped fresh Italian
 parsley
6 to 8 carrots, peeled and
 sliced on the diagonal

For Friday night, I make roast chicken or a fish dish, or, if there is a big crowd, I always make brisket, a recipe I promised Lexy Bloom, my editor at Knopf, to include here exactly the same as it appears in *Jewish Cooking in America*. It was my mother's family recipe, and I love to make it to this day—of course riffing on the original, as all cooks do.

It's best prepared in advance and refrigerated so that the fat can be easily skimmed from the surface of the gravy. When making this, serve with farfel, egg noodles, potato latkes (page 263), or Kasha varnishkes. A colorful salad goes well with this, too.

---

1. Preheat the oven to 350 degrees, and scatter the onions in a 9-by-13-inch Pyrex pan.

2. Sprinkle the brisket with salt and pepper, and rub it with the garlic. Lay it, fat side up, on top of the onions. Top this with the tomatoes, red wine, celery, bay leaf, thyme, and rosemary. Cover and seal with foil, and bake for about 3 hours, basting every ½ hour with the pan juices.

3. Add half the parsley and the carrots, and bake, uncovered, for about 30 minutes more, or until the carrots are cooked. To test for doneness: Stick a fork in the flat (thinner or leaner) end of the brisket. When there is a light pull on the fork as it is removed from the meat, it is fork-tender. Bring the meat to room temperature, then remove it to a cutting board and trim all visible fat from the brisket. Place the brisket with what was the fat side down, on a cutting board. Look for the grain—the muscle lines of the brisket—and, with a sharp knife, cut slices across the grain.

4. Return the sliced brisket to the roasting pan with the sauce, and refrigerate overnight or freeze. When you're ready to serve, reheat it in a preheated 350-degree oven for 20 minutes. Some people like to strain the gravy, but I prefer to keep the onions, because they are so delicious. If the gravy needs reducing, put the meat on a serving platter and reduce the gravy in a saucepan until it has the correct consistency. Pour some over the meat, and put the rest in a gravy boat. Cover the meat with the carrots and the remaining parsley, and serve.

Entertaining at Our Home

From the beginning of my marriage, we always had a special meal for the start of the Sabbath. When the children were little, they knew that Allan would be home, and they could invite their friends over; as we got older, it became an evening when we could assemble interesting friends and family. Unlike at a bona fide dinner party, we dressed more casually, and often invited people who appeared in our lives seemingly out of the blue. Since Allan always liked there to be just one conversation around the table, I tried to have between six and eight guests, also the number of servings I like to make in my recipes; guests have always been a natural testing ground for them. But since our dining-room table held more, we often reached ten or twelve, including last-minute guests—something spontaneous that we both loved.

Unlike for a regular family dinner, I always included a seating plan, and these days purposefully bcc: guests when I am sending out an informational email about the dinner. A successful dinner party, like an experience in a restaurant, is a form of good theater. And as with good theater, not letting them know who or what is coming raises their anticipation.

Although Allan and I were not particularly religious, we were rather traditional. Each week, we started the Sabbath meal with three long breaths, something added to our ritual by my daughter Merissa. Then I covered my eyes and recited the blessings over the candles to separate the hectic work week from the Sabbath. After all, in the Jewish religion, the Sabbath is the holiest day of the week; the table is like an altar in the Temple of Jerusalem. Allan would say the blessing over the wine and hold in one hand a hot-from-the-oven challah, which I enjoyed making every week. We all would hold the challah or touch someone holding the challah, say the blessing over bread from the earth, and then rip pieces off the bread to share with all our guests. Rarely was there any bread remaining. Then Allan talked about the portion of the week from the Bible with the guests who would often discuss it.

Then the meal began. On Fridays, unlike dinner parties on other nights, we started directly with the meal, and served no appetizers other than soups or salads. And in our home, Friday night was the only time we always had a homemade dessert, not just fruit.

When our children were very little, we would also have Friday-night theater: they would put on a play between the main course and the dessert. While they figured out their lines, the adults discussed what had happened during the week. Then the adults would go upstairs to a stage in a loft above the kitchen, where the children would perform for us, and, finally, we would all return for dessert.

20.

Motherhood and Raising Children

For Mother's Day in 1981, I wrote the following note to my mother:

"As I sit here watching my beautiful Daniela sleep, I am thinking of my own mother. How wonderful, how complicated, and how unpredictable is motherhood. We all started nestled and nurtured in your womb. Once divided, you showed each of us your love as I so eagerly give it to my own daughter. With love in your eyes and heart you watched us develop and grow, grow away from you as is the human condition. How hard it must be to become the mother of adults who must now go it on their own. Thank goodness for grandchildren who start the cycle over for you and can appreciate and be appreciated in still a different way. And what joy it must be for a grandmother to see her own child give birth. Supposedly grown up I am the better for our short visit with you. Still a child, Daniela glows when she talks about her 'grandma in Providence who knits.'"

When Daniela was about nine and Merissa four, I wrote *The Children's Jewish Holiday Kitchen,* opening our house to some of their friends so they could learn to cook the dishes after school. Instead of numerical steps, I wrote the directions by showing what parents could do and also what children could do. Published in 1987 and still in print—a revised edition prepared with my grandchildren as helpers is forthcoming—it is, I think, so popular because I tested the recipes with the children and put their voices in the book. And it meant I could have a really meaningful activity with my children in the process.

When I look back, I don't know how I did it: one, then two, then three children, with a husband working in New York at the United States delegation to the United Nations in those early years. Even with some help, it was hard, juggling everything. I was lucky: I worked at home before it became popular and could work when I wanted. But that did not prevent me from feeling guilty. Mothers have never had it easy, whether they work from home or in the office—or even if their job is "only" to take care of their children. Striking a balance is never simple or guilt-free.

Fortunately, my writing did not take all day; when I watch Daniela with her children, I am amazed how well she and her wife, Talia, do it all. With full-time jobs as an immigration journalist and immigration lawyer, they have an additional distraction that I did not have: the Internet and everything about it, so overwhelming that it makes them work seemingly twenty-four hours a day. They try their hardest to be present for their toddlers, reading with them, not staying engrossed in their cell phones when they are not working. When I watch them, I am hopeful for this next generation and their children.

I remember that, when Daniela was in her senior year of high school, Jean Harrison, the wife of the then headmaster, gave a speech at a mother-and-daughter banquet in which she said that the most important relationship that any woman has is with her mother, whether she likes it or not. Since then, I have thought so often about Jean's words, which hit me hard; I realized that, throughout our lives, daughters listen to and watch their mothers, taking cues from them and reacting to them.

When Merissa was about seven months old, in September 1982, I got a call from the last live-in logging camp in America saying that if I wanted to include it in a book that eventually became my *American Folklife Cookbook*, I should come quickly, because the camp was closing for good. I really didn't want to go alone, because I was nursing Merissa, so I brought her with me.

On another trip that year for the same book, Merissa and my mother accompanied me to Louisiana to interview a chef in Cajun country. The high point was going to K Paul's restaurant, in New Orleans's French Quarter, where Paul Prudhomme gave Merissa and my mother, rather than

With my children, Daniela, David, and Merissa, 1985

me, stars for good behavior. I have always enjoyed bringing my children with me on these tours—it was a way for them to learn about customs and traditions from around the country. And, fortunately, the celebration of food makes it so much fun to take this type of trip.

Of course, Allan and my parents couldn't help all the time. We were fortunate to have assistance throughout the years from au pairs, nannies, and cleaning people from so many different countries: Gambia, Haiti, Austria, Germany, France, the Philippines, Vietnam, Brazil, and El Salvador. As they were learning about us, we were learning about them and their cooking. I see the influence of these women continuing for my twin grandchildren, who speak an early mishmash of Spanish and English, and love beans and rice. Once, when I cooked a chicken for Aviv and Alma, Aviv said to me, "Grandma, we don't like chicken, we like beans and rice." For them, this recipe will always be the real comfort food.

Maria's Rice with Herbs and Zucchini

Serves 4 to 6

2 cups (400 grams) basmati
   rice
1 teaspoon kosher salt
¼ cup olive oil
¼ small onion, diced
4 baby or ½ large zucchini,
   cut into rounds
¼ cup fresh herbs, like
   cilantro, Italian parsley, dill,
   chervil, or tarragon

I try to cook on Thursdays, the day Maria comes, and then she cleans up afterward and sets the table for Friday night. That way, everything is ready for the next evening, making it almost stress-free. Through the years, I have taught Maria how to make brisket and challah, which she now serves her family from El Salvador at Christmas and Easter. But I have learned so much more from her. She has a quiet calmness that captivates me and all my friends. What she does not say is more important sometimes than what she does say. For my family, Maria's dish of beans and rice shows how immigration has only enhanced our food. More than her beans and rice, my favorite dish is her exquisite yet simple rice with tiny zucchini rounds, fresh cilantro, and parsley plucked from my garden. She made it before the premiere of David's first documentary film, *The Story Won't Die,* about Syrian refugee artists. Her method comes from her Salvadoran beginnings, and also from friends from Brazil and Iran; I suggested flavoring the already flavorful dish with vegetables and fresh herbs.

1. Put the rice, salt, and 3 cups water in a saucepan, bring the water to a slow boil, and cook for 10 minutes, uncovered.

2. Drain the rice, and rinse it with cold water. Then put it back into the saucepan with 1 tablespoon of olive oil and, using a knife or stick, poke 3 half-inch holes in the rice to help it steam. Mix 2 tablespoons of oil in ⅓ cup water, pour this over the rice, return the pan to the stove, cover, and cook over low heat for 20 more minutes, until the rice is cooked.

3. Meanwhile, sauté the onion in a tablespoon of olive oil until golden. Add the zucchini, and stir-fry for a few minutes until it's golden. Chop the herbs you have selected, and mix them with the zucchini and onion. Just before serving, sprinkle the vegetables on the rice, and stir in.

Note To make the accompaniment of red or black beans: Start with 1 pound of dried beans. Cover them with water to soak for a few hours or overnight. Then bring the water to a boil, add three mashed garlic cloves, half a diced onion, and salt and pepper to taste. Cover and simmer for 1 to 2 hours, until the beans are soft. Serve with the rice.

In addition to Friday-night entertaining, I was big on start-from-scratch birthday parties, celebrated according to the season. Because my mother had fun making my birthday parties for me, I wanted to carry on the tradition for my daughters. Merissa's birthday is around Valentine's Day, so her parties were easy to create, with grilled pizzas in the shape of hearts and a very good ice-cream cake with an Oreo or Hydrox crust; and, once, a fortune cake for the Chinese New Year with almonds for intelligence and a penny for prosperity.

Once, when Daniela was about seven or eight, in 1984 or '85, she wanted to have Kraft's boxed macaroni and cheese for her birthday party dinner. This was way before Annie's organic macaroni and cheese was on the market. In any event, Marian Burros had just published a recipe in *The New York Times* for homemade macaroni and

Merissa's birthday

cheese. I was sure the children would love it, and it would be in keeping with my cooking credo. No matter that Daniela had specifically asked for the boxed variety—this had to be better. Well, I thought it was better, but my daughter didn't. Poor Marian has forever been associated in my children's minds with disappointingly homemade macaroni and cheese.

When our children were little, we liked opening our home for potluck dinners for their classmates and parents at Sidwell Friends School. We also made a sukkah on our back porch for the children's classes at Adas Israel Synagogue's Sunday school.

The biggest event of each year in the 1980s and '90s was a Memorial Day potluck bash, first at our house in Chevy Chase, and then in D.C. The party was immortalized in an article I wrote for *The New York Times Magazine* in 1990, "The Great Outdoors: A New Twist on Potluck." Each of our children was allowed to invite six families, all the members of whom would be involved in the preparations for the event. The dishes, which were served on our long dining table, brought outside for the occasion, might include a Persian string-bean-and-meat stew, two-pepper soup, or onion bread. Most were homemade. When a guest who did not like to cook arrived shamefacedly bearing a store-bought food offering, he or she quickly learned to put the gift on a beautiful plate and just keep quiet about its provenance. At the height of this celebration, the year when *The New York Times* had me write the article, we had about 140 guests of all ages in our back and front yards, from both sides of Washington's political divide.

Rhubarb Strawberry Crisp

½ cup (1 stick/113 grams)
   unsalted butter, melted,
   plus butter for greasing
   the pan

3 pounds (1⅓ kg) fresh or
   frozen rhubarb, cut into
   ½-inch-long pieces

1½ pints strawberries, hulled,
   left whole, or halved if large

1 cup (200 grams) granulated
   sugar

1⅓ cups (170 grams)
   unbleached all-purpose
   flour

½ teaspoon ground cinnamon

1 cup (213 grams) packed
   dark-brown sugar

½ cup (45 grams) rolled oats

1 cup (120 grams) chopped
   pecans or walnuts

Vanilla ice cream or whipped
   cream, for serving

Yesterday Barbara Aledort outdid Martha Stewart with the ultimate tea party for about 35 women for my 40th birthday. Her Victorian home was filled with flowers in gorgeous bouquets. The tea table included quails' eggs, apple terrine, orange brioche, scones, rum birthday cake, vanilla and Grand Marnier butter, chocolate bread, port, sherry, wine and a Victorian bouquet for me. Elinor Dunn gave me another bouquet composed of 40 fresh carrots. As one guest said, "Thank you for inviting me to your fantasy land."

—*Letter to my parents, 1983*

My birthday fantasy land was converted, as were so many experiences of my life, into an article for *The Washington Post Magazine* on Barbara Aledort's perfect tea party. Then and now, a favorite dish was her rhubarb-strawberry crisp, which I have made throughout the years, and which Barbara also brought each year to our outdoor potluck party. Use strawberries and blueberries later in the springtime, blueberries and peaches in the summer, apples and cranberries in the winter, or whatever seasonal fruit is available.

1. Preheat the oven to 375 degrees and generously butter a 9-by-13-inch rectangular or oval baking dish.

2. Mix the rhubarb, strawberries, granulated sugar, ⅓ cup (45 grams) of the flour, and the cinnamon, and put this mixture into the prepared baking dish.

3. Using your fingers, pinch together the remaining cup of flour with the brown sugar, oats, nuts, and the ½ cup of melted butter. Sprinkle this topping over the rhubarb-strawberry mixture.

4. Bake for 35 to 45 minutes, or until the rhubarb is bubbling and the topping is crisp and browned. Remove it from the oven and cool slightly. Serve it with vanilla ice cream or whipped cream.

Yemeni Food in Brooklyn

In 1986, while Allan was still working at the United Nations and David was just an infant, born in 1985, our family went to New York for my birthday in January. I was eager to try the Yemen Café, which our friend the Yemenite artist Benjamin Levy had told us had just opened in Brooklyn. Although I thought that going to Brooklyn to visit all the Arab stores on Atlantic Avenue and eating Yemeni food would be an adventure and a learning experience for the family, neither of the girls wanted to go. Why did they have to go to a Yemeni restaurant? They wanted to go to the Hard Rock Cafe or Planet Hollywood.

As we walked up the steep steps to the restaurant, in a brownstone building on Atlantic Avenue, I so vividly remember Allan saying to the girls, "It is your mother's birthday. If she wants to go to a restaurant that serves food from Yemen, then that is where we are going." Eventually, they settled down, but probably only ate the rice. The main thing I distinctly remember about my first visit to the place was the metal mixing bowls that served as plates.

Fassolia
(Yemeni White Beans with Onions and Tomatoes)

Serves 4 to 6

1 cup (185 grams) dried Great Northern or cannellini beans, or 3 cups canned beans, saving the liquid

¼ cup (60 ml) olive oil

1 medium onion, cut into ½-inch dice (about 2 cups)

½ teaspoon chopped garlic

One 14.5-ounce (411-gram) can crushed tomatoes

2 tablespoons tomato paste

Kosher salt, to taste

½ teaspoon curry powder

½ teaspoon ground cumin

¼ teaspoon freshly ground black pepper

2 scallions, cut into ½-inch slices, including the green parts

2 teaspoons finely chopped Italian parsley

When I returned to the café recently, more than thirty-five years later, the mixing-bowl plates had disappeared, but the water cups were still made of metal. The décor and the food, very different from the Jewish Yemenite food I had tasted in Jerusalem many years ago, had not changed at all, only the prices. Fortunately, the fassolia, a delicious white-bean vegetarian mash with sautéed onions, tomatoes, and scallions, tasted exactly as it did before.

1. Cover the dried beans, if using, with water, and let them soak overnight. The next day, drain them, cover them with new water in a saucepan, and simmer them for about an hour, uncovered, until they are soft.

2. Meanwhile, heat the olive oil in a large sauté pan, add the onion, and sauté it for a minute or two. Then add the garlic, tomatoes, and tomato paste, and continue sautéing until the tomatoes cook down, about 5 minutes.

3. Add the cooked beans (the dry ones will have expanded to about 3 cups) and a few tablespoons of their cooking liquid, the salt, curry powder, cumin, and black pepper, and continue simmering, squishing the beans so that they are infused with the flavors. Add the scallions and parsley, and cook a few minutes more, until the scallions are soft and the flavors blend; add a little water if needed. Adjust the spices, and serve alone or with rice.

21.

My Holiday Is Passover

And they shall eat the flesh in that night, roast with fire, and unleavened bread; and with bitter herbs they shall eat it.

—*Exodus 12:8*

Allan and I hosted our first Passover Seder in 1980. The tradition is an awesome one, a continuation of history in modern times, a gathering of people who form a community if only for a few hours. And it requires so much planning and preparation!

At the time, Daniela was two years old, and my in-laws were staying with us. Little did we know that Allan and I were embarking on a tradition that would last for the next thirty-nine years of our lives together. As I remember, it was very small: Allan's brother Sam, his parents, his aunt Ruchsha and uncle Henik—who had survived four concentration camps, including Auschwitz—and our good friends Cathy Sulzberger and Joe Perpich, their toddler, David, and our Daniela; the two little ones were surely put to bed shortly after it started.

Passover is the defining event of Judaism, commemorating when the Jews went from slavery in Egypt to freedom in the Promised Land as they passed Mount Sinai and became a united people. It is many-faceted and exciting when little children are present, because the heart of the Seder is to pass on the story from generation to generation. The Seder can go on for hours, so through the years we, like so many others, have tried to include events to sustain everyone's attention, especially the children's.

Passover is a holy day where the table becomes the altar, as it does on the Sabbath. As such, it becomes personalized by each family's singular voyage, bringing their own customs and culinary adaptations of recipes. My family loved everything about it, from Allan's leading the reading of the Haggadah—the narration of the freedom story—to the discussions, to the guests (both regular and pop-ins), and of course, to the food.

Then and now, the Seder is a particularly joyous accomplishment for anyone doing it for the first time. It's the hardest but most rewarding thing I do all year. First of all, you spring-clean the house. Some, like the Orthodox, take it much more seriously than I do. They change dishes and remove every bit of chametz—food that ferments or rises—from their house. If you're strictly following Jewish law developed by the rabbis, fermentation was one of the things that presumably the Jews learned when they were in Egypt, so we rid our houses of all active fermentation, such as yeast and yeast products, to distinguish ourselves from the idolaters.

As a game, I used to have my children read the ingredients of the products in my kitchen, eliminating those that are not permitted during the eight-day holiday. Sometimes I give regular flour and yeast away, sometimes I keep them in my garage, sometimes I just close the flour bins with tape. Very observant Jews go so far as to have their rabbis sell the chametz that remains in their homes during Passover, and then buy it back after the holiday.

After my house and kitchen are ready, I start cooking. I set a section of my kitchen apart to prepare some of the meal, like the chicken soup, the brisket, even a few desserts, all of which I freeze in advance.

On the Seder plate are the symbolic, metaphoric foods that are meant to awaken interest in us all, but especially the children. "Seder" means "order"; the show-and-tell, with so many stories and visuals, is used to keep both children and adults engaged. Many of my visual props have been given to me by various friends throughout the years, and I cherish them all, especially one large brass Seder plate that Allan and I found in Morocco.

As my mother used to say, it's a *ganze* produc-

The Seder and its components, ready for Passover

tion. Take the Seder plate, for example. The hard-boiled egg, burnt in the oven or with a match, represents birth and rebirth in the spring—as well as the sacrifice at the Temple and the roundness of the circle of life. A roasted lamb or beef shank bone, chicken leg, or, for vegetarians, broiled beet represents the Passover sacrifice offered before the Jewish people left Egypt and each subsequent year on the day before Passover in the Temple of Jerusalem. Parsley or karpas, representing the fruit of the ground that awakens in spring and the initial flourishing of the Jews in Egypt, is dipped in salt water to represent the tears of slavery there and the sadness, even for enemies like the Egyptians who drowned in the sea. Maror—bitter herbs, like romaine or chicory lettuce—symbolize the bitterness of slavery. (In the tenth century in

Alsace and southern Germany, the maror became horseradish.) Finally, haroset, though not part of the Biblical Seder, is the fruit-and-nut paste representing the mortar used by the Jewish slaves as they built Egyptian cities.

Throughout my adult life, I have put several haroset dips on the table as a first course, to be eaten symbolically with bitter herbs on the matzo, called the Hillel sandwich. Each dip is different, depending on its geographical and historic journey to our table, and I try to tell its story as part of our Seder. This is truly one of the most awesome aspects of the historic dinner, once held outside, on the hillside in Jerusalem, with a lamb roasted before dawn, unleavened bread, and bitter herbs, as stated in the book of Exodus. To me, haroset, although it is not mentioned in the Torah, explains more than any other food the wandering of the Jewish people in a Diaspora that extends around the world.

I try to serve at least three, sometimes five varieties of haroset. The oldest is probably the Iraqi date syrup sometimes served with walnuts, which represents Jews who come from throughout the Middle East. Many years ago, I watched Bombay born Mozelle Sofaer, who as a volunteer for Gandhi took him messages in prison, and her husband, David Meyer Sofaer, born in Rangoon, slowly cook down the dates with a little anise in a large pot, then strain them in cheesecloth all day, resulting in a smooth, thick, sweet silan, or date molasses—the original honey in the "land of milk and honey." You can now buy it already prepared. I love it throughout the year, especially with halvah and ice cream.

⌁⌁═◯═⌁⌁

I love to experiment with my menus all year long, but not necessarily at Passover. I feel strongly that in the world we live in tradition is important, because it reminds us of where we come from and where we belong, differentiating each of us, in a good way, from everyone else. Our recipes, like our genetic backgrounds, define us. And yet sometimes we can find better recipes for certain things. For example, Allan's family always started the Seder with a saltwater soup with a hard-boiled egg—salt symbolizing tears, eggs the renewal of spring. But it has been replaced today, thanks to strong requests from my children, by the following recipe, made so delicious with long-cooked hard-boiled eggs, spinach, and other greens. It's like what everyone, Jews and Gentiles, ate in the ancient world.

Garosa (Haroset) from Curaçao with Dates, Prunes, Raisins, Tamarind, and Peanuts

One haroset I always include is a ball of dates, raisins, and nuts, representing the journey of the Sephardic Jews fleeing Spain during the time of the Inquisition, and where they have taken it: to Portugal, Morocco, France, New Amsterdam via Brazil, and the Caribbean. Depending on where the Jews landed, the filling for the balls changed; they're always shaped in the size of large marbles or walnuts. This one, adapted from *Recipes from the Jewish Kitchens of Curaçao*, includes locally grown peanuts and tamarind. Then the balls typically are rolled in cinnamon. Dates, which came from the Middle East to Spain, were probably sent each year to South America as a treat for Passover. There are so many more variations, as my many books will show you—and way more than that!

1. Put the dates, prunes, raisins, figs, grated zest, peanuts, cashews (if using), dark-brown sugar, honey, and 1 tablespoon of cinnamon in a food processor fitted with a metal blade. Process until roughly chopped, then add the wine and tamarind or orange juice and process until the mixture sticks together when pressed. Taste it, and add more brown sugar or honey if needed.

2. If you want, put ¼ cup of cinnamon in a bowl. Form balls of the mixture into the size of walnuts, about 1 to 1½ inches in diameter, and roll them lightly in the cinnamon. I don't bother as I feel the balls are sweet enough without the extra cinnamon.

3. The haroset balls can be made days ahead of time and kept wrapped and refrigerated until the Seder.

Makes about 64 haroset balls

4 ounces (113 grams) pitted dates, about 1 cup

4 ounces (113 grams) pitted prunes, about 1 cup

4 ounces (113 grams) golden raisins, about 1 cup

4 ounces (113 grams) dried figs, about 1 cup

2 tablespoons grated lemon or orange zest

8 ounces (226 grams) unsalted roasted peanuts, about 1 cup

4 ounces (113 grams) unsalted roasted cashew nuts, about 1 cup (optional)

4 ounces (113 grams) dark-brown sugar, or to taste, about 1 cup

2 tablespoons honey, or to taste

1 tablespoon cinnamon, plus ¼ cup for rolling (optional)

3 tablespoons kosher red wine

2 tablespoons tamarind or orange juice

Huevos Haminados with Spinach, Beet Greens, and Kohlrabi Greens

☞←
Serves 12
☞←

12 eggs in their shells,
    at room temperature
1 teaspoon leftover coffee
    grounds
1 teaspoon leftover tea leaves
As many onion peels as you
    can find
1 tablespoon white-wine
    vinegar
3 tablespoons olive oil
2 cinnamon sticks
1 large red onion, diced
2 pounds (907 grams) mixed
    cold-weather greens,
    such as spinach, Swiss
    chard, kale, and greens
    from beets or kohlrabi
Kosher salt and freshly
    ground black pepper,
    to taste

Eggs, a symbol of the cycle of life, are truly the spring symbol for most religions. No wonder. Hens lay more eggs in the springtime, when there is an abundance of new grass.

Sephardic Jews—and all Jews once upon a time—have a way of making a delicious Sabbath-morning or holiday dish, huevos haminados, cooked eggs, which actually involves some recycling. The eggs are simmered in water overnight, using leftover onion skins, tea leaves, coffee grounds, and cinnamon sticks to create a lovely color, creaminess, and aroma. Or they are nestled in their shells in a rice-and-meat Sabbath stew called dafina (page 414) in Morocco and t'beet in Iraq. The difference between Jewish and non-Jewish overnight eggs is that, because of the prohibition of working on the Sabbath, the Jews briefly cooked the eggs in water and peeled them before the Sabbath began, then put them into the pot to cook slowly, thereby creating the taupe color and added flavor given by all the other ingredients surrounding them. Recently, I saw whole eggs sitting in the embers of an Arab bakery in Jerusalem, reminding me of this ancient custom.

When I was in Rome researching my book *King Solomon's Table,* I met a woman whose family came to Italy from Corfu, Greece. She shared with me her recipe for huevos haminados with spinach. I have added Swiss chard, beet tops, and kohlrabi tops, delicious greens that enrich and flavor the spinach, and were no doubt included in ancient forms of this dish.

---

1. Put the eggs in a soup pot, and cover them with water by at least 2 inches. Stir in the coffee grounds, tea leaves, onion peels, vinegar, 1 tablespoon oil, and cinnamon sticks. Bring the water to a boil, then lower the heat and simmer for 4 hours, adding more water if needed to keep the eggs covered. Let the eggs cool in the broth, and then remove them with a slotted spoon, and wash off the froth that will have formed. Discard the cooking liquid and solids, or pour this into your compost, and wipe the pot clean. Tap the eggs gently against the counter, and peel them under cold running water, keeping them as nearly whole as possible. Put them into a bowl.

2. Set the pot over medium heat, add the remaining 2 tablespoons of oil, then add the diced onion, and cook until golden. Add the greens and ½ cup water and cook, wilting them and stirring frequently, until they are soft and as cooked as you like. Add salt and pepper to taste, roughly chop, and serve a dollop of greens with each egg as the first course of your Seder.

Another must at Passover is gefilte fish, an unfortunate guttural title for a dish that can be so delicious. I've learned many ways to make it over the years, from my mother-in-law and my gefilte-fish ladies, with whom I have been making this fish the day before the Seder for at least a dozen years. We shape the ingredients of our family recipes into oblong patties, some using more or less carp, pike, and whitefish, salt, egg, whatever. But these recipes are all infused with memories and laughter, and of course served with horseradish sauce, homemade if possible.

My traditional recipe for gefilte fish is in *Jewish Cooking in America*. At Rosh Hashanah, I do not make patties, opting instead for this lighter and easier version made in a springform Bundt pan, with dill and halibut. And during COVID, I made this as a main course for Passover.

I also include in my Seder lots of brightly colored Sephardic salads, like roasted pepper, beet, carrot, and always asparagus, symbolic of spring. My many desserts, too, have meaning: the chocolate roulade, the lemon-almond torte, all in my cookbooks. But if I had to select my two favorites, they would be a schaumtorte with bittersweet chocolate and hazelnuts, a Danish dessert made for us by my daughter-in-law Liv's mother, Eva, when we visited Copenhagen (see page 55), and this pecan torte with a lemon-curd filling.

Halibut Gefilte Terrine with Fresh Herbs

Serves about 12

Cooking spray
2 large sweet onions,
   like Bermuda
   (about 2 pounds/
   907 grams)
2 large carrots, peeled
3 tablespoons olive oil
3 pounds (1⅓ kg) halibut,
   cod, or grouper fillets
4 large eggs
6 tablespoons matzo meal
2 teaspoons kosher salt,
   or to taste
2 teaspoons freshly ground
   white pepper
2 tablespoons sugar
½ cup chopped fresh dill,
   tarragon, and/or chervil
¼ cup chopped fresh Italian
   parsley, plus more for
   garnish
Horseradish sauce,
   for serving

Preparing the gefilte fish in a mold or a springform pan omits fussing with the bones and skin to make a fish stock that you need when making patties, which creates more work and odors in the kitchen. In addition, the white of the fresh fish contrasts beautifully with the fragrant green herbs and the orange carrots, creating a more appealing and colorful dish. Gefilte fish is usually made from a freshwater fish, as found in Eastern European lakes. But saltwater fish is just as flavorful, and easier to find. As usual, Jewish dishes vary according to what is available. Living part of the year in New England, I was surprised at how delicious northeastern halibut could be in this dish.

---

1. Preheat the oven to 325 degrees, and grease a 12-cup Bundt pan with cooking spray.

2. Dice the onions, and shred the carrots on a box grater. Sauté them in the oil over medium-high heat until the onions are golden and soft. Set them aside to cool.

3. If you can have someone at the fish market grind the fish, all the better. Otherwise, you can pulse it in a food processor fitted with a steel blade, making sure you remove the membranes that may attach themselves to the blade—or use the grinding attachment of a stand mixer.

4. Put the cooled onions and carrots into the bowl of a stand mixer fitted with the paddle, along with the ground fish and the eggs, matzo meal, salt, white pepper, sugar, ½ cup (118 ml) water, and herbs. Mix at medium-low speed for about 10 minutes, or until everything is well blended and smooth.

5. Pour the mixture into the prepared Bundt pan, and smooth out the top. Set the filled Bundt within a larger pan with 2 inches of warm water up the sides of the Bundt. Bake for about an hour, or until the center is solid and a toothpick inserted near the middle comes out clean.

6. Cool for about 15 minutes, blot away any water on top, and run a knife around the edges of the pan. Swiftly invert the gefilte fish onto a flat serving plate.

7. Refrigerate it for several hours or overnight. Slice it as you would a torte, garnish the slices with parsley, and serve with horseradish sauce, either red or white. Leftovers keep for about 5 days.

I like to make my own horseradish sauce—the sine qua non for gefilte fish. I grate enough peeled raw red beetroot into grated white horseradish and add a little vinegar, salt, and sugar until it turns a pleasant pinkish red. If you are doing this in your kitchen, make sure to wear goggles to avoid the fumes from the horseradish!

Passover Pecan Lemon Torte with Lemon Curd Filling

Torte

¼ cup (29 grams) matzo
meal, plus more for the pan

8 large eggs, separated

1 cup (200 grams) sugar

¼ teaspoon kosher salt

Grated zest of 1 lemon

½ tablespoon fresh lemon
juice

1 cup (100 grams) pecan
halves, coarsely ground

Lemon Curd Filling

3 lemons

¾ cup (150 grams) sugar

3 large eggs

¼ cup (½ stick/56 grams)
unsalted butter, vegan
butter, or coconut oil

Fresh blueberries, for serving

Many years ago, in Jerusalem, I was given a recipe for an almond-lemon torte. I loved the tartness of the lemon but wanted it even more lemony. I was reminded of my love for lemon curd, which started when I'd go from bakery to bakery in Paris, tasting each lemon-curd tart. For this torte, I changed the almonds to pecans (because Passover already has so many almonds) and added my favorite lemon curd, which I learned from Suzanne's, a long-gone restaurant on Connecticut Avenue in Washington. It's not hard at all: make the curd a few days in advance and, if you want, freeze the cake up to 2 months ahead.

1. Preheat the oven to 325 degrees. Dust a 9-inch springform pan with matzo meal.

2. Beat the egg yolks with the sugar and the salt until they're smooth and pale lemon yellow. Gradually add the ¼ cup of matzo meal, the lemon zest, and lemon juice. Fold in the pecans.

3. In a separate bowl, whip the egg whites until stiff but not dry (by hand or using a hand mixer or stand mixer). Gently fold them into the yolk mixture.

4. Scrape the batter into the prepared springform pan and bake on the middle rack for 45 minutes, or until a toothpick comes out clean when inserted. Let it cool while you make the lemon curd.

5. To make the filling Grate the rind of the lemons to get 2 tablespoons zest, then juice the lemons to get ¾ cup of juice. Whisk the sugar and the eggs in a medium saucepan. Gradually add the lemon juice and zest. Add the butter or coconut oil, and cook over medium heat, stirring constantly and being careful not to boil, until the lemon thickens into a curdlike custard, about 5 minutes. Set aside to cool.

6. Once the cake is cool, split it into two round layers. Spread the lemon-curd filling, reserving a few tablespoons, on the cut side of the bottom round. Add the second round, top side up, then spread the remaining curd, dot with blueberries, and serve.

But what makes our Seder different from others is the play we have done for more than forty years. It is always the same: God, sheep, grown Moses, baby Moses, Miriam, and Aaron and his siblings. The children leave the table a little after the main course to rehearse and raid our closet for costumes. Although it used to be only children acting, many of the "children" are now in their forties, and some guests, in their nineties, also perform. It is always the same, always hilarious, and the crowning joy for all of us.

I remember one year, when the play was over, this crowd had become a community, and there was silence. I sensed that no one wanted the evening to stop. It wasn't just a dinner party. It was a sacred space, and I loved it. Even though it's so sad that many of our participants are gone now, I feel they will live on in the stories told and the strength we take from the lives they lived—from Allan's uncle Henik, who celebrated life after being in Auschwitz, to Allan himself, who was the leader of our Seder and my partner in life for so many years.

Since the mid-1970s, I have been writing about Passover every year for various newspapers, magazines, and now Web sites. Through the years, I'd go out to a second Seder, because our family's custom is to host only the first night. As a result, I have observed so many traditions new to me, like that of Persian Jews, who hit each other with scallions during the service; or Iraqi Jews, who put on a play in which the children pretend to be paupers, with sacks on their backs holding matzo wrapped in handkerchiefs. The leader asks where they have come from and where they are going. They say they were slaves in Egypt and are going to freedom in Jerusalem. I especially like the marvelous Moroccan custom of holding the Seder plate over every guest's head so that each will relive the Exodus, feeling he is personally going from slavery to freedom.

As I taste and experience these old traditions that are new to me, I am so excited to be able to put them into articles and books, sharing them with my readers. Memories come together—things our fathers and mothers taught us, like the story of the Exodus, that we in turn will pass on to our children. In addition, in my small way, I feel that my visits to people's kitchens all over the globe have taught us all about the diversity of Judaism, enriching our minds and our holiday tables.

As I learned these customs and the delicious foods that accompanied them, so different from my own, I wanted to share the knowledge I had gained. I had an idea to make what became known as *Passover: Traditions of Freedom,* now an evergreen documentary, aired in 1998 by Maryland Public Television and around America for a whopping twelve years.

To make the film, which I produced with Charles Pinsky, we and the crew went to Israel and replicated a very early Seder, but not in Jerusalem. Instead, our Seder took place in a Bedouin village where, to this day, when they slaughter a lamb or goat, they rub their tent post with the blood to keep away the evil spirits. The Bedouins also made bread for us as visitors—from flour and water, no leavening. Why not? They explained—through the Bedouin expert Clinton Bailey, our translator, and the person who brought us to this village—that they wanted to give guests nothing but pure food, and yeast was a contamination, of civilization and cities. Therefore, they mixed the flour and water, quickly rolled out what became a very thin round dough, and slapped it onto the sides of a *taboun* oven (which looked like an upside-down wok) to bake. It was delicious, and similar in shape to what we know as shmura matzo.

Of all my explorations of Passover Seders, I think that the most trendsetting article I ever wrote was for *The New York Times* in 2006. Entitled "It's Passover, Lighten Up," it debunked many practices that we used without thinking. Emily Moore, a food writer and chef in Seattle, tipped me off that baking soda and baking powder, for example, are both kosher for Passover. I was shocked. When I interviewed Rabbi Moshe Soloveitchik, a member of a prominent rabbinic dynasty who oversees ritual observances for Streit's Matzos, he confirmed it. "They're just minerals. What do we care about minerals?" For the Orthodox, they just have to be marked "Kosher for Passover."

To my further surprise, Rabbi Jeffrey Wohlberg, told me that, as of 2015, it is now permissible for Conservative and Reform Jews to eat legumes, including soybeans—called kitniyot in Hebrew—which are so important for the lactose-intolerant and others.

Jews in medieval Europe began to keep beans and lentils, as well as grains, from the Passover table because until modern times they were often ground into flour. The use of rice and corn were later restricted, too, by some Jews. But Sephardic Jews of the Middle East continued to eat them at Passover.

Partly because of the increased intermarriage between Sephardic Jews and Ashkenazi Jews in Israel, legumes have become accepted for Passover by the Israeli Army. When my article appeared, there was quite a lot of confusion; several rabbis around the country said that their phones were ringing off the hook with questions from their congregants.

I can't wait to hear what people think of my homemade matzo. I don't make it for Passover, but theoretically I could, using wheat grown by Jewish farmers around the country who grind it separately from other flours. It is not stamped "Kosher for Passover," but it is made from the Biblical emmer or einkorn wheat.

Homemade Matzo

Recently, I was asked to lead a matzo-baking class for an organization called Reboot that my daughter Daniela is a member of in Los Angeles. I used ancient emmer wheat, the so-called mother of wheat, which Glenn Roberts, the owner of Anson Mills in South Carolina, is growing in South Carolina, Arizona, and the Pacific Northwest. According to Glenn, it is even older than the twelve thousand years that are usually cited today—researchers are finding, as they do better seed archaeology and evaluation of the genetic material, that it likely dates back forty-four thousand years.

Round matzo (*pain azyme* in France), baked in an oven, was the norm at the beginning of the nineteenth century, until an Alsatian Jew named Alex Singer created the first mechanized matzo-dough rolling machine in 1838, which cut down on its preparation time and made mass production possible. Then, in 1886, Dov Behr Manischewitz arrived in Cincinnati as a part-time peddler and shochet for the Orthodox community. The next year, he started a small matzo bakery, which eventually grew to become B. Manischewitz Baking Company, the largest maker of square, machine-made matzo in the world.

When making your own matzo, try to find einkorn or emmer wheat flour, so you can be really authentic. For the Seder, you should make your matzo of just flour and water. If you like it as much as my family does, you can embellish it later—even during Passover week—with a little kosher salt and some sprinkled rosemary or other herbs, and lighten the dough with a teaspoon of kosher for Passover baking powder, and a few tablespoons of olive oil.

Makes 5 matzot

2 cups (about 250 grams) whole-wheat, unbleached all-purpose, or emmer or einkorn flour, or matzo cake meal, plus more for work surface

---

1. Fifteen minutes before you plan to begin, position an oven rack as high as it goes, turn on the oven's broiler to high, and put a brick or a pizza stone on the bottom rack. Preheat a baking sheet on the top rack.

2. When you are ready to begin, set a timer for 18 minutes, the amount of time from start to finish for a correct Passover matzo (otherwise, the matzo will theoretically ferment and is therefore not kosher for Passover).

3. Quickly mix the flour with ¾ cup (178 ml) water. Sprinkle a pastry surface, preferably marble, with additional flour. Then knead the dough with the heel of your hand for about 3 minutes, until it is smooth, →

adding more water if it's too dry and more flour if it is too sticky. (Humidity will affect it greatly!)

4. Using a dough cutter, divide the dough into five equal pieces. (At this point, the more people helping, the better.) Have each of your helpers knead the pieces of dough until they're elastic. Then use the rolling pin to make the dough very thin and very flat, in a circle, 6 to 7 inches in diameter; sprinkle the dough with flour if it is too sticky.

5. Roll the dough out one more time, and prick it all over with a fork to prevent any rising. Remove the baking sheet from the oven, and cover it with parchment paper. Carefully transfer two pieces of the flattened dough onto the parchment-lined baking sheet; then put the sheet back into the oven, and bake for 3 to 4 minutes, until the matzo is dark brown and crisp. Watch through the oven's window to make sure the matzo isn't burning; if it does, lower the oven rack a notch. Repeat with the remaining dough; I hope you will have prepared and finished baking within 18 minutes!

Matzo Brei (Fried Matzo with Eggs)

Serves 4

6 tablespoons unsalted butter

2 large onions, diced

2 matzo squares

4 large eggs

Kosher salt and freshly
ground black pepper,
to taste

1½ cups chopped fresh
mushrooms and/or spinach

1½ cups diced smoked salmon

¼ cup chopped fresh dill

In my house, besides the lightness of matzo balls, there is no dish more contested or discussed than matzo brei. My family debates as to which is better: sweet or savory. And, if sweet, should it be made with one matzo per one or two eggs, then sprinkled with honey, cinnamon sugar, or maple syrup? Should the matzo be softened in hot or cold water, should it be whole, or broken into little pieces, and if so, how big? And if we're making it savory (my preference, not my late husband's), how long should the onions be cooked? And what kind of mushrooms should be used? Should we use schmaltz or butter? (We use butter.) One Passover, we had a matzo brei cook-off between my brother-in-law Sam and Sheila Lukins, co-author of *The Silver Palate Cookbook*, who was our guest for the weekend. Each thought they won, but this one, a savory version, is my favorite.

---

1. Heat 4 tablespoons of butter in a large skillet over medium-low heat. Add the onions, and cook, stirring occasionally, until they're golden brown, 15 to 20 minutes.

2. Submerge the matzot in cold water for 30 seconds, and remove them.

3. In a large bowl, whisk the eggs, and add salt and pepper. Break up the matzot into bite-sized pieces and add to the egg mixture with the onions and the mushrooms and/or spinach.

4. Melt the remaining 2 tablespoons of butter in the skillet if needed. Add the egg mixture, and let it cook until the eggs are just set, 2 to 3 minutes. Right before serving, sprinkle them with the smoked salmon and the dill.

Note If you prefer it sweet, then try my daughter Merissa's rendition, with three eggs, 1 teaspoon vanilla, ½ teaspoon cinnamon, ¼ cup milk, a pinch of kosher salt, and two matzot crushed in little pieces and soaked for a minute or two in cold water.

22.

Leo Lerman and *Gourmet* Magazine

In the fall of 1985, as Schocken Books was starting to gear up for the publicity campaign for *An American Folklife Cookbook,* the publicist called me, excited.

"You have arrived," she said.

I couldn't figure out what she meant until she said that Leo Lerman, a longtime editor at *Mademoiselle* and *Vogue,* then interim editor in chief of *Vanity Fair,* and at the time Condé Nast's editorial adviser at large—where he was working with the newly acquired *Gourmet* magazine—wanted to have lunch with me. She also said that he adored *An American Folklife Cookbook* and that it would be the lead book for his *Gourmet* cookbook roundup in December. He wrote that the book was "full of love, streaming from these raptly narrative pages studded with recipes, comes to us full force from Mrs. Nathan and from the people she sought out for some eight years." What astounded me in the review was his likening my book to the works of two of my favorite regional writers, a "gastronomical and social field trip that Mrs. Nathan reports with a sensibility as keen as Sarah Orne Jewett's and Kate Chopin's." I had tried, in this book, which started with experiences I had with the Smithsonian Folklife Festival and a few articles in *The Washington Post* and *The Boston Globe,* to show how everyday people around the country, in places where folk traditions were fading fast, were holding on to what they loved best.

In the 1980s, food was beginning to be taken seriously in this country, as more than representing fuel for the body. As one of the cooks I visited—Eddie Washington of Seebert, West Virginia, a slight Black woman stooped over with arthritis, who cooked on a green-and-white Kalamazoo wood-burning stove—told me, "Cooking is just a song to me. It is just one of those things I like to do."

Unfortunately, because of a delay in the production of my book, there were no books to sell to anyone who had seen Leo's sterling review. Nevertheless, the appointed book-launch was still on, and in its honor I bought a new bright-red wool Marimekko dress to wear when I met Mr. Lerman.

Leo and I were to meet in the Grill Room at the Four Seasons, the high-and-mighty restaurant designed by Philip Johnson in the Seagram Building. When I arrived, the elderly balding man with a rabbinic beard was already seated, dressed in a dark suit and what I would later learn was a signature lavender-dotted tie and purple socks. When I sat down, he looked intently at me and said that I was younger than he'd thought. There was a calmness about him that I liked. I felt at ease right away.

Although this was the first of many lunches I was to have at the Four Seasons, many of them with Leo, it was clear from the way he was treated that the restaurant was his regular haunt for Condé Nast, most probably to garner gossip for Si Newhouse, who, as Ruth Reichl later wrote, never ate garlic. As such, Leo was given "his" table for people watching. He told me that, since several of his relatives were hearing-and-speech-impaired, he had learned to read lips at an early age and could read any conversation in any room. Plus, he was farsighted—all the better to see at long distances. The Four Seasons was a perfect place for him to collect gossip from powerful people.

He didn't beat about the bush. By the time I finished my first course—leeks vinaigrette, a Four Seasons classic and a favorite dish for me— he had told me that Susan and Robert Lescher would be my agents, Judith Jones would become my editor, and I would start writing for *Gourmet*. Within months, everything he predicted happened because of his intervention.

*

I later learned I was in good company: there were other women in the food world whom Leo had helped. One of his "girls" was Dana Cowin, who, straight out of Brown University, was his personal assistant at *Vogue*. "I thought he was so ancient," Dana told me. "His hands didn't work so well, he didn't see well, but Mr. Lerman was magnificently connected to everybody, had impeccable taste, and was permanently interested in the next new thing. I answered the phone from Glenn Close, Marlene Dietrich, and Greta Garbo and worked with Richard Avedon and Irving Penn on photo shoots." Soon Dana was at *House & Garden,* where Leo advocated for her to be promoted from associate editor to managing editor, and later to become editor of *Food & Wine.* "He really is partly responsible for my wonderful media career."

Barbara Kafka, plucked from *Mademoiselle* by Leo and one of the smartest people I have met in the food world, was also at *Vogue* at that time, developing recipes. He warned Barbara to forget about writing about art, her first love, and stick to cooking. She followed his advice, suggesting three ideas to *Vogue*. Thus began her august cooking career.

Nothing was really easy. As my father used to say, introductions can help, but it is up to you what you make of these opportunities. In addition, though, interest in the food world was mounting; once the American Federation of Chefs changed their designation from blue- to white-collar worker in the Department of Labor in 1968, being a chef had become an acceptable career. Between 1982 and 1989, when food sections and advertisements were expanding, some publications, like the *Los Angeles Times* and the *San Diego Evening Tribune,* grew to have forty-four pages in their food sections. The number of food magazines was increasing, and interest in healthy and gourmet food was growing everywhere.

After the first of many lunches with Leo, I received a phone call from a friend of his at the New York Public Library asking if I would like to give a lecture in a series also featuring the Indian cookbook writer Julie Sahni and the Japanese cookbook writer Elizabeth Andoh. My lecture was to be "What's Really Cooking in American Kitchens." The tickets were five dollars apiece, and people could sign up by sending checks to the library with stamped self-addressed envelopes. Of course, I said yes. I thought it was such a great idea to speak about the stories of people in a cookbook, and at what better stomping ground than the New York Public Library, where I had done so much research for *The Jewish Holiday Kitchen*. The Trustees Room was packed, and I loved the experience of giving a lecture on food as a phenomenon of culture and history, talking not so much about the recipes as about the people who made them and their cultural context.

When I returned home to Washington, on a high, I immediately suggested to Janet Solinger, then the head of the Smithsonian Associates, that the Smithsonian follow suit with a lecture series. This was late 1985. Janet listened skeptically, then mulled it over, and finally got back to me, asking if I would put together the first of many lecture series. I chose "America's Great Masters of Cooking: Trends in American Cuisine," with Julia

Child, Craig Claiborne, Paul Prudhomme, *The Washington Post*'s then restaurant critic Phyllis C. Richman, and people from Plimoth Plantation. It was such a success that the Smithsonian has been doing food programs ever since.

But my meeting with Jane Montant, the editor in chief of *Gourmet*, was not so successful. While Leo was trying to bring new talent to *Gourmet* after Condé Nast bought the magazine in 1983, Jane was very resentful of someone giving her suggestions from the parent company. To make it even worse, I had the audacity to bring my very active two-year-old daughter, Merissa, to the office, something Jane did not look on very kindly.

In the end, she did assign me a piece for a column called City Dining. I wrote about three Washington restaurants in April 1986, around the time when Allan became deputy assistant legal counsel of the Department of Justice. Leo, who was coaching me, suggested that I choose two restaurants that were predictable and one unpredictable. So I chose Jean-Louis at the Watergate as number one, then the tiny Galileo Italian Restaurant with another young chef—Roberto Donna, from Turin—as the second, and, finally, the off-the-mainstream, family-run Caspian Tea Room, located in a local strip mall, as the third. I loved the Caspian Tea Room's atmosphere and its fesenjan, a Persian pomegranate-and-walnut stew that I have been enamored of my whole life. I love it so much that I've included different versions in several of my cookbooks. The Caspian Tea Room's cucumber salad was also a treat.

Leek Salad with a Beet Vinaigrette

Years ago, when I was to appear on *Live with Regis and Kathie Lee* with Henry Winkler, I was told not to prepare anything and just to follow what Henry did. I was making a leek-potato kugel, so it must have been before Passover. First Henry put the leek in his ear, then he threw it at me, then he asked me why there are leeks in what was basically an ordinary potato kugel. I told him that in the Bible it says that when the Jews were in the desert they missed the leeks, garlic, and onions from Egypt. He said, not missing a Jewish beat, "You mean even in the desert Jews were kvetching?"

Well before my encounter with Henry Winkler, leeks had a special place in my heart, and whenever I see leeks vinaigrette on the menu, I order it, especially in the winter. I love the soothing taste of cooked but not overcooked leeks, and I yearn to go to Macedonia, where leeks are king.

But a recipe that I truly love is the appetizer at the Four Seasons, which I have adapted, adding a slurry of sweet bright-red beets; they go beautifully with the slightly vinegary leeks.

Serves 6 to 8

1 medium red beet
2 teaspoons kosher salt, plus more for the pot
3 medium leeks, including dark greens
2½ tablespoons Dijon mustard
½ teaspoon thickly sliced garlic
¼ teaspoon freshly ground black pepper
3 tablespoons sherry vinegar
½ cup (118 ml) vegetable oil
Hazelnuts, roasted and chopped, for garnish

---

1. Preheat the oven to 450 degrees. Wrap the beet in aluminum foil, put it on a baking sheet, and roast it for about 1 hour, or until it's easily pierced with a knife.

2. While the beet is cooking, bring a large saucepan of salted water to a boil. Trim the leeks, discard the tough outer leaves, halve them lengthwise, and wash them to remove the grit. Cut the leeks into about 2-inch lengths and boil them for about 10 minutes, or until they're soft. Strain, and put the leeks on a serving platter.

3. Whisk the mustard, garlic, the 2 teaspoons of salt, pepper, vinegar, and 1½ tablespoons of water together in a medium bowl. Slowly drizzle in the oil, whisking until the dressing is emulsified.

4. When the beet is cool enough to handle, slip off the skin and slice it into two or three pieces. Purée them in a food processor or blender with the vinaigrette. Taste, and adjust the salt, pepper, and vinegar as needed; then chill until you're ready to serve.

5. Then, making sure the leeks are salted to taste, cover them with a line of beet vinaigrette, sprinkle with hazelnuts, and serve.

Persian Cucumber Salad with Yogurt and Walnuts

Now that Persian cucumbers are available, those of us who love cucumber salads can pursue our passion year-round. Similar tasteful, refreshing, and simple salads come from many cultures, but I think this one is the best I have ever tasted.

Serves 4 to 6

---

1. Dice the cucumbers, the onion, and the radishes, and put them into a ceramic bowl. Add the currants, apricots, and walnuts with half the mint and half the dill, and salt and freshly ground pepper to taste. Spoon the yogurt on top just to cover, and stir it in. Cover, and let the salad sit in the refrigerator for a few hours or overnight.

2. Just before serving, sprinkle the salad with the remaining mint and dill and, if you want, cilantro. Serve it chilled.

2 small Persian cucumbers

1 small onion, or the white
   parts of 2 scallions
   (about ¼ cup diced)

2 radishes

⅓ cup (48 grams) currants
   or dried cranberries

⅓ cup (63 grams) dried
   apricots, diced

⅓ cup (43 grams) walnuts,
   roughly chopped

6 sprigs fresh mint, chopped

4 tablespoons chopped
   fresh dill

Kosher salt and freshly
   ground black pepper,
   to taste

About 1 cup (240 grams)
   plain yogurt

2 tablespoons chopped fresh
   cilantro (optional)

Later in the 1980s, I wrote my favorite piece ever for *Gourmet*, when Gail Zweigenthal, who had been under Jane's tutelage for many years, became executive editor. The piece was about marrons glacés, the candied chestnut confection that I have adored ever since a young Frenchman popped a plump piece into my mouth.

Before I did my research for the article, Allan and I were visiting Annecy and Mégève. At the time I remember Madeleine Kamman's advice to me when I had asked about marriage. "Pay attention to your husband when he is with you and do what you want when he leaves."

As soon as Allan took off from the Geneva airport, I felt as free as a bird. I drove through the Alps, stopping in tiny villages along the way. In one charming roadside restaurant, I tasted a crique, a paper-thin potato pancake with no filler, which Daniel Boulud showed me how to make when I returned to New York. I have enjoyed crunchy rather than dense latkes ever since. After my lunch, I finally arrived in the city of Privas, in Ardèche, the marrons glacés capital of France, to learn how to make the confection.

I've loved everything about chestnuts ever since childhood, when I tasted warm ones that had been roasted on the streets of New York by an Italian vendor, and which my mother and I plucked from a small paper bag. I can't resist Mont Blanc, a sundae with vanilla ice cream, topped with a purée of the sweetened chestnuts put through a ricer and served with a dollop of whipped cream. But nothing tastes quite like a carefully made candied chestnut, a Christmas holiday specialty in both France and Italy. In 1982, after Merissa was born, while I was still in the hospital, Allan brought me a box of them; he knew how much I like them.

23.

Moroccan Food—
A Long Love Affair

My love for Morocco started when I lived in Jerusalem and tasted the memulaim (stuffed vegetables) and cooked the salads I learned from my cleaning woman. I loved the flavors, sophistication, and earthiness of this cuisine conceived at the very end of the spice route. After North African nations gained independence, Israel had a huge influx of the poorer Moroccan Jews; most of the wealthier immigrated to France. Fortunately, Morocco has officially welcomed back their Jewish population.

In February 1982, when I was very visibly pregnant with my daughter Merissa, a friend glanced at me and said, "Joan, you've got to get a more stylish haircut." She immediately called Jean-Paul Amsellem, her hairdresser. (It seemed that most of the hairdressers in Washington in those days were Moroccan.) As he styled my hair, the two of us chattering in French, I learned that he also owned a French restaurant called Bistro Français (now closed) in Georgetown that served couscous on Thursdays. After I got my hair cut, I promised that if the baby did not come the next week I would visit for couscous. Not missing a beat, Jean-Paul replied, "And if you're in the hospital, I'll bring you some couscous." As I was nursing Merissa in the hospital the next week, the scent of Moroccan spices wafted through the corridor. Jean-Paul had sent it over for me. Until he retired, Jean-Paul cut my hair and also taught me to make his wife Nicole's preserved lemons, harissa, and a multitide of Moroccan salads—and even taught me a little bit about the stock market.

In Ouarzazate, Morocco, with the family on a camel ride

Preserved Lemons

I have been making my own preserved lemons for almost forty years. The bottled kind you can buy in stores are mostly cured in water with some acidic preservative; the final result is just not as good. I am a purist and do not put in sugar, garlic cloves, or anything other than lemon, salt, and fresh bay leaves if I can find them, for color. These lemons are one of the absolute staples in my refrigerator.

Makes 8 preserved lemons

About 16 lemons
About 1 cup (240 grams)
  kosher salt
4 fresh bay leaves (optional)
2 tablespoons olive oil

---

1. Cut off the very ends of eight of the lemons. Slice each one lengthwise into quarters, cutting to but not through the opposite end. Gently open half the lemon over a bowl, and sprinkle a scant tablespoon salt into it; then open the other half and add another tablespoon.

2. Put the lemons into a large jar—it's fine if you have to pack them in, because they will shrink. Juice the remaining lemons, and completely cover the cut ones in the jar with their juice. Slip in the bay leaves, if using. Let the lemons sit for a day, lightly covered with a towel.

3. The next day, pour a thin film of olive oil over the lemons and their juice. This will help keep them sealed while they are being preserved. Now cover the jar tightly and put it into the refrigerator, or store at room temperature, allowing the lemons to cure for 3 to 4 weeks, or until the rinds are soft. They will last for at least a year.

Since those first tastes, I have always looked for Moroccan cooks and was naturally drawn to them when I started to write a series about food in embassies for *The Washington Post Magazine*.

Through Jean-Paul, I met Ali Benjelloun, the ambassador from Morocco, and his wife, Jackie. Thanks to my fluency in French, and because of my love of Moroccan food, I invited Fatima El Maaroufy, the Benjellouns' cook, to come to my house to give a cooking class for my friend Cathy's thirty-fifth birthday in 1984. Fatima dazzled us by making b'stilla, the celebratory pie filled with nuts, chicken, spices, and egg custard.

Usually, a banquet at the residence of the Moroccan ambassador begins with a huge display of a b'stilla, which in Morocco is traditionally baked in outdoor public ovens as the sign of a wedding or a birthday. Why have just a bite of b'stilla to start? we thought. So, instead, we offered it as the main course, with a panoply of colorful salads—spinach, red pepper, carrot, and beet—as the first course.

Allan's and my relationship with Morocco was solidified a decade later, in 1994, when I was asked to be a speaker there at an Oldways conference on olive oil. Oldways was the organization that, by bringing journalists and others to Mediterranean countries, sparked the whole notion of the healthy Mediterranean diet. On this trip, sponsored by the olive oil industry, more than one hundred chefs, journalists, cookbook writers, and scientists crawled like a camel caravan throughout the country. The cast included, among many others, *Vogue*'s Jeffrey Steingarten; the still-to-become celebrity chefs Todd English, Gordon Hamersley, and Bobby Flay, as well as the cookbook writer Paula Wolfert. I'll never forget how excited Paula got when we were watching teachers at the Touarga National School for the Culinary Arts demonstrating their craft outside the Royal Palace in Rabat, making crunchy and delicious warka, a uniquely Moroccan crust for b'stilla, by deftly putting flour and water on a griddle and peeling the dough off. (Most Americans today use store-bought phyllo to make their b'stilla.)

Allan and I and a few others visited the Mellah in Casablanca. We went into a 19th century synagogue, a butcher shop where cows' feet were ready to be bought for the Sabbath, dafina and angel hair noodles were sold. About 5–6,000 Jews live in Morocco. Before 1956 there were almost 400,000. We came back to the hotel and went to the American Embassy, where Marc Ginsberg, the Ambassador, and Janet, his beauty queen wife from Arkansas, greeted us. We tasted traditional Moroccan Jewish delicacies—dafina with grains, meguina (an omelette with brains), turkey stuffed with couscous, pescado blanco (a white fish with red pepper sauce), and fijuelas for dessert. I met the head of ORT whose mother-in-law supervised the cooking.

—Journal entry from the trip

Perhaps the most delicious meal was in Meknes, where Moulay Messaoud Agouzzal, a tiny Berber man and the so-called king of olive oil (at the time he owned 80 percent of the olive groves in Morocco), invited us all for a luncheon on the lawn outside his very large house with three kitchens. Greeted by Berber dancers, we all sat at low tables on floor cushions while a whole roast lamb was ceremoniously brought to each table, all carried on huge silver platters.

I described it all in my diary: "The b'stilla was the best I ever tasted, flaky, not too sweet, perfect balance of cinnamon and sugar and chicken and nuts, then the lamb mechoui and free-range chickens with preserved lemons and olives and more. It was a fabulous meal all eaten Bedouin style with our right hand."

We also visited Fez, Morocco's culinary capital, where Allan and I spent the day with the local rabbi. "The rabbi showed us the Jewish cemetery and the local mellah and gave us a sense of what life was like for centuries until 1956," I noted at the time. "Only the depression in the doors with signs of the mezuzahs gave us a clue to times past. The communal bakery with bread, pierced with special holes marking whose it was and a tiny talmud torah gave us a sense of what was left of Jewish life and how vibrant it once was, in what was called the Jerusalem of Morocco. We visited Maimonides' home where he lived for six years and taught at the university before going to Izmir and then to Egypt." Maimonides was, among other things, an astronomer, a physician, and one of the greatest Torah scholars ever.

But Allan's and my most lasting connection with Morocco came later that year, when we met Mohamed Benaïssa, the new ambassador from Morocco to the United States, and his wife, Leila. It was at a program at Sidwell Friends, sponsored by the Moroccan government, with President Bill and Hillary Clinton, whose daughter, Chelsea, a few years older than Merissa, was also at the school. We had heard from an attaché at the French Embassy that Mohamed was a cultured, educated, charming man; and that he was. He spoke excellent English and was also slightly offbeat—perfect for Allan. The two hit it off immediately, as I did with Leila. Other than official dinners at the residence, we sometimes met for a "casual" lunch at their home, and they came to our Passover Seders and Shabbat dinners with their children. This relationship was like so many throughout our lives, intertwining food and politics.

At the time, Allan, who had left government for private practice, was working on bringing the perpetrators of the destruction of Pan Am Flight 103 to justice. Mohamed and he thought that King Hassan II might be able to urge Libya to admit their culpability and resolve the impasse. Unbeknownst to me, Allan was summoned to Rabat by the king to speak with him. Of course, while Allan was visiting with the king, I was given no idea what he was doing, for security reasons. All I knew was that he told me the food was marvelous. Now I wonder what impact their conversation may have had on Qaddafi's willingness to admit Libya's guilt.

Later that same year, we brought the children to Morocco on their spring break from school for a "study tour." Other than booking the airplane tickets, we had no idea what the plans were. The king's van met us at the airport, and after a nap at a hotel, we flew to Ouarzazate, the gateway to the Sahara, in the High Atlas Mountains. When our airplane arrived, there was the king's van again. It seemed that, wherever we had a meal, we might be served the same food as others, but rose petals and other delightful decorations were strewn on our table. Needless to say, none of us ever forgot that trip, and Morocco has been part of our life to this day.

Throughout the years, we have visited the Benaïssas in Asilah, a charming port town on the former Spanish Moroccan Atlantic coast, where Mohamed is the mayor. He holds a unique annual Cultural Moussem (Festival), bringing artists and intellectuals from around the globe to workshops and inviting scholars and politicos from around the world for discussions.

Allan participated almost every year, and I would often accompany him. Each time, we stayed at the Raissouni Palace, built in the nineteenth century by a wealthy warrior who became Asilah's governor, right in the center of the tiny seaside town that has white stucco walls.

During the day, while Allan was at political sessions, I would spend time either talking with the artists or wandering through Asilah, trying to imagine it when there was a large Jewish presence there. Once, my son, David, and I followed the aroma of couscous through the warrens of this ancient seaport. After we located the source, we knocked on the door and were invited in to taste. Lost in conversation, we forgot the time and had to rush back to the Benaïssas' home, just in time for lunch.

Another time, I spent an entire day at the public oven in the town, trying to catch the rhythm of it as the heartbeat of cooking—women coming early in the morning with kneaded dough on trays set atop their heads, giving the baker a few dirhams in advance to bake their bread, the most sacred of foods. The women left, and returned a half-hour or so later to pick up their golden rounds. This public space was where the pulse of the town once beat; the Jewish oven, now boarded up, was only a few feet away from the Muslim one. I imagined women and men, wandering back and forth from their homes to the oven and the marketplace, sharing new recipes for tagines, fish, and b'stilla, the mark of a festive life-cycle event in each family. I wrote an article about this, which appeared originally in *The New York Times,* but later also in *Le Monde* and a local Arab newspaper in Asilah; after that, Mohamed, who had seemed to tolerate my culinary questions, started taking my profession a little more seriously.

The last time I was there, a few years ago, Mohamed surprised me by having found a women's couscous cooperative in a nearby village. His secretary took me there with a driver, and we watched women, from nine years old to ninety, first searching for herbs and drying them, then sifting the semolina, putting it through wire strainers, and making the most heavenly herbed couscous I have ever tasted, all the while sitting on the floor and talking. It was a beautiful sight, a service for which these women earned so little. At one time, most women made their own couscous. But since a couscous-making machine was invented in 1963, most couscous, even in Morocco, is processed.

When you live in Washington, most relationships with foreign diplomats end with their next posting. But not ours with Mohamed, who went on to become the foreign minister of Morocco, but always the mayor of Asilah, and stayed with us whenever he came to D.C. And when Allan passed away, every single member of his family either called or wrote me a beautiful note.

Moroccan Chicken with Almonds, Chestnuts, Cinnamon, and Couscous

Serves about 8

4 pounds (1.8 kg) boneless,
   skinless chicken thighs,
   halved
Juice of 1 lemon
1 tablespoon kosher salt,
   plus more to taste
5 tablespoons olive oil
3 small onions, diced
   (about 2 cups)
Pinch of saffron threads
1 tablespoon ground ginger
1 tablespoon plus ½ teaspoon
   ground cinnamon
1 teaspoon freshly ground
   black pepper
¾ cup fresh Italian parsley
   leaves and stems, chopped
¾ cup fresh cilantro leaves
   and stems, chopped
2 cups (473 ml) chicken broth
   or water
1 cup (130 grams) roasted and
   peeled chestnuts
½ cup (71 grams) currants
1½ cups (210 grams) blanched
   whole almonds
⅓ cup (66 grams) sugar
2½ cups (488 grams)
   couscous

Of all the delicious meals we have had with the Benaïssas, there is one couscous dish that I especially relish. It's not a dish served for diplomatic functions but, rather, one eaten at home. To me it recalls some of the taste elements of the more complicated b'stilla. Mohamed told me that in Morocco they traditionally make this with small chickens, stuffing them with the couscous, nuts, sugar, and cinnamon, and surrounding them with chestnuts and currants.

---

1. Rub the chicken with the lemon juice and salt. Allow to marinate for 30 minutes at room temperature. Heat a Dutch oven over high heat, and add the oil. When the oil is hot, brown the chicken pieces in it in batches, cooking for 2 to 3 minutes per side, taking care not to crowd the pan, until the chicken is golden brown, then remove the chicken pieces to a plate. Drain all but 1 tablespoon of oil from the pan.

2. Add the onions, and sauté until they're beginning to soften. While they are cooking, add the saffron to a cup of warm water and allow it to bloom. Add the ginger, 1 tablespoon of cinnamon, black pepper, ½ cup of parsley, and ½ cup of cilantro to the onions. Cook for 1 minute; then return the chicken to the pan, and toss to coat it in the onion mixture. Add the saffron-water mixture and the chicken broth or water. Bring the liquid to a boil, reduce to a simmer, and cook, covered, for about 30 minutes, or until the chicken is cooked. Just before serving, add the chestnuts and currants, and stir to warm everything through.

3. While the chicken is cooking, toast the almonds for 5 minutes until golden brown in a 350-degree oven, watching closely and stirring to make sure they do not burn. Allow them to cool for 5 minutes, then mix them with the sugar, a tablespoon of water, and the remaining ½ teaspoon of cinnamon in a food processor. Pulse 15 times, until most of the mixture is finely ground but there are still some larger pieces of almond for crunch.

4. Cook the couscous according to package instructions, fluffing it up with a fork; when it's done, stir in the almond mixture. To serve: Spread the couscous across a large serving platter, and mound the chicken pieces on top. Garnish with the remaining parsley and cilantro.

24.

My Work Writing for
The New York Times

Like many people of my generation, I grew up with *The New York Times* delivered to my family's front door, to be read at breakfast. When I was a young woman living in Jerusalem, it was my job to get to know all the foreign correspondents, but especially those from *The New York Times*. I met so many, including James Reston, Abe Rosenthal, Richard Eder, James Feron, Charles Mohr, and Peter Grose.

When *The Jewish Holiday Kitchen* came out, in 1979, Mimi Sheraton, one of my cooking and writing heroes, contacted me to ask if the *Times* could excerpt the passage of the book on honey cake for Rosh Hashanah. I was also assigned an article on the food of the Yemenite Jews in Jerusalem. I wrote about the meal before the fast of Yom Kippur at the home of the Zadoks, a family whom I knew when I lived in Israel and who were known for their jewelry store across from the King David Hotel.

At the time, I was writing for *The Washington Post Magazine,* and my editor did not look kindly on my writing for both papers, so I stopped writing for the *Times*. When a new editor came to the *Post* in the mid-1980s and removed all food writing from the magazine, saying that the Food section had more than enough, I thought that this would be a good time to try to write for the *Times*.

In 1986, I bumped into the then managing editor, Abe Rosenthal, at the cocktail party the *Times* used to throw at the Army Navy Club before the annual Gridiron Dinner, and I thought about mentioning my wish, but didn't. So I wrote Abe anyway, telling him that I was following up on his suggestion at the Gridiron cocktail party. Nothing happened, so I wrote to the food editor, Margot Slade. She immediately called me, and said that she had been expecting my call: Abe had sent a note to her weeks before, saying that I would be contacting her and that she should try me out.

One of the first articles I pitched and wrote for the Food section was about the foodways at the Museum of the Iron Range in Hibbing, Minnesota, a mining town with a large immigrant population. The *Times* sent me to Hibbing, where I stayed overnight to watch the women cook. When the piece came out, Arthur Ochs (Punch) Sulzberger, the publisher, congratulated Margot on the story. She found it curious that he was even interested and called to let me know. I told her that one of the women that I wrote about was Mary Perpich, the mother of Punch's son-in-law, Joe. At that point, I was still learning the intrica-cies of ethics in journalism—I never even thought it might be a conflict mentioning the mother of the publisher's son-in-law, for that wasn't the point of the story.

This recipe is a tribute to Joe. Although he may have left the Iron Range, I feel that, as for so many other people from Minnesota who moved elsewhere, the place, his past, and the potica never left him.

At Mary's Cafe in Hibbing, a luncheonette with oilcloth on the tables and an old-fashioned counter, the Irish cook makes chicken soup with German dumplings, Yugoslav sarma (stuffed cabbage) and Cornish pasties. The Italian-owned Sunrise Bakery opened in 1913 to provide hard rolls for miners' lunch pails. Today, it sells ethnic breads—French, Italian, Russian, Finnish and Jewish as well as a Norwegian sweet bread called julekake, German stollen and a jellyroll-style pastry known in Yugoslavia as potica (pronounced po-TEE-tsa).

—Joan Nathan, "Sarma and Strudel," The New York Times, February 25, 1987

Potica
(Croatian Pastry Stuffed with Nuts)

For the Dough

2¼ teaspoons active dry yeast

¼ cup (50 grams) granulated
    sugar

¾ cup (178 ml) whole milk,
    lukewarm

½ teaspoon vanilla extract

Dash of salt

1 large egg

3 to 3½ cups (375 to
    438 grams) bread flour or
    unbleached all-purpose
    flour, plus more for
    stretching

¼ cup (½ stick/56 grams)
    unsalted butter, melted,
    plus butter for greasing
    the bowl

Potica is really a culinary memory of the Austro-Hungarian Empire, a rolled pastry with nuts, sugar, and honey; similar desserts are found today in Austria, Hungary, Slovenia, and Croatia. The filling is similar to that of baklava, because soft fruits would have spoiled in hot climates more readily than nuts and honey, which has been a traditional preservative. In Central Europe, fruit fillings like apples and cherries were more common. Unlike strudel, also a stretched dough, potica has a softer, cakelike crust made with yeast, making it easier to stretch. The final result is worth the fuss. Choose a good friend or family member to help stretch the dough.

---

1. Dissolve the yeast in ¼ cup (60 ml) of warm water along with 1 tablespoon of sugar in the bowl of a stand mixer. Then add the milk, vanilla, salt, egg, and the remaining sugar, and mix well. Slowly add 3 cups (375 grams) of the flour and mix; work in the butter until the mixture forms a smooth ball. Add the remaining ½ cup (63 grams) of flour if the dough seems too sticky. Scrape the dough into a greased bowl, roll to coat, then cover and let it rise for about 1½ hours, until it's doubled. Do not punch it down.

2. To make the filling Mix the walnuts, melted butter, both sugars, honey, the whole eggs, and ⅓ cup (79 ml) of the heavy cream in a bowl; add more cream gradually until the mixture is the consistency of honey.

3. Preheat the oven to 325 degrees, and line a 9-by-13-inch baking pan with parchment paper.

4. On a table or other flat surface that is at least 3 feet by 5 feet, spread a clean bedsheet so that the edges hang slightly over the sides. Sprinkle it with flour, roll out the dough to form a rectangle, and then, starting from the middle and working your way out, carefully stretch and pull the dough until it is about 2½ by 3 feet; it should be thin enough to see through, but try not to let it tear.

5. Dollop the filling on the dough and spread it as thinly as possible along the 2½-foot side and as deep as it will go (the filling will not entirely cover the dough), leaving a 1-inch border. Starting at the 2½-foot end, carefully roll up the dough. Cut it into three equal-sized rolls, press the ends together to enclose the dough, and transfer the loaves to the pan, separating them with aluminum foil.

6. Mix the egg yolk with the remaining tablespoon of heavy cream in a small bowl, and brush this over the potica. Bake the rolls for about 1 hour, or until they're golden brown.

For the Filling

1¼ pounds (567 grams) walnuts, finely ground

¼ cup (½ stick/56 grams) unsalted butter, melted

¾ cup (150 grams) granulated sugar

1 cup (213 grams) packed dark- or light-brown sugar

¼ cup (84 grams) honey

2 large eggs, plus 1 large egg yolk

⅓ to ½ cup (79 to 118 ml) plus 1 tablespoon heavy cream

Genius Latkes with Chives

In addition to not having to squeeze or mess with onions, a major benefit of this recipe is that everything but frying can be done in advance. I like to sprinkle chives or scallions into the grated potatoes, giving them color and flavoring the oil, so oniony-latke lovers will have one less complaint to make.

Makes 8 latkes

4 large Idaho or russet
  potatoes, washed and dried
1 teaspoon kosher salt
½ teaspoon freshly ground
  black pepper
½ cup snipped fresh chives
Vegetable, canola, or avocado
  oil, for frying
Crème fraîche or sour cream,
  for serving
Smoked salmon, for serving

1. Preheat the oven to 350 degrees, and put the rack in the middle of the oven. Bake the potatoes directly on the rack for 30 minutes, then flip and bake them for another 15 minutes, or until they are hot throughout but still raw in the middle. Remove them and let them cool for about 30 minutes.

2. Slice the potatoes in half widthwise, and begin grating the cut side on the large holes of a box grater. (As you grate, the potatoes should open up, leaving the skins intact; save them to prepare potato skins if you like.)

3. Sprinkle the grated potatoes with the salt and pepper, then stir in the chives. Taste, and adjust the seasoning if necessary.

4. Take about ½ cup grated potato in your hands, and gently squeeze between your palms to form a patty. Press the patty until it's about ½ inch thick, and carefully set it on a plate. Repeat with the remaining grated potatoes, to make about eight latkes. Cover, and refrigerate them for at least 2 hours, or up to 24 hours.

5. Just before serving, pour about ¼ inch of vegetable oil into a large, heavy skillet set over medium-high heat. (When it is hot enough, a shred of potato dropped into the oil should sizzle immediately.) Working in two batches, gently fry four latkes until they're crisp and deep golden on both sides, 3 to 4 minutes per side. Transfer them to paper towels or a wire rack to drain. Repeat with the remaining latkes.

6. Serve them hot, topped with crème fraîche or sour cream and smoked salmon.

I n 1988, I wrote about one of my favorite people ever: Mattie Ball Fletcher. The chef Patrick
O'Connell had introduced us in the early 1980s,
when I was doing a story for *The Washington
Post* about his Inn at Little Washington. Mattie
Ball, who died at 107 in 1996, was the oldest living descendant of Martha Washington. She was
quite a character, quite a cook, and quite a gar-
dener. She lived her whole life in Rappahannock
County and remembered a time when oysters
came up the river on blocks of ice: "When the
oysters arrived, the postman would deliver them
to us, all for a dollar a gallon. Then we would cut

Mattie Ball Fletcher at a hundred, in Little Washington,
Virginia

up a block of ice from the river and put them in
the icehouse."

The article I wrote was on her one hundred
Thanksgivings. "I used to raise turkeys, and
I thought I was right rich when one fetched
seventy-five cents a pound," she told me at the
time. She kept the feathers to make pillows and
feather dusters. Mattie Ball was also concerned
about how I would portray her. "Don't make me
too domestic," she warned. "I know a lot, I read a
lot, I garden a lot."

For another *Times* article, in March 1996, I covered a feast for the three thousandth anniversary
of the city of Jerusalem. Seven three-star Michelin
chefs, from France, Belgium, and Italy, came to
cook a kosher dinner for six hundred people.
Two American chefs, Paul Prudhomme and Jean-
Louis Palladin, were also invited. Jean-Louis—
whom I had written about for *The New York Times
Magazine* in 1987 and whom I had known for years
before that—was to cook the foie gras course, for
which he had earned a worldwide reputation.
His plan was to stuff foie gras into quails, one of
the birds eaten in the desert during the Exodus.
(This was before Israeli foie gras was prohibited,
as a result of a campaign against the cruelty of
force-feeding animals.)

Jean-Louis thought he figured out a way to use
the laws of kashrut that dictate that first salting,
then washing, then broiling foie gras just a bit
releases the blood and still makes good foie gras.
In fact, there is so much blood in the liver that
people in the ancient world thought that the liver
was the soul of a man. But Jean-Louis decided
to broil the outside ever so slightly, cut off the
outer layer, then use the inside. He did so, but the
shomer, the rabbi who "watches" over the cooking process, pronounced the foie gras not kosher

and dumped forty pounds of it into the garbage. When Jean-Louis saw what had happened, he almost cried. The rabbi said that these laws had been around for three thousand years. Jean-Louis asked him politely and respectfully if it was not time to change the laws just a bit.

He started over. Since broiled goose liver becomes rubbery, he roasted the liver in a 400-degree oven for 12 minutes to get rid of the blood, while Rabbi Moshe Pashkoss, one of the event's three *mashgiach*s (ritual supervisors), watched closely.

"I don't think that King David would have eaten such a rich dish," mused the rabbi, referring to the king who founded Jerusalem. "He was a shepherd who came from the people. But at least I am glad that they are having a feast that tastes good and is kosher."

That trip was extraordinary for me: sitting in a bus driving up to the Galilee, with the pastry chef of Taillevent seated next to me, and the rest of the Michelin chefs chattering all around, relaxing as chefs do on these jaunts abroad. In a way, I felt that this trip and this dinner were the pinnacle of my career, in a country I love, with French chefs with whom I could speak in their language, and given the honor of writing about it all for *The New York Times*.

Then, to my shock, someone else from the *Times* got hold of the story and covered the event first—not for the Food section, but another section. When I called Trish Hall, my editor, just after my plane landed in New York, she was furious. "Write your article," she said. "And make it the best piece you have ever done." I went to my hotel room and wrote, and my story made it into the paper.

It is strange. Even after all these years, I still get that rush when an article comes out. And you never know when an article will spark attention.

In 2001, just after 9/11, the *Times* food editor forgot to assign an article for Rosh Hashanah. On the Monday before the holiday—which would start on that Tuesday night—I received a call, frantically asking if I would write one. My daughters were coming home for the holiday and didn't want me to be writing instead of concentrating on them, but a gorgeous challah had just come out of my oven, and I told the overwrought editor I could write something on how making bread is comforting during times of crisis (a lesson we collectively relearned during COVID). I also told them that, after a certain time, they would not be able to reach me because of the holiday.

The creative tension of being under deadline pressure helped me write very quickly. I called the article in to the New York bureau (which is how you turned in copy in 2001 if you weren't in the newsroom). The next day, my article came out, with a gorgeous picture of my lusty challahs appearing on the front page of the Food section. But my glee was short-lived. When the phone rang and the *New York Times* 111-111-1111 number popped up on my telephone, I knew there must be some sort of error in the article. In those days, it was the job of the standards editor, a man named Al Siegel, to ferret out inaccuracies that appeared in the paper.

My heart sank. It appeared that someone had transcribed the article incorrectly, writing that the amount of oil, instead of water, was 1½ cups, making the resulting dough like "a Valdez oil spill," as one reader wrote. (In the *New York Times* style sheet, water never appears in the ingredient list.) Thank goodness, it was not my mistake. However, the *Times* repeated the entire corrected recipe—and the photographs—in the Food section the following week, because it seemed everyone was making bread.

Now you tell me ½ cup! I had wondered when I saw that 1¾ cups of oil if
you had mixed up the bread recipe with the one for deep-fried turkey. . . .
I was hoping that making my own challah this year would be a soothing
experience, and that the scent of baking bread would help us forget the
smell of fire and soot. I had not counted on giving my family a good laugh,
something we all needed even more than a perfect, round challah. Thanks!

—Note from a reader, September 27, 2001

Dear Joan: Thank you for your concern. Your advice was too late as I had
made the challah over the weekend so could not add more flour. After baking
on Wednesday, found it was heavy and had an undeniable greasy taste but
edible nonetheless. You're right—I should have more compassion for the
people at the paper and will try the recipe again.

—Note from a reader, September 28, 2001

I have now been writing for the *Times*, mostly about Jewish holidays, for about thirty years. Editors like Trish Hall, Sam Sifton, and now Emily Weinstein and Pete Wells have been respectful and have taken chances with me, accepting articles about Jewish food from such faraway places as India, Yemen, and Nova Scotia, following me on my travels around the world. And for one Passover article I wrote a checklist that people seem to have clipped to pull out each year.

During COVID, I wrote an article about what the *Times* titled "genius latkes" that went viral, as it could only do in the Internet age.

It is a given that most people love potatoes, and particularly preparations in the potato-pancake family, like rösti, crique, hash browns, and latkes. I had learned a way to bake the potatoes, cool them, grate them, squeeze them into patties, and refrigerate them before frying. This method keeps the potatoes from turning gray, and makes grating easy; plus, you don't have to squeeze out the water released from the potato or collect the potato starch. Fans of this recipe tell me the house does not smell of oil frying, nor their hands of onions.

I could not believe the frenzy of slightly more negative comments. "What, potato latkes with no onions!"; "I have been making potato pancakes for 50 years and they are never any trouble"; "How could I tamper with latkes . . . no onions, no egg, no filler?" The comments were vehement. All about latkes!

But most of the readers who made them—and there might have been millions, since there were 770,000 hits for the article around the world—said they would never again make anything else.

25.

A Trip to the Soviet Union

In 1987, I participated in the first ever culinary trip for food writers to the Soviet Union.

It was quite an ambitious trip. There were eighteen of us, including Bill Rice (my former editor at *The Washington Post*), Paula Wolfert, Arthur Schwartz, Susan Friedland (an editor at HarperCollins), and Alice Waters. I bonded with Alice at the Rostov-on-Don Airport, a stopover in southern Russia between Riga and Tbilisi, as we looked over the rabbit coats and hats on display for her daughter, Fanny, and my daughter Merissa.

The trip took place in October, two years after Mikhail Gorbachev became the de facto Soviet leader as the head of the Communist Party. He became president in 1990 after encouraging perestroika, economic, political, and social reform within the Communist Party as well as glasnost, a new openness in policy reform. He became the unintended catalyst for dismantling what had taken nearly three-quarters of a century to erect: the Marxist-Leninist-Stalinist totalitarian state. When we arrived, the old regime was still in power, but within just a few years, by 1991, the fifteen member republics of the Union of Soviet Socialist Republics would go their own ways; and we had visited five of them, watching the process. In the course of twelve days, we visited Moscow, Vilnius, Kaunus, Riga, Tallinn, Tbilisi, and Leningrad. When we reached Tbilisi, Alice, the queen of fresh food, could finally smile because the vegetables and fruits were plentiful and the markets beautiful.

Our leader, Algis Grigas, was a Lithuanian tour manager living in Chicago, an operatic baritone who wanted his country to secede from the Soviet Union. He was thrilled with what was happening and did everything he could to make us fear the old regime.

When we flew into Sheremetyevo Airport in Moscow, the customs officers immediately took away from me the VHS tapes of the movie *Exodus* that I had brought for Jewish refuseniks, as well as baby formula to be sent to people in Pripyat, Ukraine, who were affected by the Chernobyl nuclear power plant explosion the year before.

Then, later, the *dejournaya*s (officers of the day), the older, babushka-like women stationed at desks on each floor, took our keys when we left our rooms, probably to check through them when we were gone; they watched our every move at the huge Cosmos Hotel.

Life, like the food we were eating and seeing, was dismal almost everywhere. Without the choices we had in the States, the food was merely at the subsistence level. In Moscow, there were bread lines at bakeries that offered hardly any bread inside. Butchers had very little meat, and what they had was very expensive. Chickens looked rancid. Where were the eggs? We didn't see any. It also looked as if all fish was canned. Gorbachev wanted to encourage competition to create more choice, but it was still just beginning. I did notice at local markets that enterprising people from Azerbaijan were hawking grapefruits and oranges they had stuffed in suitcases and flown to Moscow on dirt-cheap Aeroflot flights.

Each of us writers on the trip had a separate agenda besides food. Mine was to visit refuseniks, dissidents whose names I had been given; I wanted to hear their stories and resurrect the Jewish food traditions in this country that disavowed religion. The first night, I left dinner at 10:00 p.m. with my roommate, Iris Bailin, who worked for *The Plain Dealer* in Cleveland. We descended into the bowels of the Moscow subway system and arrived eventually at the home of Igor and Inna Uspensky, who had been refused exit visas to Israel for fifteen years, and who, despite their doctorates, could work only in menial jobs. They served us a second dinner of a gruel of pumpkin and hot millet, and we talked until 1:00 a.m. about the difficulty of living in Moscow and the Uspenskys' dream of going to Israel.

The next day, I took off from the group to find Café Yosef, which someone in D.C. had told me

was the only "kosher" cooperative in the Soviet Union at that time. Finding the restaurant was practically impossible. Taxi drivers had never heard of it. I had the street number, but when I finally located the restaurant there was no sign outside. Inside, it was very simple, with oilcloth-covered tables, homemade curtains over the windows, and piped-in Israeli and Yiddish music.

The food was certainly not kosher, but the closest thing to public Jewish and Israeli food at the time. Anyway, what was Jewish food in the Soviet Union and what was Russian food? Chopped herring, p'tcha (calves' foot jelly), classic Russian cabbage soup, matzo-ball soup, and carp floating in a pool in the back kitchen of the restaurant, waiting to be made into gefilte fish, were all there. When I asked Yosef how, at a so-called kosher

Alice Waters in front of a vegetable-and-fruit store in the Soviet Union, 1987

restaurant, they served carp in cream sauce with meat on the same menu, he replied, "We have gefilte fish and matzo-ball soup, don't we?" To a Jew who grew up in the Soviet Union under the communists, I presumed, that was as kosher as they could get.

Our next stop was Vilnius, the capital of Lithuania, where Algis pointed out the Lithuanian flag flying at the city's ancient fortress. Had we been there only two weeks earlier, he also pointed out, flying the Lithuanian flag would have been considered anti-Soviet treason.

At a luncheon at Bociu, the state-sponsored cooking school and now a restaurant in Vilnius, a whole stuffed carp, called gefilte fish, was one of the many dishes prepared for our group on a twenty-foot table laden with carefully crafted dishes. Gefilte fish was considered a delicacy—chopped, then stuffed back into the skin "the way the Jews used to teach us to do it," Irena Cereskiene, a cookbook writer, told us.

Like their Christian counterparts, the Jews of Lithuania discovered ingenious ways of creating special dishes from meager ingredients, like transforming potatoes into puddings, breads, and pancakes. And although the Jewish presence has faded today, Jewish dishes have not. In an article in *Vakarinės naujienos,* an evening newspaper, a journalist bemoaned the taste of bread in the 1980s. "Whatever happened to challah?" the reporter asked. "It is a pity. It was such a good kind of bread."

Kichel and Herring

At the end of the nineteenth century, a huge mass of Jews from Lithuania immigrated to South Africa. I looked eagerly for a South African Jew to tell me about dishes like kichel and herring. I have found that when a mass of people immigrate to a new place, their native foods comfort that first generation, but the next generations often abandon them. For a while, I had thought of going to South Africa again to find a great kichel maker, until I gave a speech in West Hartford, Connecticut, a few years ago. An elderly woman named Marcie Wolman shyly came up to me to say that she enjoyed making kichel. I later learned that Marcie, now in her nineties, was born in Durban, grew up in Johannesburg, went to Israel in 1948, lived on a kibbutz, and then returned to South Africa, where she married a dairy farmer. She and her husband later turned the farm into a caravan resort called The Rocks. And, according to her daughter Sheila Mann, Marcie made the thinnest kichel imaginable.

Kichels, meaning "cookies" or "crackers" in Yiddish and German, come in all shapes and sizes: airy bowtie cookies (see *Joan Nathan's Jewish Holiday Cookbook*) and kichel crackers cut into various shapes depending on the cook and the place she lives. Kichels can be shaped like biscuits, probably cut with a Yahrzeit candleholder in Lithuania, or like Florentine crackers. They can be sprinkled with anise, toasted fennel and orange, rosemary, poppy seeds and onion, or, as was done in South Africa, sprinkled with a tad of sugar and served as a sweet and salty snack with a herring paste, or just a piece of herring on top.

⌐⊶

Makes about 160, depending on how you cut your kichel!

⌐⊶

3 large eggs

3 to 4 tablespoons vegetable oil, plus more for brushing

2 cups (250 grams) unbleached all-purpose flour, plus more for rolling

1 teaspoon kosher salt, plus more for sprinkling

1½ teaspoons baking powder

1 tablespoon sugar (optional)

---

1. Using a food processor equipped with a steel blade, or a stand mixer fitted with the whisk attachment, whip the eggs with 3 tablespoons of the oil to get plenty of air into them. In a small bowl, mix the flour with the salt and baking powder, then add to the eggs and the oil and process until a dough forms. If the resulting dough is a little too dry, add a bit more oil; if it's too sticky, add more flour. Let it rest in the refrigerator for about 30 minutes or overnight.

2. Preheat the oven to 425 degrees, and line two baking sheets with parchment paper. Then cover with a rack brushed with oil.

3. Cut the dough in half, and mold each piece into a sausage shape; roll the dough out on a lightly floured surface as thinly as you can, to →

⅛ inch or thinner. You can also use a pasta machine for this, using the #3 setting first, then #6. Prick the dough with a fork all over to let air in.

4. Now the shape. You can use 2-inch biscuit cutters, you can roll the dough into a thin pizza shape, or you can use a pie crimper or sharp knife, as I do, and then cut the pieces into rough 2-inch diamond shapes, as they must have done in Lithuania. Put your kichlach on the oiled racks.

5. Brush the tops very lightly with oil, and sprinkle with a little sugar and salt, if you want.

6. Bake them on the top rack for about 5 minutes, watching carefully so that they don't burn. When you smell the aroma of the cooked dough, they are nearing readiness. If you lift the pan and drop it and they are loose, then you know they are done.

Herring Salad with Apples

Makes about 2 cups

One 12-ounce (340-gram) jar
  herring tidbits with onions
  in wine sauce
1 firm, sweet-tart apple, like
  Gala or Fuji, peeled and
  cored
1 or 2 hard-boiled eggs, whites
  and yolks separated
2 tablespoons chopped fresh
  Italian parsley
Sliced pickles and cherry
  tomatoes, for garnish

Drain the herring and onions, and pulse them with the apple into bite-sized pieces in a food processor fitted with a steel blade. Scrape the mixture into a serving bowl. Grate the egg white and the yolk, and sprinkle both on top of the herring. Top with the parsley, and garnish with pickles and cherry tomatoes. Serve on kichel.

Jews have lived in Vilnius since the fifteenth century and, as such, considered the city their spiritual and intellectual center—the Jerusalem of Eastern Europe. Eighty years ago, the city had some hundred thousand Jewish residents, who made up about 45 percent of the population; only five thousand survived World War II. In 1988, the Jewish population was about eight thousand people, most raised with little understanding of Judaism.

Here I could not escape the past. At the Kooperatyvas Stikliai, a restaurant in the Arts District, we had a relatively good meal. When I asked, I learned this area was once the Jewish ghetto, and that 80 percent of its population were sent in trains to Auschwitz.

On a short visit to the most depressing farmers' market any of us had ever seen, we found some wonderful dried mushrooms to take home for soups. But aside from that, for us food writers, the lack of food at the almost empty October market, where the oversized root vegetables like leeks, potatoes, beets, carrots, and onions were the only things still growing, was heartbreaking. When Iris wanted to take a picture of the almost empty market, she was detained by men in brown shirts. Later, her camera was taken from her room. And when Alice saw the drab produce, she fled the market, almost sobbing: "I can't stand this."

That night, we had a wonderful treat, courtesy of our tour guide, who loved opera—front-row seats in the state opera house to hear *Norma* by Bellini. During the intermission, we followed the lovely Lithuanian tradition of marching around in a large circle sipping the thickest hot chocolate I have ever tasted, almost puddinglike.

On the bus from Vilnius, with quick stops in Kaunas, Riga, and Tallinn, our Lithuanian tour guides fed us on propaganda, telling us that the KGB was after one of us, to arouse fear in the members of the group, a common method used in the Soviet Union at the time to build distrust.

Our next stop was Tbilisi, Georgia, to which we flew on Aeroflot. The seatbelts didn't work, and the backs of the seats were not stable, which you felt when the flight was bumpy. The only thing served on these internal flights was water, from a few shared collapsible tin cups; the stewardesses brought them around for all passengers, wiping them after each person sipped from them.

Georgia was the fiercely independent home of Stalin and one of the first states to break away from the Soviet Union and achieve independence in 1991. It was also the only place we visited where there was any fresh food, in part because of its climate and proximity to Turkey, Iran, Armenia, and Azerbaijan. In the two-storied open marketplace, we found wonderful nuts, chickens, Georgian flatbreads, whatever we wanted.

Arthur Schwartz and I went to a synagogue there, in a building where there were two congregations: an Ashkenazic and a Sephardic, both including only men on Friday nights because the women were all at home cooking. Afterward, I went to the home of the cantor of the synagogue. In the kitchen, as in many homes I have seen since, beds were our seats, used for sitting at the table during the day. I ate an eggplant dish that taught me how food and recipes have traveled throughout history. This exact recipe, tiny squares of thinly sliced eggplant still with its skin, flash-fried, and then seasoned with salt, pepper, and local spices—a distinctly Jewish dish—has appeared in many guises throughout my career, from Georgia to Italy, where it is called melanzane alla giudia; it followed the paths of the merchants of the Silk Road. In a sense, the recipe mirrors the journey of the eggplant itself. (See my *Flavor of Jerusalem, Jewish Cooking in America,* and *King Solomon's Table* for various recipes.)

Before I left Washington, Esther Coopersmith, a well-known hostess who learned that I was going to Tbilisi, told me to visit Zurab Konstantinovich Tsereteli, a famous painter, architect, and sculptor of large-scale monuments. I didn't want to go alone, so I asked my roommate, Iris, to accompany me. When we arrived at the artist's sprawling home, a man greeted us and mysteriously gave each of us a pile of two hundred rubles (about three hundred dollars at that time). We didn't know what to do with it.

When we entered the dining room, we found a long wooden table groaning with zakuski (appetizers)—smoked salmon, caviar with buckwheat blini, eggplant caviar, radishes in sour cream, marinated mushrooms, and the ubiquitous salat Olivier (made with carrots, peas, potatoes, and hard-boiled eggs, bound with mayonnaise and named after a Belgian chef living in Moscow in the 1860s).

We noticed that the artist, our host, was in his pajamas, as was his wife, a Georgian princess, who sexily sauntered off to bed. After a few toasts with vodka, Iris and I, suspecting what was coming next, were afraid we were the women of the evening. Why else would the artist's sergeant-of-arms give us money? We sat down at the table and tried to eat, but politely left as soon as we could.

At the end of our trip, in Leningrad, I met another refusenik couple, Vladimir Raiz, a mathematician who worked in biology, and his wife, Karmela, a concert violinist, who had also been trying to leave the Soviet Union for fifteen years. We walked outside, for fear that our conversation indoors was being tapped. He told me about how Jewish foodways, abandoned a generation ago, were slowly coming back from the underground, in memories of baranki, or bagels; kugelis, potato kugel; koldunai, potato dumplings; latkes; challah; and mandeburczinik, potato bread. Vladimir, who had the distinction of being the longest-waiting refusenik in the Soviet Union, was given permission to emigrate with his wife to Israel in 1990.

By the time we reached Leningrad, the last city on our journey, Iris and I were sure we were the ones that the KGB was tracking, in part because of the rubles we had received at Tsereteli's house. My guess is that everyone else thought it was them, for whatever reason.

Despite my apprehensions, this trip was amazing for so many reasons: I got to meet some extraordinary people, I learned so much about the plight of the Soviet people, I saw the paucity of food. We witnessed a civilization shutting down right in front of our eyes. And as I write this today, after Putin's invasion of Ukraine, we see echoes of this past come to life again.

But most of all, I realized how lucky we all felt in 1987—and today—to be Americans, even with all the weaknesses in our system.

Mandeburczinik/Potatonik (Crispy Potato Onion Bread)

Many years ago, a moving story came to me from the *Haaretz* food columnist Nira Rousso. She had received a letter from an elderly man asking for a recipe for mandeburczinik, which meant "potato bread" in Ukrainian. Slightly heavier than a kugel and thicker than a latke, it was also called "potatonik" and "bulbovnik," and it was the symbol of Galicianer food, from the southeastern corner of Poland and western Ukraine, which was part of the Austro-Hungarian Empire cuisine before World War II. According to Nira, this man wrote that he "wanted to re-create the flavor of his childhood kitchen, which was wiped out in one day by the Nazis." She published his request because the letter was charming and she was touched by it. To her surprise, accounts of pre-Holocaust memories piled into her office. One man poignantly wrote that mandeburczinik was baking in the oven when the Gestapo invaded his house and took his mother away to a concentration camp.

For most of us today, fortunately, food does not carry such sad stories. When someone gave me a recipe for mandeburczinik, I eagerly tried it. Since it was summertime and I had rosemary in the garden, I added that—and, wow, did it bring out the potato flavor. You can also add other vegetables to the batter, like corn or chopped broccoli.

I first baked this bread in muffin tins, with onions on the bottom, but as I tested it I realized I liked the ease of a baking dish, resulting in a focaccia-like bread. The woman who gave me the recipe said that her husband remembers 5-by-2½-by-1-inch pans in Poland. However you bake it, the bread is a real winner.

Serves 8 to 10

- 1½ scant tablespoons active dry yeast
- 1½ teaspoons sugar
- 2¾ cups (343 grams) unbleached all-purpose flour
- 1¼ pounds/566 grams (about 1½ large) russet potatoes
- 1 small onion
- 1 large egg
- ¼ cup (60 ml) plus 1 tablespoon vegetable oil
- 1½ tablespoons kosher salt
- 1 teaspoon freshly ground black pepper
- 2 tablespoons chopped fresh rosemary (optional)
- 1 cup chopped chard or baby kale (optional)
- 2 medium onions, sliced into thin half-moons

1. In the bowl of a stand mixer fitted with the paddle attachment, mix the yeast, sugar, and ¼ cup of the flour with ½ cup lukewarm water at low speed. Let the dough rise while you prepare the potatoes.

2. Peel the potatoes, and shred them using the large holes of a box grater (or the shredding disc on a food processor). Shred the small onion, too. Put the potatoes and onion into a clean kitchen towel or cheesecloth, hold this over a small bowl, and squeeze out as much liquid as you can into the bowl. Put the squeezed mass into the stand mixer bowl. Pour →

Mandeburczinik/Potatonik (Crispy Potato Onion Bread) *(continued)*

off and discard the liquid from the bowl, reserving the layer of starch that settles at the bottom; then scrape that starch into the mixer bowl.

3. Add 2 cups (250 grams) of the flour, the egg, the ¼ cup (60 ml) of vegetable oil, the salt and pepper, and the rosemary and chopped greens, if using. Mix at low speed just until the flour is incorporated. The batter should be sticky. Slowly beat in the remaining ½ cup (63 grams) of flour, just until incorporated. Cover, and let the dough rise in a warm place for 1½ to 2 hours, until it's about doubled in size.

4. Meanwhile, warm the remaining tablespoon of oil in a large skillet set over medium heat. Add the sliced onions, and cook, stirring more frequently toward the end, until they're soft and translucent, 15 to 20 minutes.

5. Preheat the oven to 400 degrees, and grease a 9-by-13-inch baking pan. Scrape the dough into the pan, and press it gently with your fingers so it spreads over the entire surface. Scatter the cooked onions over the top, and bake for 30 to 35 minutes, until it's browned. Let it cool for a few minutes, then cut it into squares and serve with smoked salmon. If you're making this ahead, reheat in a 350-degree oven for 10 minutes, until warm, when you're ready to serve.

26.

A Legendary Editor

As Leo Lerman had predicted in 1985, a Lescher, not Bob but Susan, did become my agent. One day in the late eighties, she called to say that Judith Jones wanted to get together about an idea that she thought might interest me. For Judith, who always liked to cook, Julia Child's manuscript had been "an answer to a prayer," she told me. "I had been looking for something like this for years. I had not edited a cookbook, not that anybody edited cookbooks in those days." Julia Child was one of my heroines. And now Judith Jones, her editor, whom I had talked to around six years before, wanted to see me again.

I took the subway to the Knopf offices at Fiftieth Street and Third Avenue, not knowing what to expect from this conversation. Judith, a slight, very attractive, and spunky woman, met me wearing a bright-yellow St. John suit that went well with her shoulder-length gray hair streaked with blond. I later learned the suit, which she wore so often, came from Saks Fifth Avenue, one of the few that she didn't get from a tiny consignment shop called Tatiana's near Bloomingdale's—a woman after my own heart.

Like Jeane Kirkpatrick and my mother, two rather formidable women in my life, Judith didn't beat about the bush. She told me she was launching a series entitled "Knopf Cooks American" and asked if I would be interested in writing a book on how Jews influenced food in the United States and how living in America affected Jewish food. I loved the idea. I would have my work cut out for me: I had written a book on Jewish holiday cooking, but not about American Jewish cooking and the story about how restaurants, cookbooks, food businesses, and trends began intrigued me: I immediately said yes. Even before we signed a contract, I started thinking about how I could learn what I needed to know to write this book.

In this time before the Internet, the first thing I did was apply for a scholarship to the American Jewish Archives in Cincinnati, where I met the nonagenarian Jacob Rader Marcus, seated in his home office with a Chicago White Sox baseball cap atop his head. This human encyclopedia of American Jewish history met with me several times each week to answer any questions and to send me off to study books that he knew intimately—sometimes even the page number of a particular topic by heart—to show me the progression of Jewish food in America. I spent whole days in the vast archives, which Jacob Rader Marcus had spent his entire adult life assembling.

He taught me about Jewish peddlers, called "egg eaters" by Gentiles, who crossed the country afoot armed with hard-boiled eggs and cured herring wrapped in newspaper, proteins these kashrut-observing immigrants could eat. He also told me about how Jewish communities sprouted up around the country in towns like Poultney, Vermont, and Wheeling, West Virginia, where peddlers first from Germanic lands and later Eastern Europe would fan out around the countryside during the week to sell their wares. These peddlers then came back to a central place, even-

tually assembled ten members to form a prayer minyan, and settled there with their families.

I also learned about the importance of Jewish communities in river towns like Little Rock, Arkansas. Peddlers, picking things up from the boats, would put their wares on their backs to sell around the country. "Mercantiles," as Jewish merchants were called in the nineteenth-century South, would sell the goods in their grocery or general stores. Jewish communities, spread throughout history and the Diaspora, followed this template.

In addition, I wrote *Hadassah Magazine* and the local Jewish press around the country, letting them know that I was looking for recipes, stories, and ephemera about immigrants and food. To my pleasant surprise, letters flooded in from everywhere, and I was off to the races.

In addition, I was in touch first with Myron Weinstein and later his successor Peggy Perlstein, someone whom I called my "secret weapon," the head of the Hebraic Section at the magnificent

Judith Jones and me

Library of Congress. Through the years, they and others have been essential for checking facts for Jewish holiday stories.

For *Jewish Cooking in America*, Peggy suggested that I look at the early Yiddish ads from the *Forward*. A visit to the library gave me the idea of using the photos of these advertisements as endpapers, which were unfortunately eliminated for cost reasons by Knopf in the sixth edition of the book. Peggy also suggested that, since ordering the prints from the Library of Congress would be very expensive, I go to the National Yiddish Book Center in Amherst, Massachusetts, to gather the material myself and have the ads photographed locally. Since we spent a month in the summer on Martha's Vineyard in those days, I packed David (age six), Merissa (nine), and Daniela (thirteen) into our white Volvo station wagon, and took them on a photo-foraging foray to find food images.

After driving about six hours from Washington, we trudged up the four flights of stairs in the warehouse, which was packed with Yiddish books gathered from all over the world. We pulled out tomes of bound copies of the *Forward* and, as I remember, sat on the floor, rummaging for Yiddish images for Jell-O, chicken fried in Spry, Maxwell House coffee, Borden's milk, Quaker Oats, Royal baking powder, and Baby Ruth candy bars, to name just a few.

For the most part, these products reached the Jewish press through an advertising genius named Joseph Jacobs, who encouraged companies to target their marketing to reach the new immigrant Jewish public who did not speak English. Some of his work had high-reaching results. When he approached Maxwell House, he had a brilliant idea. Because immigrants from Eastern Europe assumed that no beans, including coffee beans (which are technically berries), were kosher for Passover, he suggested Maxwell House sponsor a Maxwell House Haggadah. By juxtaposing this text read at every single Passover Seder right next to cans of Maxwell House coffee, he not only erased the superstition against using coffee beans at Passover but created a whole generation of Americans who associated the holiday with their well-smudged Maxwell House Haggadah.

Jacobs was not the only one to see the potential in buyers. When Procter & Gamble produced Crisco, they advertised that Jewish women had been waiting four thousand years for this white vegetable shortening that looked like lard to make American pie crusts and Southern fried chicken.

Since I envisaged the book as a history of American Jewish food, I divided it historically. Still intimidated by Judith, I had only vaguely discussed the organization of the book with her. In any event, I sent in what I thought to be the finished manuscript in the fall of 1992. With no email in those days, Judith called me immediately with some urgency in her voice. I remember precisely where I was at the time: in my study, the Monday after Thanksgiving. Judith's voice was icy and crisp. I could just imagine her tossing her head. "I don't understand what you are trying to do," she said. "You'd better come to New York."

The minute I hung up the phone, I understood what I had done wrong. This was a cookbook, not a history book. Readers may like the history, but they want recipes. The book had to be divided, like a proper cookbook, into breakfasts, appetizers, and so on. I was so grateful for the word processor, because I could cut and paste, which I did, putting the bulk of the history in the introduction, following that with the chapters of recipes, including quotes and sidebars throughout the book. Judith agreed with my plan; we only had to delay the publishing process by six months, so the book came out just before Passover of 1994.

Dear Joan,

Here are the Poultry and Meat Chapters. I haven't been keeping copies of the edited chapters I've sent back to you, partly because my green pencil is hard to read when xeroxed. But it occurs to me that it might be helpful for you to return the pages that are heavily edited when you send back your revised version. That way I can check easily to see how you have taken care of various queries and suggestions. Otherwise, with the pristine new pages that the word processor turns out, I will have to read from scratch all over again.

Please don't get discouraged. This is a difficult book because you are working with so many different people's recipes and different styles of cooking. For the most part you've seen them make some of these tricky things but it's harder for the reader who hasn't. In some instances when I can't visualize the process I am simply asking for a more explicit translation.

And then there are my quirky edits. As you know, I am trying to get away from the formula recipe writing that everyone has subscribed to and to make food writing more direct and more literate. I don't like starting sentences with "In a bowl, place . . ." No one talks that way. You put something in a bowl. And the overuse of "mixture" drives me crazy. Why not refer to it as the batter or the filling of the dough, giving it a name? Mixture upon mixture gets confusing and sounds so unappetizing. So I hope you will bear with me on these refinements. . . .

As you well know, this last phase of editing and fine-tuning the manuscript are essential to a good cookbook. I have done my part turning the chapters around as quickly as possible but there is always further work to be done by any author in response to the editing. I know some houses don't bother today with this kind of editing and just turn everything over to the copy-editor. But I don't think you get a reliable, well-written cookbook that way.

I want to talk to you more about photographs when we have the completed ms. in hand, know how long it is, and can do new estimates. Our marketing people tend to think, as I do too, that cookbook buyers want to see finished dishes that are appealing and that tell them how a particular recipe will look.

Love,
Judith

I wrote three more books with Judith.

A few years later, in March 1999, we flew to Israel together with Judith's stepdaughter Bronwyn Dunne to shoot photographs for my next book, *The Foods of Israel Today*. I had decided to write it the night when Prime Minister Yitzhak Rabin was assassinated. I was on a book tour, leading customers through a grocery store in Highland Park, Illinois, to teach them how to decipher which foods were kosher. When the news came on, I realized that I desperately wanted to do a book showing the positive, human side of most people—and their food—in Israel.

Judith and I really got along, which was surprising to many in the food world because of our age and life differences but I think that we were alike in very real ways. We were both Francophiles and spoke fluent French; we were hard workers and risk takers; and we liked to have fun. I remember fondly taking her to a cheese farm in the Judean Hills where she gulped down a bottle of fresh goat milk. Another time, we visited a man who baked his bread on shiny black stones retrieved from the bottom of the Sea of Galilee. She insisted that we bring those stones home, as well as a wooden paddle from his oven, for her to make pita in Vermont and me bread on Martha's Vineyard. Despite Bronwyn's admonition and the annoyed looks from flight attendants who thought we were really nuts, we did it, and my paddle, a great memento, is nailed on the wall in my study.

I also liked that Judith was a person without prejudice, taking everybody for who they were. This was evidenced at the beginning of her career at Doubleday, when she found a copy of Anne Frank's diary tossed into a pile on an editor's desk in Paris. Her recommendation was that the New York office see it, because, as she said, "American people need to read this book." Her charm won over the editor's reluctance to publish the book by, as Judith told me he said, "that girl."

Later, when I was in France working on *Quiches, Kugels, and Couscous*, Judith invited me to dinner. She told me that Knopf had given her a first-class ticket to France and dinner for two at the three-star restaurant of her choice to celebrate her fifty years at the company. Judith selected the Auberge de l'Ill, in Illhaeusern, Alsace. We met in Strasbourg and drove for about forty-five minutes, to stay overnight. When we got to the restaurant, Judith was very careful that we eat the *plat du jour* so that the meal wouldn't be too costly for Knopf.

Despite her toughness and idiosyncrasies, the editing process was the real treat when writing for Judith. For every book, I would spend several days at Bryn Teg, her home in Stannard, in the Northeast Kingdom of Vermont, to edit and cook recipes from the forthcoming book, or to cook whatever was seasonal from her garden.

Our day would begin with an 8:00 a.m. icy dip in the swimming pond that Judith's late husband, Evan, had dug for her a short walk down the hill. It was nestled beneath the house, designed and built by a young Carlos Montoya, who became a friend of mine on the Vineyard. Judith's post-and-beam framed house featured a large kitchen and extraordinary views over the Green Mountains. In the kitchen, which doubled as a dining room, Judith and I would sit under the chandelier over the table and have breakfast together, a civilized, sit-down affair, and plan our meals for the day, as was her ritual, before we began the editing process.

Judith always used her green pencil, evoking such a grin for her writers on the rare occasion when she wrote the four letters that formed the word "nice." She made me more critical and a better writer. We'd sit for three hours going over the manuscript, then make lunch that might be leftovers from her fridge—she was notorious for keeping every bit of leftovers, a trait she shared with my mother, and, I admit, me. At the same time, she always loved walking down into her garden and plucking salad greens or rhubarb and other home-grown vegetables, to ensure that everything was as fresh as possible.

Afternoons would include visiting a cheese farm like Jasper Hill, or mushroom hunting with Nova Kim—known as the wild-mushroom lady of northern Vermont—and her partner Leslie Hook, who helped Judith find some chanterelles on her property. The two not only dressed exactly alike but had his and her outhouses, right next to each other, so they could look at the Green Mountains together as they sat on the toilet.

Or we edited some more. Then, before making dinner, we would take another plunge in the pond. Most nights, dinner was at home, and in the later years it often began with her own grass-raised beef, a project she started at age eighty-two with Bronwyn. And, if the season was ripe, she would make her delicious rhubarb tart with tiny local strawberries, a recipe that I put in my *New American Cooking*.

meant in our lives. We were three people with distinct memories of the same ingredient.

I said that I had first learned about chickpeas when I was living in Jerusalem in 1970 through a delicious dip called hummus that few in the United States had even heard of before then.

Madhur, an elegant and articulate woman, told us the term for chickpea in Hindi is "kabuli chana," meaning the bean from Kabul, Afghanistan. They were smaller when Madhur was growing up in India, but over the years chickpeas have been hybridized. As a child, she ate them mostly as chaat, a spicy snack, and at home in chana bhatura, a round leavened bread rolled out and deep-fried that is served with very spicy chickpeas with dried pomegranate seeds. And she lamented the lack of green chickpeas, so delicious when picked fresh off the bush.

Then Lidia, who grew up in Istria, Italy (before it became Croatia), chimed in with her usual great gusto. "My grandmother grew chickpeas," she said. "We ate them green, right off the plant or in salads. Then, when they were mature, she would let the pods dry on the plant and we would all sit under the mulberry tree in the courtyard and shuck them. Grandma would keep them in a burlap bag in the cantina. Once they were dry, she would use them to make soups and pasta sauces, and toss them in salads when they were cooked."

As we dipped our spoons into the delicious spring vegetable soup with leeks, fennel, peas, and ricotta that Lidia served that day for Judith, we all continued to share memories of our own spring potato soups and of the chickpeas that sometimes went into them.

———✦———

When Judith retired in 2013, at age eighty-nine, I didn't know what to do. My husband and my wonderful new agent, David Black, told me just to wait it out. How right they were! Lexy Bloom, who is about the same age as my daughter Daniela, has taken over some of Judith's authors; today she's the editorial director of Knopf Cooks. As the mother of a young child, Lexy is a different kind of presence from Judith, and in so many ways I feel liberated without Judith's green pencil and resistance to putting money into professional photography in books. After all, Julia Child's *Mastering the Art of French Cooking* sold millions of copies without photographs. But it is a new era, and Lexy is hands-off until editing time. I worked with her on *King Solomon's Table*, and what a pleasure it was.